One Young Fool
in
South Africa

Joe and Victoria Twead

Also available in Large Print and e-Book editions.

The Old Fools Series

Victoria Twead

- Chickens, Mules and Two Old Fools (Wall Street Journal Bestseller)
- Two Old Fools ~ Olé!
- Two Old Fools on a Camel (Thrice New York Times Bestseller)
- Two Old Fools in Spain Again

- One Young Fool in Dorset: The Prequel
- One Young Fool in South Africa: The Prequel

Para Beaky

**who constantly urged me to write,
then improved and polished this,
my first clumsy effort.**

* * *

"Thank you, Joe. Am I allowed to improve and polish this dedication?"
"Certainly not."

* * *

Contents

Part One

Beginnings

1

Ma

July 2014, El Hoyo, Southern Spain.

Joe and I sat at the kitchen table. It was a balmy summer's evening and the door was open wide. Cicadas buzzed in the vine outside, competing with our neighbours, the Ufartes, who sang and danced a flamenco in the street. Dogs barked and children shouted.

"Hmm..." I said, taking a sip of Paco's homemade wine. Paco was another neighbour, and he had insisted that this particular batch of red wine was his best yet. "Not bad. Not bad at all."

"I agree," said Joe.

We sat in companionable silence for a little while, listening to the village noises.

"You know," I said, perhaps a little fuelled by Paco's wine, "you really should write about your childhood. From what you've told me, I think people would find it very interesting. Anyway, isn't it about time you carried out your threat to write your great masterpiece? Your, um, what is it you call it?"

"Magnum opus," Joe answered with a smile and took a generous slurp of wine. "It's not really a happy story, though."

"It doesn't matter. I think people would be fascinated. More interesting than that other heavy tome you were threatening to write."

"Perhaps you have a point, Sweet Pants," he said, treating himself to another slurp. "You know, I might just do that. Now BURMA."

"BURMA? What's BURMA?"

"It's 'be upstairs ready my angel'. It's what we boys used to snigger about."

"Poor Joe. You live in a fantasy world, don't you? Now concentrate on your story and start writing."

* * *

South Africa, 1951

I have no idea exactly when I was born or indeed where. Perhaps it was a home birth or perhaps I was delivered in a maternity hospital, I cannot be sure. What is certain is that it was somewhere in Johannesburg, a major city within the Union of South Africa, a colony of Great Britain. The 11th July 1951 was the date given to me when I was old enough to understand such things. But I have never seen any confirming documentation.

My very first memory of the world was when I was about two years old. I was standing in a sunlit kitchen, the bright light streaming through a large-paned window that overlooked a sink. I am with a man and a woman and the man is bending over me.

"This is for you, Robert," he said quietly, and placed a tiny object in the palm of my hand.

I didn't know what it was but it was red and shiny and I found it very attractive. I closed my fingers protectively around it, reserving it for a later, more leisurely inspection. Without saying another word, the man left. The moment he had gone, the woman pounced on me, easily relieving me of my trinket.

"Your name is *not* Robert," she hissed, "it's Joe!" and she tossed the object into a bin.

I did not pine its loss for long. The man might have been my father but I am not certain. If I did see him again it was all too brief and he remains an indistinct figure in my memory. I would not properly meet him again until I was in my mid teens.

The woman, on the other hand, I knew was very important to me and that her word was law. She had informed me that my name was Joe and I accepted that. I have done so ever since, even to the present day, more than six decades later.

Unfortunately her decision to change my name has caused many problems. The paperwork that recorded the first eighteen years of my life insists that I am Robert, not Joe. But I am resolute: it is Joe, not Robert.

The woman was my mother and I would call her Ma. She called me Boy.

Ma smoked incessantly. Her movements were slow, her actions unhurried. There was always a dreamy look in her eyes as if she was looking deep within herself. I never could fathom her thoughts. When I interrupted them with one of my endless questions, she would give me a long look before slowly lifting her hand to drag on a ubiquitous cigarette. The look was invariably one of mild surprise, as if questioning my very presence. It was almost as if she had forgotten who I was and why I was there. She seldom answered my questions. In fact, she seldom spoke to me.

I didn't mind. I soon accustomed myself to her ways and accepted her and them with that infinite capacity that is gifted to all very young children. In return I was given absolute freedom. And what freedom!

I could roam wherever I wanted and do whatever I pleased. Often the police, after first giving me a plate of food which I ravenously devoured, returned me to my house. Whether this affected Ma's behaviour, I do not know. Soon enough, however, I would be off again only to be returned by the police or by a perfect stranger.

"Now don't touch anything," one stranger said, leaving me alone in his car before disappearing into a store.

Of course I immediately searched everywhere for something to touch. My eyes settled in the centre of the steering wheel which was bright red with a gold rim. I touched it. Nothing happened so I decided to give it some proper attention. I discovered that the gold rim screwed off, releasing the red centre which sprang out at me. The instant it was free, the car horn blared continuously and, terrified, I shot back to the passenger seat. The man appeared and quickly repaired my vandalism, but not before giving me a malevolent look.

Soon we were on our way and looking for my house which was amongst identical houses, situated in identical streets.

"There's my house!" I would shout.

"Are you sure?"

"No, that's not it."

"What about this street? Is your house here?"

"Yes! There's my house!"

But it wasn't, so we carried on searching.

We would find it eventually and I would be handed over to Ma.

My memory at this age is only reliable enough to portray the kitchen, the man, the trinket, Ma, the police, the plate of food, the man in the car, the horn, and the search for the house. I don't know exactly what age I was, where I lived, or for how long.

* * *

"I hope you're not going to mention the little bird," I said, trying to read over Joe's shoulder.

"What bird?" Joe said somewhat defensively. He clearly had something to hide.

"You know what I'm talking about."

Joe did. The event, like so many others in his life, greatly mortified him.

"I must," he said reluctantly, "I have to be honest."

* * *

My second memory of the world around me occurred not long after that.

I was alone in a small backyard overlooked by the window that belonged to the sunlit kitchen. The yard was completely enclosed with stone slabs underfoot. Except for a small tree in the centre of the yard, I saw no other plants or greenery.

Not far from the tree, a small bird hopped on the ground. It hopped away when I approached but made no attempt to fly. I caught it easily and picked it up. It was tiny and comfortably fitted in the palm of my small hand. I could feel its warmth.

I stared at the fledgling. To my astonishment it chose not to escape, preferring to nestle down in my palm. It even closed its eyes, probably enjoying my warmth.

I should have been delighted in the absolute trust this tiny creature had shown me, but I wasn't. An inexplicable rage overwhelmed me and, with all my might, I threw it to the ground, killing it instantly. I immediately regretted my action but had no time to ponder the consequences.

Ma appeared from nowhere and slapped my face so hard it took my breath away. She must have witnessed it all from the kitchen window. Her face was dark and her expression thunderous. I made no sound, too shocked to say or do anything.

For some time we stared at one another. In my heart I knew that I had done something dreadful and dearly wished I hadn't. But Ma's reaction affected me profoundly. From then on I viewed her as formidable, someone to be greatly wary of.

In fact, it was the first of very few slaps I would get from her, and they were all richly deserved. Always delivered in anger, they would only follow after much provocation. I had simply to learn the boundaries that defined her limits.

After staring wordlessly at me, she turned on her heels and walked away.

Now, six decades later, the memory of that day still pervades my thoughts. I doubt I will ever know why I killed that tiny bird. I am still plagued with remorse and wish I could rewind the clock and undo the past.

I believe that, deep down, Ma never forgave me for what I did and would henceforth view me with doubt and mistrust.

2

Dogs, Locusts and Birds

Being returned by strangers and the police must have alarmed Ma because we suddenly moved to another location. We travelled everywhere by train, which I loved. Powered by steam locomotives, the compartments were comfortable, having two long seats facing each other over a middle table that folded away.

While Ma sat on the seat opposite, I would kneel on the other and watch the scenery pass by. The railway network was a narrow-gauge affair that restricted the train's speed to below 50 mph, which it rarely (if ever) achieved. It afforded me ample opportunity to enjoy the passing countryside. If I saw something of interest, I would swing around and tell Ma who would respond with a look of disinterested surprise.

On one occasion I witnessed an event that greatly shocked me.

Very often the rail track ran alongside a tarred road and I would watch the motor cars easily breeze past our slow-moving train. Being the fifties, the vehicles were solidly constructed and, almost without exception, black.

My eyes scanned the road ahead and I spotted a large black dog lying in the middle. It appeared to be in no distress and I could not understand why it chose such a precarious spot to take a rest. It was panting in the heat, its head raised and its front paws stretched out parallel with the white dividing line.

Naturally I scanned the road in the opposite direction and saw a black car approaching. The dog was facing the other way and appeared to be entirely unaware of it.

To my horror the driver deliberately manoeuvred the car to run over the dog. Had the dog simply turned its head, it would have seen the car and quickly moved out of harm's way. But it didn't.

How can it not hear the approaching car?

I believed that there was still some hope, a small chance that it would swing its head around, perceive the danger, and make its escape. But it didn't.

All too soon the car was upon it. From my vantage point I saw the dog roll beneath the car, two or three times, before being left dazed and in an almost identical pose to the one it was in before being run over. It was still panting but disorientated, its head spinning from side to side.

During the incident, the black car did not change its speed. Whoever was behind the wheel, he (I cannot believe it was a woman) deliberately aimed the vehicle at the animal with the sole purpose of harming it. Having run over the dog, the driver unhurriedly steered his vehicle back onto the left hand side of the road, as if nothing unusual had happened.

I turned my attention back to the dog, now fast disappearing from view. As far as I could tell, other than possible internal injuries, it was unharmed.

I breathlessly related all I had seen to Ma: how the dog had not seen the car, how the car had callously driven over the dog, how the dog had somersaulted beneath the car, how the driver had behaved as if nothing had happened, and how the dog was left dazed, but alive, its head spinning and in almost the same position it was in before the incident.

I was rewarded with a stony look and silence.

* * *

I remember being on a farm. To this day, I do not know its location or who the people were that surrounded me. Neither do I recall seeing much of Ma. I did not mind. I felt safe there, and with hindsight, I suspect I was related and felt I belonged.

I do not know my exact age but perhaps between three and four. And I don't know how long I lived there but the memories are vividly etched into my brain. The utter freedom to do what I liked, when I liked, made it one of the most wonderful periods of my life.

I knew it was a farm because there was a farmhouse and fields where neat rows of crops grew. Long green leaves hung down from tall stalks with white tufts at the top. I would learn that the crop was maize, or mealies, as we called corn on the cob in South Africa.

Above these, black birds trailed long tails. They flapped furiously to keep airborne, seemingly unable to fly more than a few feet before dropping into the green foliage.

I dearly wanted to catch one and was convinced that their apparent inability to fly would make them easy prey. No matter how hard I tried I never got near a single one. Off they flew with a squawk, staying just out of reach. I soon tired of my efforts and decided it was best simply to admire them from a distance.

In front of the farmhouse was a large dusty clearing where dust-devils, small whorls of tornado-like winds, were a common sight. In the middle of the clearing, an ancient dun-coloured dog lay. It had large black callouses on its elbows. When standing, it was huge, almost as tall as me.

I was aware that it was very old. Whenever it lay down in the dust, it did so with a loud groan. Its large dark eyes, now turning white with age, stared at me when I stroked its head and its thick tail thumped the ground raising dust.

Also alongside the house was a barbed wire fence that separated the property from an area of woodland. The trees beyond were plentiful and tall and easily accessed by climbing through the fence.

Hanging from the fence were skinned rabbits, their pink flesh drying in the hot sun. In addition, there were a number of black birds that hung by their feet, their wings loosely open in death.

"Crows," a young man explained to me. "We hang them there to warn other crows not to steal our crops. We eat the rabbits. Nice."

He was about ten years older than I was and I followed him everywhere. He was infinitely patient with me and never minded my presence. I think his name was Niels but I cannot be certain.

Niels never went anywhere without a pellet gun. During all my time with him I never once saw him miss anything he aimed the gun at. His primary targets were the pigeons that proliferated in the woodland. I asked him why he shot them.

"Is it to scare away other pigeons?"

"No. These are for eating."

I would watch, fascinated, as he levelled the weapon at a bird sitting high on a branch. The sharp crack of the released spring was instantly followed by a louder crack as the pellet slapped the bird's chest. The bird had no chance. It attempted to take flight but instead it tumbled from its perch, landing not far from where we were standing.

I retrieved it, holding its still-warm body in my hands, its head lolling lifelessly. I would search its chest for the wound that had killed it. There was very little blood, just a tiny hole where the pellet had entered.

* * *

"I love these warm summer nights, don't you?" I asked. "It's not just the village noises, but it's seeing bat silhouettes against the moon, and watching the stars popping out."

"And the scents," Joe added. "The jasmine smells wonderful."

"And so does next door's dinner. I suppose we'd better go inside and start on ours. You peel the potatoes and I'll sort the salad, okay?"

Joe nodded and we both stood up and headed back to the house.

"Anyway, the mosquitoes are beginning to feast on me. They're the only downside of Spanish summer nights."

"You've just reminded me of something," said Joe.

"I did?"

That evening I cooked alone as Joe rattled away on his computer.

* * *

I stood on the edge of the mealie field. It was a warm sunny day, and Niels and a black farmworker were with me. Whilst looking at the black birds with long tails, flying in and out of the mealies, a huge bug-eyed creature landed close to me. Its eyes were red and it had long bright green wings that folded neatly back over its back and abdomen. Its abdomen was hooped in green and yellow stripes. I had no fear of the creature and picked it up with my thumb and forefinger. It made no effort to escape. I look up inquiringly at Niels and the workman.

"A locust," Niels explained.

Suddenly, another arrived. Then another, then hundreds. A swarm of them surrounded me. I began to scream.

Niels and the farmworker laughed as they rescued me from my predicament.

* * *

I was standing in the clearing in front of the house on a bright sunny day.

The large dog is dead. Its eyes, completely opaque now, stare at nothing. I marvel at the stillness of death. All around there is activity, the vitality of life, and in the midst of it the huge dog lies perfectly still.

A pickup truck appears and a man slings one end of a heavy chain around the dog's hind legs and attaches the other to the back of the truck.

As the dog's carcass is slowly dragged away, its head is the last thing to move and, when it does, its snout points at me. Its eyes stare sightlessly back at me in one final farewell. It leaves a wide smooth trail in the dust.

* * *

All too soon, this idyllic existence had to end. Ma appeared and I did my best to escape her.

"I'm not going!" I screamed from within a mens' public lavatory.

Somehow I knew she wouldn't follow me inside and I was right. Instead, she employed a young black boy to come and fetch me. I stared at the boy who was my age. A feeling of delight enveloped me and all I wanted to do was play with this newfound playmate.

"Your mother wants you," he said and turned to leave.

Forgetting my purpose for being in the lavatory, I followed him out.

Ma nabbed me.

3

Partings

I am asleep and awakened by a man, almost certainly my father, who lifts me up and carries me to another bed.

I am approaching four years of age. I cannot identify my current location but it is not the farm. Ma is bending over me.

"You have a baby sister!" she whispers.

"Where is she from?" I ask.

"The stars!" she replies.

Satisfied, I fall asleep again.

* * *

We are in a train. Ma is holding Lizzy, my baby sister, and glaring at me. I am in my usual position, kneeling on the seat opposite, watching the scenery pass by.

The reason she is glaring at me is because I won't allow Lizzy to kneel at the window with me. I want it all to myself.

"Let your sister look out of the window too," Ma says and grudgingly I make room for her. When Ma isn't looking, I squash Lizzy against the window's edge. This makes her howl and Ma comes over to take her away.

I fear the consequences because Ma has a mighty hand. The expected slap is certainly deserved and I await the blow to fall, but it does not.

Content, I resume watching the countryside slowly pass by.

* * *

We are at the seaside and walking along the beach. A fierce wind is blowing, whipping up the sand which stings my legs. Despite this, I gaze in wonder at the vast ocean of blue. The wind, however, drives us into one of the open-fronted shelters that have been erected along the sea front.

Ma looks down and sees that one of Lizzy's little red shoes is missing.

"Go look for it, Boy," she commands me.

I retrace our steps but cannot find it. Ma is bitterly disappointed.

* * *

The house we are living in is dark and smells. I don't mind because Ma is always close by. I do not know the people with whom we share the house but suspect that they, like the people on the farm, are related to us.

The house is probably located somewhere in Johannesburg. My probable age is between five and six but, again, I am not sure. As on the farm, I am free to come and go as I please.

Ma, Lizzy and I share the bed. The bed cover fascinates me. It is pink and patterned with raised cotton squares. The small squares are numerous. It's almost as if a pink net of inch-sized squares has been superimposed upon a smooth pink sheet.

But what intrigues me most isn't the quilt's structure. It is the fact that the centre of almost all the squares has been burned out with a cigarette. The result is part-quilt and part-net, albeit with a lot of blackened edges.

It must have taken whoever did this a very long time and at the expense of very many cigarettes.

* * *

I am still in the city. It's afternoon and I am sitting on a kerb, watching the traffic in a busy street. I stare down at my bare feet and listen to a man who is talking to passers-by who invariably return his friendly chatter. I do not understand their language but that does not concern me. I have heard it spoken many times in the past.

The man is black and in his hands he has a knife and piece of wood. He towers above me and, while he laughs and talks, he uses the knife to whittle away at the wood. It is, in fact, the reason I am sitting there because I am enthralled by his handiwork.

Ever so slowly, a shape is emerging from the foot-long narrow plank of pale wood. Already I recognise the appearance of the butt end of a rifle. He niftily carves out a trigger and moves on to shaping the barrel.

Although I am also watching the traffic, my eyes are constantly drawn to his work above me and I must shield them from the sun. At last he completes the rifle and I stare with admiration as he rubs the finished article with his hands, feeling for any rough edges.

With one final inspection, he bends down and wordlessly hands it to me. The action takes my breath away. In a flash I realise that the entire project was for my benefit. I doubt I possessed the breeding to thank him and can only hope that, in some way, I did show my gratitude. It is more likely that he understood and accepted a child's nature which in itself is reward enough. But, to this day, I still marvel at his generosity.

This might be the moment to say that I was kept away from the society of the many black people who lived in South Africa. It most certainly was not by choice for I would have befriended and played with any number of children, whatever their colour, had the opportunity arisen. Unfortunately, it never did.

As a final aside, never once during the twenty-two years that I lived in South Africa, was I ever treated with anything but friendliness and respect by the many black people with whom I worked and met.

* * *

Still in the city and it is a very bright and sunny day.

I am walking barefoot on a pavement alongside a busy street and desperately need to go to a lavatory. I successfully fight the urge to release my bowels.

With clenched buttocks I tread warily, hoping to get home (wherever that is), before disaster strikes. I tread on something sharp and the resulting pain distracts my concentration. A foul yellow mess runs down my legs and fills my short trousers.

I burst into a loud wail, hoping somebody will come to my rescue, but nobody does.

* * *

It is night time and I am with Ma and a strange man.

We are in a small white van and travelling along an isolated road. The van is typical, with a cabin for the driver and passengers and, in the rear, a separate windowless compartment for transporting goods. We occupy a single seat and the driver and I sandwich Ma in the middle.

We pull over and stop. The man gets out and walks around to my side. He opens the door and leads me to the back of the van.

"If you see anyone coming," he says, "I want you to come back here and bang on the doors. Like this," and he demonstrates the action. "Do you understand?"

I nod.

He leads me back to the front of the van. Ma is now waiting outside. I climb in and the door is closed behind me. Ma and the man disappear around the back and the van rocks as they climb inside. I hear the back doors close and then I am left alone in the silence and the dark.

I stare through the windshield, anxiously anticipating the arrival of another vehicle. I have no idea what Ma and the man are doing in the back and, frankly, I don't really care. Adults behave in ways that are entirely alien to me. All I want to see is the glimmer of another vehicle, so that I can execute my commission.

After a very long time I see a pair of headlights approaching. I jump out and bang on the back doors.

"Someone is coming! Someone is coming!" I shout.

By the time Ma and the man have exited the van, the approaching headlights have come and gone. We return to our places in the front of the car and drive away.

On the way back, Ma giggles like a young girl. I have never heard her behaving this way before and decide that some secret, known only to her and the man, is responsible.

The man doesn't say a word and I never see him again.

* * *

I am in the heart of a great city. I am in a room with high ceilings and many people surround me. The purpose of this room, and my reason for being there, is unknown to me. All I can see are adults' legs. I am trapped. I am probably between five and six years old.

I attract the attention of the person standing closest to me, a stranger, who bends down.

"I need the toilet," I whisper.

He leads me through the throng to the room entrance. We pass into an impressive foyer that ends in a corridor that parts left and right.

"Do you see that door?" he says, pointing at the door in the right limb of the corridor, and I nod. "That's the toilet," he says.

I make my way to the door and pass through. I am greatly surprised to see a white man sitting at a wooden desk just inside this room. On the desk is a large black telephone. We briefly look at each other and I turn my attention to the room.

Ahead of me is a row of urinals, tall ones with a step in front for patrons to stand upon while they complete their business. To my left is a row of cubicles housing flushable toilets. I only need the urinals and step up with my back to the man.

I am just finishing up when I hear a commotion outside. The unmistakable sound of Ma screaming reaches my ears and I quickly pull up my trousers. At the same time the telephone rings and the man lifts the receiver to his ear. The moment I am alongside him, he lifts a huge hand to prevent me from passing outside. Somehow I am able to evade him and make my way through the doorway. I am shocked by what I see.

Ma is in the main entrance and screaming.

"Leave my baby! Leave my baby!"

She has Lizzy's arms and another lady has her feet. I can see that they are having a tug of war with Lizzy as the rope. Before I can say or do anything, someone pushes me past the commotion and out of the building.

We pass down a broad flight of grey stone steps and I look back, trying to catch sight of either Ma or Lizzy. I only see Lizzy who is in the arms of the lady. Evidently she won the tug of war. Lizzy and I are bundled into a car that is waiting outside.

We cannot see out because we are in the footwell of the back seat. I look up and see a man sitting there, staring impassively ahead, paying us no heed. I quietly play with Lizzy in the footwell.

My halcyon days of freedom are at an end.

* * *

When I was twenty-two, and had lived in Johannesburg city centre for the better part of two years, sharing a flat with another boy my age, I walked past a large grey building that I had often seen. It had an impressive dome set above an equally impressive façade. A central inset arch framed the entrance which was guarded by eight stately columns, four on the left and four on the right.

I had no notion of its purpose but it looked official, perhaps serving some public function. I decided to investigate. I mounted the broad stone steps in front and passed unopposed through the front doors. Immediately I was transported back to the time that I stood in this very foyer, so many years ago. Ahead of me was the corridor that branched left and right.

I stepped forward and there, on the right, was a room down the right-hand corridor. I entered and was confronted by urinals ahead and cubicles on my left. The manned table and telephone were gone.

From the toilet, I retraced my steps to the foyer. I faced a door with gold writing and was reminded of this very door being opened for me and a finger pointing out the WC behind me.

I read the gold writing on the door: *Court Room No. 1.*

The building was the High Court in Johannesburg.

4

A Place of Safety for Children

I remember very little about the journey in the footwell of the car. What I do most vividly recall is the destination.

I don't know what became of Lizzy but I was shown into a large darkened room containing about six metal beds, each with a small open-fronted metal locker. One of these would house the clothing I would be provided with: shoes, black socks, shorts, a shirt, and a belt with a neat s-shaped buckle for fastening around my waist.

The bed was unmade. A thick red rubber sheet covered a thin mattress and a striped pillow was placed on a folded grey blanket. I would learn that this was the only bedding provided. I did not mind. I had slept in far less comfortable conditions in the past.

It's what happened next that taught me to fear the place I had arrived at. I felt a stinging pain on the back of my legs and, with a cry, whipped around to see who, or what, was responsible.

A white woman towered above me, wielding a thin bamboo stick. Tearfully I gazed questioningly at her, wondering what crime I had committed. In answer she babbled at me in Afrikaans, a language with which I was entirely unfamiliar. Because I didn't understand, she raised the stick to hit me again. I did my best to evade her but to no avail. The blows rained down, always on the backs of my legs.

Clearly I had to learn this language, and fast, otherwise my existence here would be miserable indeed. With the sponge-like capacity of a child to effortlessly absorb anything new, I did quickly master it.

Sadly, what I failed to appreciate was that the women in charge (there were three) enjoyed hitting me. They would creep up on me and whip the backs of my legs when I least expected it. And they were unremitting.

Sometimes they found an excuse to punish me. One of their favourites was after I had pulled on my black socks. It should be noted that I had never before donned a pair of socks and had no idea whether they were inside out or not.

Of course I should have recognised that a sock is correctly worn with the seam on the inside but nobody told me this, certainly not the ladies. For them it was too much fun to whip me for my failed efforts.

When one considers the permutations of a pair of socks, with both seams on the inside being correct, and my lamentable lack of knowledge of this fact, it isn't difficult to conclude that I was often beaten. I do believe I was caned even when I wore them correctly. I soon detested the sight of the socks.

Naturally I came to hate the women and the institution that I will forever term 'The Afrikaans Place'. Every day when I awoke, rising from my bed with its distinctive rubber smell, I feared the future and the three ladies who would soon descend upon me.

Of course other children occupied the dormitory too, but I never spoke to them and they never spoke to me. I was simply too miserable, dreading when the next blows would fall.

There was some relief, however, in the form of afternoon playtime. We were seated on a patch of grass not far from the entrance to the main building. At a distance from where we sat, I could see a wire fence. It was about four feet high and surrounded the entire property. Beyond the fence was a sidewalk that skirted a busy main road.

We were not permitted to wander from where we sat. Staff members patrolled us, ensuring we obeyed this rule. To my surprise, Lizzy was dumped next to me. I had no notion of where in the building she had been kept and frankly didn't care. She was not much more than a year old and, in my opinion, still a baby.

Lizzy and I had had very little interaction whilst we were with Ma. At that time the world around me was just too interesting for me to be concerned about a sister who was nearly four years younger than I. Needless to say there had been very little sibling bonding between us and we certainly had nothing in common.

Until now.

To my amazement, young as she was, she recognised me. Her baby features broke into a smile, the first kindness I had been shown since arriving at this dreadful place. A drowning man, breaking the surface of the water and taking a lungful of fresh air could not have been more grateful than I was. I was enchanted and from then on grew to love her as a brother should. I began to long for the playtimes when we would be together again.

We always played the same game, aeroplanes. I would lift her in the air on the soles of my feet, my hands holding hers to steady her, and she would gurgle with pleasure above me. Neither of us tired of this and it always delighted me to see her face light up.

Generally, after playing with Lizzy, I would look around, inspecting my surroundings and those with whom I sat. I noticed that the other children always seemed to be sitting as quietly as I did, having little interaction with one another. The patrolling staff seldom interfered in our activities and this surprised me.

Young as I was, I was aware that my play with Lizzy was potentially dangerous. However, no attempt was ever made to stop me. And neither was I beaten. That was reserved for when I was alone and in the dormitory. I was grateful.

I don't know how long I had been at the Afrikaans Place but it was during one playtime when I saw a figure walking slowly on the sidewalk beyond our fence. I instantly recognised her.

Ma!

Salvation!

She had come to rescue me!

Without hesitating, I jumped to my feet and sprinted as fast as I could towards her. Behind me I could hear a staff member giving chase and shouting for me to stop. It only encouraged me to run faster. Soon only the wire fence separated Ma from me.

"Ma! Ma!" I shouted, hoping she would reach over and lift me to safety.

But she didn't.

She took a slow drag on a cigarette and, other than the briefest glance, did not look at me all. She chose, instead, to stare at something over my head. I spun around, following her gaze.

Lizzy. She had come for Lizzy.

In a flash I fully appreciated my predicament. I realised that all was lost and I would never be rescued. By now the staff member had arrived and had grabbed and turned me away.

"It's my mother!" I said in Afrikaans.

She ignored me and led me back to the group of children sitting on the grass. I wondered if I would be punished but I wasn't.

Lizzy was oblivious of all that had happened and, as always, smiled when she saw me again. I looked back at Ma who had not moved from her spot. She was still smoking and her movements were unhurried. For a long time she remained there, staring in our direction.

From then on, every day, she would slowly walk along the sidewalk, smoking, occasionally stopping to look in our direction. I would stare back at her, always aware that she was there for Lizzy. But I also felt comforted when I saw her. Her presence gave me hope that this nightmare might end and we could return to our carefree existence.

Then one day, Ma disappeared.

My sense of the helplessness of my situation can only be imagined. I believed I was doomed to spend the rest of my life in this awful place, subject to unexpected whippings and, other than Lizzy, without a friend in the world.

* * *

Every morning we attended an Afrikaans primary school, located within walking distance, which also accommodated local children. I remember being placed in a pre-school class where I doubt I learned anything, but welcomed the opportunity to escape the Afrikaans Place.

When the school day ended, we walked back and into the clutches of the waiting staff. Would I be beaten? I could never be sure but I was always fearful and lived in a state of perpetual terror. Sometimes a few days elapsed in which there were no punishments. Relieved, I would relax, only to be jolted back to reality when I felt a stinging pain on the backs of my legs. Screaming, I would unsuccessfully attempt to flee from my persecutors.

I will never know who these women were and why they behaved as they did towards me. These events occurred in the mid fifties and no doubt they are all now dead. But I do wish I could ask them why they treated me so. Was it because I was English speaking? Maybe. I am aware that children can be objectionable but, even so, it did not warrant such cruelty.

One day at the school I picked a fight with an older boy who bloodied my nose. I remember lying on the ground and crying, nestling my head in the crook of my elbow. Blood spilled from my nose and onto the ground. This fascinated me but not as much as the children's legs I could see surrounding me as I lay there. None of them said a word. They simply stared down at me.

When eventually I stood up, there was blood down the front of my shirt. The teachers at the school were not in the least concerned and treated the matter as an everyday event. But I feared the reaction of the staff at the Afrikaans Place.

Walking back that bright sunny day, I knew I was in for a beating. I was the centre of attention as I approached the main entrance. The ladies silently inspected me.

"Your punishment is that you wear this shirt for the rest of the week," one of them said. "It will teach you to keep it clean in future."

If that was to be my only punishment, I was prepared to wear the shirt for the next twenty years. But at least I was not beaten.

Then one day I returned after school to find a clean set of clothing awaiting me in my locker. Surprised, I stared down at them.

"You're leaving tomorrow," a voice said behind me.

I turned around to see one of the ladies. For once she had not delivered a surprise whipping to the back of my legs. But that was insignificant when compared with the profound relief I felt at learning that I would be leaving. I did not care where they sent me as long as I didn't have to stay there.

I could not wait for the morrow and I dressed very early, awaiting my departure.

I had finally escaped.

"What a truly terrible place," I said.

"It certainly was," said Joe. "I didn't tell you, but I searched for it on the Internet."

"Really? Did you find it?"

"Well, everything has changed, so I'm not sure exactly what it is now. But I did learn one thing. Something pretty ironic."

"What was that?"

"It had an alternative title. They called it 'A place of safety for children'."

Part Two

Johannesburg Children's Home

5

Uncle Gussy

As the sun dipped down behind the Spanish mountains, Joe and I sat in the garden watching the sky turn peach, orange, then red. In the coop, the last chicken jumped up onto the roost to join her sisters.

"Vicky, do you think it's too dark?" asked Joe.

"Too dark for what?"

"I meant the first part of my book, not the evening. Do you think it's too dark?"

I paused, considering.

"No, I don't think so. You told it as it was, and it was definitely a dark time in your life. Those women at the Afrikaans Place were unspeakably awful. It's unforgivable what they did. Nobody should treat little children like that."

We sat in silence for a while. A scops owl hooted, answered by another on the other side of the valley.

"I'll start writing about JCH tomorrow," said Joe. "That period of my life was much lighter. What's for dinner?"

"Patatas a lo pobre," I said, getting up. "It won't be long."

I headed for the kitchen, ducking under the vine where bunches of ripening grapes dangled low.

Joe remained in the garden, deep in thought.

* * *

Johannesburg, 1957

I am on a train. The train is not like those in which I travelled with Ma. This one has open carriages and a number of other passengers are travelling with me. We are seated on hard but comfortable seats and I am with a strange man who barks orders.

"Get on the train."

"Sit there."

"Get off the train."

I follow his instructions to the letter, fearful of the possible consequences if I don't. The Afrikaans Place has trained me well. Other than an occasional glance, I don't even look out of the window. Neither of us says a word. The journey takes about an hour.

We return to Johannesburg. We arrive at an enormous train station, larger than any I have seen before. We board an electrified tram which delivers us to a suburb not far from the centre of the city.

Soon I find myself in a building and am sitting on the top step of a flight of stairs, drawing a picture. The paper is resting on the linoleum and my nose is not far from what I am drawing: a crazy-looking trapezium-shaped object with parallel lines drawn across.

"That's a stupid picture he's drawing," I hear a child's voice declare and I tense but do not look up.

A lady's voice gently scolds the child.

"Leave him alone. He's enjoying himself."

I look up and a woman is smiling down at me. She is wearing a nurse's uniform which is white and spotlessly clean. She is one of a number of staff members at what will be my home for more than three years: Johannesburg Children's Home, or JCH.

The Afrikaans Place was, for me, hell on earth, but JCH was heaven. Here I would once more learn to be a child, enjoying almost as much freedom as I did with Ma. From the moment I looked up into the kindly eyes of the nurse, I knew I was safe again. This feeling never left me all the time I was there. Quite simply, I loved the place.

It was run by a husband and wife team who had no children of their own. Mr and Mrs Flottow were responsible for some one hundred children, aged between two and eighteen. Mrs Flottow was addressed as Matron and the children addressed Mr Flottow as Uncle Gussy. Only girls remained after the age of nine. At that age the boys were sent to a boys' home, located in another suburb of the city.

Other than Uncle Gussy, the staff were all women and were addressed as Nurse. We saw very little of Matron. She was a large woman and her uniform was dark, unlike the whites of the Nurses. Her headwear was triangular, like those which matrons commonly wore in hospitals in those days, whilst the staff headgear was the small nurse's hat. Matron was a formidable lady and we quaked when we encountered her.

Her husband, Uncle Gussy, on the other hand, we saw much of and he was very popular. He was of average build and height and always dressed in casual grey longs and open necked shirt. Matron undoubtedly had the most authority in the Home but Uncle Gussy was not far behind.

Only once, during all my time there, was I chastised. We were seated in the dining hall and had just finished the evening meal. I was about eight at the time and had been in the home for nearly three years.

"Now I don't want to see anybody move," Uncle Gussy commanded us and the din in the hall subsided into silence.

I could not resist it. I simply had to test if that meant *any* movement. What if I scratched my head, would that be classified as a movement? Surely that would be acceptable? And so I did.

"Joe Twead! Come here immediately!" Uncle Gussy ordered and I approached with no small trepidation.

"I was only scratching my head!" I protested.

"And I said don't move!" he replied. "Now bend down!"

Before I could utter another word, he had pushed my head down and I felt something smacking my bottom. It was so light I hardly felt it and I almost laughed. Of course I dared not in case worse might follow.

"Now let that be a lesson to you!" he said, releasing me. "Return to your seat and don't move!"

It was an unforgettable lesson. I learned that some adults were incapable of harming children and treated them gently and with respect. The ladies at the Afrikaans Place would have done well to study the ways of the staff at JCH.

Uncle Gussy's instrument of torture was a table tennis paddle and it might have been a feather, it was so ineffectual. But I have jumped ahead of myself and need to return to my initial impressions of the grounds and the infrastructure.

The property was bounded on three sides by public roads and two solid pillars marked the entrance from the busiest of these. From the entrance, a narrow, tarred road swept up and around an impressive three-story building, ending at a rear exit that led onto a residential public road. The rear exit gate comprised two stone pillars similar to those at the entrance.

The front of the building overlooked a paved quadrangle that bordered the tarred road, and just beyond this was a lawned area in which a number of fir trees grew. After the evening meals, we were allowed to play here, kicking and chasing after fallen pine cones. I can still vividly recall the overwhelming sweet smell of pine. We would study the amber coloured glue that oozed from the boughs of the trees, prying it loose to taste, and finding it nearly impossible to remove from our fingers.

The back of the building overlooked a large structure that housed wheeled trash bins as well as the vehicles that belonged to Matron and JCH. We were forbidden access to this area but nobody seemed to mind if we rummaged in the bins.

Essentially the building was rectangular in shape and part of the middle floor was where Matron and Uncle Gussy were accommodated. From their quarters, double glass doors opened onto a narrow balcony that overlooked JCH's recreational grounds.

Almost directly beneath the balcony, and leading off the tarred roadway, a cement path fell quite steeply to a fair sized playing field. Two sets of crude but effective metal goal posts faced each other at either end and our favourite time was when Uncle Gussy refereed a soccer match with everybody participating, even the older girls.

Sometimes, he would reward the players that impressed him most with a coin, usually a farthing or a ha'penny and, on rare occasions, a penny. These rewards never extended to the shiny 2½ penny coin that we called a 'ticky'. A sixpence was unheard of and I don't think any of us ever saw one.

The money we earned was spent at a store on the way to school. A penny bought four gingerbread men, a ha'penny, two, and a farthing, one. These gingerbread men were highly prized and substantial. They were colourfully decorated with smiling faces, buttons, and a belt. I would start with the head, then each arm, then each leg, and finally savour the torso, enjoying the taste of ginger.

I particularly remember one morning waiting for the store keeper to serve a girl ahead of me. I was clutching a farthing and eyeing the gingerbread man that would soon be mine. The girl attended the same school and we were both dressed in school uniform. She was a few years older than I was but not from JCH.

"A penny sheet of blotting paper, please," she said, and I gasped.

Had she just spent a whole penny on a single sheet of blotting paper? Did she not know that she could have had not one, not two, not three, but *four* gingerbread men instead of a worthless piece of paper? I marvelled at her ignorance.

"A gingerbread man, please," I said, placing my farthing on the counter and looking pointedly at her at the same time, hoping to demonstrate how a proper purchase is conducted.

She ignored me, preferring to point a superior nose at the ceiling whilst she rolled up her blotting paper. My own thoughts on the subject were along the lines that some girls just didn't appreciate the finer things in life.

Adjoining the playing field was a rockery in which plants and vegetables grew. These included rhubarb, onions and beetroot. The rockery was quite large, sloping upwards and ending at the grassy area with the fir trees. A path ran diagonally up through the centre of the rockery and joined the cement path near the top.

Two buildings stood on either side of the playing field. One was a workshop that overlooked the bowling club. It was locked when not in use and it was where we sometimes made things with an adult supervisor overseeing us. This was usually an elderly man who watched us construct, amongst other things, crude carts in which we rode at breakneck speed down the cement path. Old pram wheels were brought in and the wood was easily found from the abundant offcuts that were strewn around the large room. The carts were steered using thin ropes attached to the axles on the front wheels. Although dangerous, these rides were enormous fun.

The other building was on the opposite side of the playing field. It was large, dark, desolate and abandoned. What its purpose was, or had been, nobody knew. We sometimes entered but soon retreated, preferring the bright sunshine outside.

Almost alongside this building was a swimming pool, about ten metres by five (about thirty-three feet by seventeen), and perfectly adequate for our purposes. It was fenced off and opened only when a staff member was prepared to supervise us. It was immensely popular but closed during the winter months.

Finally, two all-weather tennis courts, rarely used and situated at the end of the playing field nearest the swimming pool, completed the available facilities in this wonderful place.

* * *

"I'm so pleased you were finally in a place where you were happy," I *said.*

"It was truly wonderful. I don't have a single bad thing to say about JCH, and I feel very lucky to have been sent there."

6

Days of Sunshine

The main building was enormous and housed everything: staff accommodation, a nursery and dormitories, the dining hall and kitchen, a sanatorium, administrative offices and even a library. All could be found within the huge three-story structure.

At the very top of the building was what we children called 'the monkeys' cage' because it looked like one to us. It was a wrought iron cage-like enclosure that ran along the length of the building between the two jutting out limbs. We never did see any monkeys in it and never discovered its purpose. When we practised fire drills, we congregated on the quad and, gazing up at the façade, always speculating about the cage at the top.

One sunny day, during one of the fire drills, it suddenly began to rain. We all looked up, bewildered, because there wasn't a cloud in the sky.

"It's a monkey's wedding," one of the nurses commented.

We children looked up at the monkeys' cage, expecting to see a bunch of monkeys celebrating, but were disappointed.

"When it rains on a sunny day," she explained, "we call it a monkey's wedding."

"Oh!" we said, still bewildered, but the phrase stuck and I still use it today.

The bathroom, in which there were three baths and three toilet cubicles, was shared by all girls and boys aged between 5 and 9. The boys were bathed first. We stood in a line, naked, awaiting our turn to be dumped in the water, scrubbed, dunked again, then hauled out and towelled down. This was performed by two or three nurses who wore rubber aprons to protect their uniforms. The same was done for the girls.

We returned to the dormitory where another nurse helped us dress in clean clothes, in preparation for the evening meal. The chatter of young voices vied with commands barked out by the nurses as they performed what must have been exhausting duties.

After ablutions, we lined up outside the dining hall on the bottom floor. Once inside, we were seated about eight to a table and our food was brought to us by African staff. I cannot recall a single meal at JCH. That we were well fed goes without saying but I am unable to say exactly what we ate.

I do recall, however, that after the evening meal, we were lined up and some of us were given a spoonful of malt. This, we were told, made up for a deficiency in our diet and the beneficiaries enjoyed the thick, dark liquid. Not being one, I was immensely envious, and begged a taste, but was peremptorily refused.

Then we were sent out onto the grassy area beneath the fir trees to romp until darkness fell, which, in South Africa, was exactly six o'clock, irrespective of the season.

Our dormitory was bright and clean with high metal beds and adjoining small metal lockers. The mattresses were protected by the same red rubber sheets as in the Afrikaans Place but now sheets, pillow cases and blankets ensured we were even more comfortable and warm. A blue linoleum floor provided a smooth surface for us to slide upon in our pyjamas, but only in the absence of staff. Using the undersides of the beds to pull ourselves along, we raced one another from one end of the dormitory to the other.

About fifteen boys occupied our dormitory and, I suspect, the same number of girls occupied the dormitory above us. I don't know how many infants were in the dormitory below on the ground floor but, during the day, I would peer through a window and see a number of high-sided beds.

Down on the playing field and between the dilapidated building and swimming pool, was a small fenced off area. Here the youngest children enjoyed the grass and sunshine and whatever toys were put out for them. It was here that I saw Lizzy again. By now she was older and could stand on her own two feet.

We would look at one another through the fence and her sweet smile still enchanted me. But in truth I no longer needed that precious support that she had provided in the Afrikaans Place. Much time had elapsed since I last saw her and the friendships I had forged with the children around me more than satisfied all my needs. Unfortunately, I no longer paid her as much attention as I should have.

* * *

"I still feel guilty about that," Joe said.

"Don't beat yourself up about it," I exclaimed. "How many little boys can be bothered playing with their baby sisters? Well?"

"Not many, I guess. Except here in Spain where families are usually big and they all look out for each other. But Lizzy and I only had each other. I should have treasured every second together."

"Small boys don't think like that. It wasn't your fault. I bet you were too busy playing with other children your own age. It's only natural."

"I suppose so."

"Cup of tea?"

"Yes, please. Nothing like tea to cheer you up. In fact I think I'll write about what Martin did to me. I can laugh about it now, though I didn't then..."

Joe smiled at me then tapped away busily at his keyboard.

* * *

The sanatorium was fun to be in providing one wasn't genuinely ill, like when I spent several weeks in there with mumps. A bout of it had afflicted JCH and a number of girls and boys occupied the high beds.

I recall one memorable day with Martin, who was a year or so older. He knew how to say a few words in Zulu and proudly boasted the fact.

"Listen, Joe, the next time the cleaner comes in, say this to him," he said, and taught me the phrase he wanted me to say.

"What does it mean?"

"Nothing, really," he said, "just 'good morning, how are you'."

Had I been a little more observant, I might have seen the gleam in the rascal's eye, but I didn't.

The African cleaner duly appeared. He was a well-built man with a no-nonsense expression on his handsome dark features. We all feared him and suspected he had a serious temper that could flare up at any moment. If he said 'jump', we did, pausing only to ask how high.

"Go on, Joe," urged Martin, "say it to him."

I attracted the cleaner's attention and he turned to glare at me. I repeated Martin's phrase, glancing at the fiend to check I had said it correctly. He was laughing and only then did I detect his treachery.

It must have been something terribly insulting because the cleaner's eyes rolled in his head while he removed the leather belt from around his waist. I was in for a flogging and I knew it. I needed to escape but his bulk blocked the doorway. My only refuge was under my bed and that is where I dived.

The enraged cleaner tried getting at me from one side but I escaped out the other. He walked around but I would disappear under again. Frustrated, he finally stood on the bed and whipped the belt over both sides, hoping the end would reach me, but it never did. Eventually he gave up and left the room, grumbling under his breath.

I later did my best to apologise, blaming Martin, but he merely scowled.

* * *

Thanks to the generosity of our delightful neighbours, we were never short of beautiful fresh ingredients to cook with. Joe chopped onions while I sliced mushrooms and shiny green peppers.

"Thanks for helping, Joe."

"That's okay. I needed a break from writing. It's so intensive, it makes my head ache."

"I know! Where have you got up to now?"

"Still describing JCH. So many memories."

We fell into silence, apart from the rhythmic chopping of vegetables.

"Ow!"

"What's up?"

"I've cut myself! Vicky, quick, get a plaster! Owwww! It really hurts!"

"Oh, for goodness' sake, they'll hear you in Barcelona! It's a tiny cut, don't be such a baby. You always make such a fuss!"

* * *

When I needed any kind of medical attention, it was always promptly administered.

On one occasion I pierced my thumb on a sharp piece of bamboo and I, together with my bleeding thumb, were swiftly carried off to a doctor who stitched me up. I can still count the seven stitches that closed a diagonal wound on the ball of my left thumb.

On another occasion I had severe toothache and was promptly taken to a dentist who removed the offending molar.

All the children in the home were regularly inoculated against various diseases, including polio and typhoid. Polio was the most popular inoculation and the least painful. At first it was a strange contraption that was placed against our upper arms and when fired, left a circular pattern on the skin. A few days later this would develop into something that looked nasty.

"Don't worry, that just means it has taken," a nurse explained. "It means it's working."

Eventually it left a circular scar on our upper arms although mine has long since disappeared.

The circular gun was administered on several occasions and eventually replaced with a sugar cube. Other than the swelling and scar left by the gun, neither method had any side effects.

The typhoid injection, however, wasn't only painful, it left all of us feeling very ill indeed. I have seldom experienced such a debilitating illness and, for a few days, we were all floored. I can only conclude that we contracted a minor dose of typhoid.

I have a lamentably low tolerance to any level of pain. At JCH, I acquired a verruca on the sole of my right foot. It was a fairly common ailment and either affected our feet or hands. The treatment was radical. The verrucas were burned out with what can only be described as a soldering iron.

At the hospital, each of us waited his or her turn. A girl, a few years younger than I, preceded me. She had a verruca on her hand. Half an hour later she reappeared, her hand bandaged, and she didn't seem any the worse for wear. Now it was my turn.

I lay on my back on the operating table and the nurse lifted my foot for the doctor to anaesthetise my foot prior to burning out the wart. He inserted a needle and pressed the plunger. Whatever the clear liquid in the injection was, it felt like liquid fire. With a scream, I pulled my leg back and kicked out, sending the injection and the doctor flying across the room.

The doctor picked himself and the injection up from the floor and slowly approached me.

"Do you want me to take that verruca out or not?" he asked, his face solemn.

Just as solemnly I shook my head.

"Very well, bring in the next patient," he said to the nurse and I was shown the door.

On the way back to JCH, the nurse was furious with me.

"You're nothing but a big baby!" she scolded. "This little girl didn't make a sound and she had the same thing done to her!"

We were on public transport and the little girl in question proudly showed me her bandaged hand. I was rightfully mortified and I hung my head in shame.

A few weeks later the exercise was repeated. This time two nurses tightly held my leg and the JCH nurse stood next to me at the table.

"Squeeze my arm when he gives you the injection," she said, and I grabbed hold of her upper arm.

The same doctor slowly squirted the fire into my foot and I squeezed the nurse's arm. It seemed to last forever and eventually the doctor unscrewed the syringe from the needle, leaving the latter in my foot. Another full syringe was screwed onto the waiting needle and the plunger pressed. But this time, no pain at all. I released my hold of the nurse's arm and could now calmly watch proceedings.

The injection was removed and the doctor began burning the verruca out. Immediately the smell of burning flesh filled the room but I felt nothing at all. I eventually ended up with a huge hole in the sole of my foot that took forever to heal.

A few days later, the nurse drew me to one side and lifted the sleeve of her tunic. A massive bruise surrounded her upper arm and I felt suitably ashamed. She didn't seem to mind though, and gave me a reassuring smile. But the pain of that injection still echoes down the decades. Some may think me a coward, but I insist I possess an incredibly low tolerance to pain.

7

Movies, Ma and a Birthday

I *looked up from reading Joe's notes while he clattered away in the kitchen.*

"Joe, you haven't mentioned your mother for ages. Did she ever visit you when you were at JCH?"

"Yes, she turned up again. I never knew when she was coming, she just appeared. Sometimes she took me to the cinema or a café where she treated me to an ice-cream."

"Have you any idea what she was doing all this time?"

"None," Joe answered, shaking his head.

* * *

The dining hall wasn't only used for meals. It also served as a theatre where, every second Friday night, a film was shown. The tables and chairs were moved aside, creating a large space for the younger children to sit on the floor. The staff and older girls sat on benches and chairs behind us.

From a very young age, I was a fan of the cinema, a place where I could lose myself for the better part of two hours. I saw my first film with Ma. It was during one of her surprise visits when she suddenly turned up at JCH to take me out for the day. We saw *Alexander the Great*, starring a blonde Richard Burton.

I very much enjoyed those Friday evenings when a film was shown in the dining hall with everyone attending.

"It's a war film, Joe," Uncle Gussy once bent down to whisper.

I hugged myself. Like most boys, I loved action films and I excitedly relayed the message to all those sitting closest to me. It was *Away all Boats*, starring a craggy Jeff Chandler.

One night *King Creole*, starring Elvis Presley, was shown. The older girls at the back screamed when he appeared on the screen for the first time, making us younger ones jump in the front. Eventually they settled down and we enjoyed what I thought was a good movie.

The best movie I saw was a realistic black and white western. Unfortunately, the title has eluded me but I have often wished I could see it again. Over the years I have searched for it but, having nothing but vague memories to draw upon, I have never found it.

Another use for the dining hall was for Lantern Service on Wednesday nights. A religious organisation would turn up and preach to us, usually illustrating the talks with pictures. I never did discover why it was called Lantern Service, but I would listen to them, not understanding much, except on one particular occasion when I was still very young.

In his exuberance to impress us about the flood that befell Noah, the speaker particularly stressed how it rained for forty days and nights and that the world was dark through all that time.

My small mind absorbed this information and assimilated it.

Lying in my bed that night, I looked out at the blackness and became convinced that there would be no return of the sunlight I so loved. I started to cry and the nurse on duty approached me.

"What's the matter?" she whispered.

"Will the sun shine tomorrow?" I asked.

Adults, I believed, knew everything.

"Oh for goodness sake, go to sleep!" she hissed and stomped off.

I did, and the sun did shine the next day.

Every Sunday, all the children were divided up and dispatched to various churches in the area. I ended up going to the Congregational Church. They treated me very well indeed.

They never foisted religion down my throat and at Christmas I was given a small gift, usually a Dinky Toy, which I loved playing with until another child liked playing with it more than I did. Then I would lose it.

Once a year the Congregationalists had their annual outing at Gillooly's Farm. This was a popular recreational facility on the outskirts of Johannesburg. Overlooked by a hill, there was a river and large grassed area for barbecues and competitive games. In South Africa, a barbecuc is called a *braai* which is the Afrikaans word for 'fry'. Gillooly's was open at all times to the general public and as a member of the Church I was invited too. I always had a lovely day out.

Ever since my time at JCH, I have had a very soft spot for the Congregational Church.

* * *

Ma was as taciturn as ever and her movements were still as languid when she appeared to take me out. Lizzy never accompanied us. The dreamy look stayed in Ma's eyes and a cigarette remained forever in her fingers. Sometimes she giggled quietly to herself, enjoying some private joke, and I never quizzed her about it. We never said much to each other but she was my mother and I felt a great affection for her. At the end of the outing she would return me to the home and I wouldn't see her again until her next surprise visit.

One evening, I was ordered to report to Matron who was waiting for me with Lizzy. She had a camera in her hand and she and Lizzy were standing on the road just below her balcony. I was perplexed.

"Stand there with your sister," she barked.

Lizzy and I stood next to each other on the edge of the tarred road, our backs to the main building. Matron stood on the opposite side of the road and looked at us through the view finder.

"Put your arm around your sister's shoulders," she ordered and I did.

There was a flash and she lowered the camera.

"Now go join the other children in the dining hall," she ordered me as she lead Lizzy away.

I was six and Lizzy was three.

A week after Matron photographed Lizzy and me on the road outside, I was in the dormitory. It was late afternoon and we were about to prepare for the evening meal.

"Hey, Joe," one of the boys said to me, "there are some people looking for you."

"Who?"

"I don't know. They're in a car. I think they adopted your sister."

By then we all understood what adoption meant but I was surprised that Lizzy was being adopted. I dashed outside, searching for the black car. I ran around the main building several times and then searched the public road outside the back gate. Apart from a black car that sped away, I saw nothing. Disappointed, I returned to the dormitory.

It would be a long time before I saw Lizzy again.

Ma suddenly appeared and took me out.

"Do you know where your sister is?" she asked.

She looked closely into my face. This was new behaviour for her and I realised that she was extremely anxious.

"I don't know," I answered truthfully. "I don't know where she's gone. I think she was adopted."

Ma quietly pondered this.

"Do you know who the people were or where they live?"

"No."

"Are you sure?"

She inspected my features closely again.

"Yes," I said, "I promise you, I don't know where she is."

Many times during subsequent outings, Ma repeated the same question.

"Do you know where your sister is?"

And each time I could only give her the same answer.

* * *

"Have I ever told you the story about my seventh birthday?"
"Only a million times."

* * *

"Joe," a nurse said excitedly to me, "it's your birthday tomorrow! Your birthday is on July the first, which is tomorrow. Do you understand?"

I didn't, not really, but was caught up in her infectious excitement.

"You will be seven tomorrow," she explained. "When it's someone's birthday, it's his special day. You will get a lovely birthday cake!"

A cake! Now that was an excellent reason to be excited. I told everyone that it was my birthday tomorrow and that I was getting a cake. I was duly rewarded with a 'oh, that's nice,' or words to that effect.

The next day I awoke, excited and pleased. It was my birthday! The nurse appeared carrying a gorgeous cream-covered cake.

"Joe, I'm so sorry, but I made a mistake. It's not your birthday. It's John's birthday and this cake is for him. Your birthday is on the eleventh, just eleven days from now."

Had it been eleven years it could not have been more distant. I was inconsolable and cried like a baby every time anybody wished me a happy birthday.

On the eleventh of July, I, too, was given a lovely cake and my past misery was forgotten. But from then on I never forgot on which day my birthday fell or, indeed, John's.

8

Boys will be Boys

The children from JCH, along with other children in the area, attended the local primary school, Observatory East. At the beginning of each school-day morning, we congregated outside the rear gate. Two nurses, assisted by the older primary girls, organised us into a crocodile of three abreast. Then off we went, one nurse in front and the other bringing up the rear.

We passed the bowling club and, after crossing a few roads, we arrived at a corner shop near the school entrance. Here the leading nurse halted the crocodile.

"Anyone want anything from the shop?" she would bellow.

On the rare occasions I was lucky enough to be clutching a coin, I and a few others would disappear inside. We then continued our walk to the school where we spent the next five or so hours. The same routine followed at the end of the school day, only in reverse and without a visit to the corner shop.

Sadly, I didn't excel at school at this time. They did their best to teach me to read and write but not too successfully. It wasn't the school's fault. I was entirely to blame. Quite simply, I was enjoying myself too much.

Everything was so refreshingly new and I had an infinite number of playmates with whom to share my experiences. I much preferred investigating the walnut tree outside the principal's office, where I was a regular visitor, than sit inside a dull classroom. The principal would verbally chastise me for not trying hard enough and then send me on my merry way.

One afternoon after school, Uncle Gussy called all of us into the dormitory. This was unusual because we always romped on the playing field after school. In the dormitory, Leslie was sitting on his bed.

Les, my age, was a quiet, thoughtful boy, the antithesis of me. I particularly liked him. He seldom spoke and when he did, it was always quietly. I would learn that he possessed a prodigious intellect.

Uncle Gussy sat down on the bed next to Les and lifted him onto his lap.

"While the rest of you have been outside playing," Uncle Gussy announced, having seated us on the floor around the bed, "I came in here and found Lesley by himself."

We looked at one another and wondered what the problem was. We knew Les was a loner who did his own thing. Why should he not sit by himself in the dormitory? Uncle Gussy must have read the expressions on our faces because he went on to explain.

"I found Leslie reading a book. Now I want you to listen to this," and he placed a book in Les's hands.

It was a Peter and Jane book. Each page had a single sentence describing their activities, accompanied with colourful illustrations. With Uncle Gussy's arm around him, Les read it fluently from cover to cover, turning each page after he read it. He had taken the book from the library.

"I'm very proud of you, my boy," Uncle Gussy said, and rewarded him with a ticky.

We all gasped. That was two and a half pennies. Ten gingerbread men. Suddenly reading and writing had a value. And school was where one learned to read and write. It wasn't difficult to conclude that school had become very important indeed.

After everyone had left the dormitory, I picked up the book and found I could read it too. The difference was that Les did it naturally, because he enjoyed it. Instead of playing outside, he preferred to be inside, reading a book. It would never have occurred to me to read a book, let alone visit the library.

During my final year at JCH, I was in Standard 1. Les and I, as usual, were sitting next to each other in the classroom. Our reading ability was being tested and we had to read aloud a section from a book. Les effortlessly read his section and now it was my turn. I was doing reasonably well until I encountered the word 'through'. I had never seen it before.

Les tried to help by prompting me beneath his breath but I chose to ignore him and sat silently staring down at the strange word. Les tried again, this time a little louder, and still I remained silent. Les's third prompt was so loud it might have been heard in the principal's office. By then the teacher had heard enough and moved on to another child. The upshot was that Les was moved to a more advanced reading group whilst I continued with the drongos.

The reason I ignored Les's help was because I was astonished that he was familiar with the pronunciation (and therefore meaning) of a word that I had never seen before. I was immediately aware that this boy was by far my intellectual superior and it was this realisation that shocked me into silence.

Typical of Les, he didn't scold me for not accepting his help, he was just not like that. In fact he never mentioned it again. I was very fond of him but he never reciprocated my friendship, at least not as much as I would have liked. He was always very friendly but stopped short of being a bosom pal. I should mention that Martin, the rascal in the sanatorium, was Les's older brother.

Other boys who, like Martin, were a year or more older, included John,

Karly, and Kevin. Kevin's mum, a nurse at JCH, was a very popular member of staff. She would continue there for a number of decades after I left, eventually becoming its Head and running the place.

Kevin, like Les, was very bright. Every night he would lie on his side in bed and gently rock himself to sleep. We became so accustomed to the sound of his rocking that we would fall asleep listening to it.

"Why do you do it, Kev?" we once asked him.

"I don't know," he said, "I suppose it helps me go to sleep."

John and Karly were not as bright as Kevin, but they were popular boys who plodded along, accepting what was thrown at them.

Apart from Les, I should also mention Joss and Mike who were also my age. Joss had an immense physical strength which he united with the nature of a lamb. I was very close to him and would spend many happy hours in his company.

Mike was an odd-ball who often played the fool and just as often found himself in trouble with Matron. On one occasion he had found a foot-long rusty metal bar near the tennis courts. He picked it up and decided to see how far he could throw it. An older girl ordered him to put it down, telling him that what he was doing was dangerous. He obeyed by throwing it at her.

What happened next was clearly unintentional, we all knew that. Mike was not vicious and undoubtedly he did not intend the bar to go anywhere near the girl. It tumbled as it flew in the air, landing some distance from her, but unfortunately it landed on its end, sprang back up and struck her on her head.

Mike blanched but went whiter still when a familiar voice bellowed down from the main building. Matron, standing on her balcony, had witnessed the entire incident.

"Michael!" she roared. "Get up here immediately!"

I don't know what his punishment was but a while later he emerged to resume his mischief elsewhere. Mike and I were not close but, nonetheless, I still liked him.

I will add mention of an older boy, the oldest among us, and who held great sway over us. His name was Marnie and he was a good two years older. He was probably about nine, or at least approaching nine, and the age difference made him very influential.

One night, for example, as we lay awake chatting in the dark, he persuaded us that he kept birds up his nose and we absolutely believed him. On another occasion he persuaded me to stay awake all night. I did and was very ill the next day.

There was a cruelty in Marnie that was not attractive. With hindsight I believe he was probably deeply disturbed because the last time I saw him, he did a dreadful thing.

I was standing on the flight of steps leading from the entrance down to the quad in front of the main building. A nurse was standing on the quad with her arms akimbo. She was angry because Marnie was being disobedient.

"Marnie!" she shouted, "come down here this moment!"

Marnie was standing on the landing near me, just outside the main entrance. There was an ominous gleam in his eyes as he returned the nurse's stare. He bent his head down and with his eyes on the ground, ran down the steps towards the nurse. He also had his right arm up, parallel with the ground, and bent at right angles. His fist was clenched.

Marnie charged down the steps and I, standing to one side on the steps, suspected he was going to punch the nurse with his fist. She, however, and much to my astonishment, suspected nothing, simply standing there with her hands on her hips. Down he came, speeding up and still she saw nothing amiss. I wanted to shout at her to be careful but couldn't open my mouth.

When Marnie had reached her she was still in the same pose, totally oblivious to the danger. Had Marnie not had his arm up he would simply have run past her. But his arm was up and his clenched fist hit her square in her midriff.

With a loud "Ooooph" she doubled over and remained like that for some time, completely winded. Marnie, having punched her, continued his run, over the road, and onto the grassy area beneath the pine trees. I don't know what became of him but none of us ever saw him again.

Most of the children at JCH were referred there by the Children's Court. Parental neglect, or drug and alcohol abuse, or just the inability of parents to support their children were possible reasons for them being there. Some parents simply had nowhere to keep their children while they were away in another country.

In the latter case, the parents paid the home for the upkeep of their children. If a child was there as a result of a decision made by the Children's Court, then the child invariably became a Ward of the State and was labelled as being 'Committed'. Committed Children were paid for by the State and the institution caring for the child was compelled to apply annually for the remittance necessary for the child's upkeep. Committed children remained 'Committed' until they were old enough to support themselves.

The State would police the institution by sending out a Social Worker who would ensure that the child was not being mistreated. The Social Worker was expected to regularly interview the child and presumably to look for any signs of abuse.

I was committed at age five and would remain a Ward of the State until December 1969, after completing my last year of high school when I was eighteen years old. During all that time I met just one Social Worker and that was when I was seventeen. She spoke to me for five minutes in her car and I told her about a fist fight I had recently witnessed.

* * *

In summer, the heat of the Spanish sun is almost unbearable, even in the mountains. If we didn't head to the beach, Joe and I often drove to the next village to cool off in the public pool, leaving our writing commitments behind.

I'd been in the pool for ages and my fingertips were like sultanas. I climbed out and looked back at Joe.

"I think you are part fish," I said, drying myself with a towel. "Are you ever going to get out of the pool?"

But Joe didn't hear me. He was racing a little Spanish boy, and the boy was winning.

* * *

It was a warm day and we were in the dormitory with a nurse.

"I think I'll take you swimming," she announced, bending over us.

I was so excited that I stretched out my arms and gratefully cupped her cheeks in my hands.

Two things happened almost simultaneously: the first was the look of alarm that appeared on her face and the second was that I snatched my hands away.

Her look of alarm was fleeting and disappeared almost immediately. But her look of alarm wasn't the only reason I snatched my hands away. It was the sense of guilt I felt, that I had done something illegal, that I had no right to touch her face. In my excitement I had forgotten myself.

Ma was totally non-tactile and I never received so much as a hug from her. But the feel of the nurse's cheeks stunned me and I ached to touch them again. I marvelled at the softness. I would have asked, but the look of alarm on her face was enough to deter me.

Nevertheless, on to the swimming pool we went and I would have been the first in. I adored being in the pool and was totally unafraid of the water. I couldn't swim properly but I had seen dogs paddling and I tried to emulate their action. Soon I could swim a short distance but always remained close to the edge. Only the older, more confident, children ventured into the middle.

It was enough that I was in water and I would have stayed there forever had I been allowed to. And I very nearly did. What happened next, I regard as nothing short of a minor miracle.

I was by myself and hanging onto the edge when it occurred to me that I had never touched the bottom. Still clutching the edge I ducked my head beneath the surface and stared down into the blue murky depths. Seeing anything underwater without goggles is difficult but I thought I could see the bottom.

Without a second thought, and without first taking a deep breath, I simply let go of the edge, expecting to plummet to the bottom. I had seen stones fall in water and I was much larger than a stone. I would be at the bottom in no time at all. Once there, I intended to spring back to the surface.

I did fall, beyond the reach of the rim of the pool, and safety, when my body became stationary, suspended some distance below the surface. I was six years old and it would be years before I fully appreciated Archimedes's Principle. Such blissful ignorance can cost one his life.

I tried to claw my way up again but, if anything, sank a little deeper. Neither could I grab hold of anything on the side of of the pool, it was too smooth. I looked down to see how far I was from the bottom but it, too, was out of reach.

The panic I felt was indescribable. I was at my wits' end what to do next and I knew my next breath would be my last. I seriously considered taking that breath and getting the whole sorry business over with. My final resort was to thrust my right arm upwards with my fingers extended. Even today I wonder why I did that, what I might possibly have gained by it.

To my astonishment, and enormous relief, the very tip of my middle finger was taken hold of and I was pulled to the surface.

"There you are," my saviour said, in a weird sing-song voice.

He was a very young boy, about four years old and he was sitting on the side of the pool. I have no idea where he came from and he certainly wasn't there before I attempted my death-defying stunt.

"You saved my life!" I gasped.

"I know," he said, again in that strange sing-song voice.

Then he stood up and ran off, leaving me to ponder my good fortune. I never did see that child again but he did leave me with a lasting memory of a near-death experience.

9

Other People's Families

Ma seldom took me out for more than a day. When she did, she always pined the loss of Lizzy, constantly bombarding me with questions that I was unable to answer. When I told her about the black car, she was fascinated, wanting to know every detail. I wished I hadn't bothered because it only reignited a plethora of additional questions.

I spent some school holiday periods at JCH but most of these times I was farmed out to kindly families who lived in towns along the Witwatersrand, often referred to as the 'Rand Towns'. These sprang up, east and west of Johannesburg, following the discovery of gold in 1886.

The towns that I recall staying in are Springs, Benoni, and Kempton Park but I also remember staying with a family in Cullinan, near Pretoria. Cullinan was where the world's largest diamond, The Great Star of Africa, was found. After being cut and polished, it measured 5.9 centimetres (2.3 inches). I believe it was donated to the Royal Family in Britain and adorns the sovereign's sceptre.

I did stay at other places, but was too young to identify them. I can state with certainty, however, that events occurred that I have never forgotten. Like those from my earliest childhood, these small islands of vividly illuminated memories are surrounded by vast oceans of dark emptiness.

The first has me sitting on the grass with three ladies who are chatting and laughing while they wash a dog with water in a large pail. They speak only Afrikaans but, because of the Afrikaans Place, I understand all that they say.

"I think I will go and have a little lie down," one of the ladies says, mopping her brow in the afternoon sunshine, and she disappears inside the house.

The other two ladies continue with the dog-washing and, when finished, they sit alongside me on the grass and continue their conversation. Then, leaving me behind, they also go into the house.

A few moments later they emerge from the house, wailing and in floods of tears.

"Just twenty minutes ago, she was washing the dog!" one of them says. "Now she's dead!"

I don't recall what happened next.

My next memory has me sitting in the lounge of a house. There is a lady with me and it is afternoon. The lounge window overlooks a shady avenue with trees growing on both sides of a street.

I am standing at the window and I see a boy walking up the avenue, approaching our house. He is my age and seems to have a purpose, but is also hesitant. I turn to the lady.

"I think there is a boy coming here," I say to her, and she joins me at the window.

We stare at the boy who occasionally pauses, as if unsure what to do next. He eventually reaches our house, opens the front gate, walks up the path to the front door and knocks on it. Only then does the lady react and she opens the door.

"I think my mother is dead," the boy says in Afrikaans.

"Go back to your house," the lady says peremptorily. "I'll call the police."

She closes the door on the boy.

I don't remember anything else except feeling very sorry for the boy and wondering what was to become of him.

On my first day with another family, I am taken to a large rectangular swimming pool. It is evening but I'm not there to swim. Instead we are to pick up a young girl who is swimming up and down the length of the pool. She is about fourteen years old.

What impresses me is that she does this effortlessly. As she glides up and down the pool, her style is elegant and smooth and after every fourth stroke, she turns her head to breathe. When she does, she looks directly at me, sizing me up, knowing I have just arrived from the home. I know this, and feel it, but I cannot take my eyes off her. The efficiency of her swimming greatly impresses me. I vow that one day I will learn to swim like that.

Now I am with a family from Benoni. They have children but I cannot remember how many and if they were boys, girls or both. My abiding memory of this family is a visit, one evening, to the town centre to see the Christmas lights. The Town Hall was wondrously illuminated with coloured bulbs that lined the building's edges. In front was a large expanse of lawn that, to my young mind, seemed to stretch to the horizon. The family parked the car next to this grassy area and we tumbled out of the car.

Of course I admired the colourfully decorated Town Hall but, the moment my feet stood on the grass, I was overwhelmed with a desire to run, and run, and run. And I did. Ignoring the shouts of the family behind me, I simply ran as fast as I could, feeling as if all life on the planet was centred in me at that moment. Never again would I experience such an exhilarating love of life. Eventually I returned to the family who didn't scold me for my disobedience.

My memories of the family in Cullinan are a little less vague. I don't recall any children but I am sure there must have been some, I just can't remember.

I do remember riding pillion on a 50cc motor bike which belonged to an older man, perhaps the father or grandfather of the family.

We drove in a car to visit the huge hole where the diamond was discovered and I was told about it. All I saw was a large water-filled crater. I was more interested in the number of brightly coloured birds that flew wildly in the lush surrounding undergrowth. Their coloured plumage contrasted vividly with the brilliant green of the vegetation. The father had brought a rifle, much more powerful than Niels's pellet gun. It fired bullets and made a loud bang when the trigger was pulled.

He pointed the rifle at one of the coloured birds and pulled the trigger. It fell from its perch and I was told to retrieve it. Like the birds that Niels killed, the head lolled as I lifted it from the ground. The greatest difference, however, was the death wound. Whereas I found it difficult to identify the pellet's entry point on Niels's birds, this bird had a huge gaping hole in its chest.

My next memory was living with a family in Springs. I was older and my memory is more distinct. They had two other children, boys, who were much older than I. I latched onto one of them, Peter, who seemed to like me. Peter shared everything he had with me. If he bought sweets, he shared them with me.

The family loved to camp and we travelled down to the Vaal Dam, a large expanse of water, south of Johannesburg. It was a popular destination and many people from the city travelled the thirty odd miles just to have a day out.

We pitched our tents on the banks of the dam and made ourselves comfortable. At night, the adults enjoyed a chat around the *braai*. I was fascinated by the fireflies that congregated every night above the flames. These bright little sparks of flying light were a wondrous sight. To me, they were indistinguishable from the sparks that sometimes flared up from the *braai*.

All day long, I swam in the muddy waters of the dam. I basked in the water's warmth, staring up at the family from where I was immersed, looking for all the world like a crocodile with just snout and eyes above the surface.

In due course I became sunburned and this developed into liquid-filled blisters. I didn't care a hoot and learned to live with the discomfort.

Upon our return to the family home in Springs, Peter and I joined a group of local children and we freely explored the area. All I wore was a pair of shorts, nothing else. We encountered a long black snake swimming in a shallow stream that had carved a route through the soft, red soil. The sides of the banks were sheer but not deep, perhaps three or four feet.

We tormented the snake and it reared, hissed, and spread a large hood. It was a perfect target against the muddy bank and we pelted it with clods of mud. It escaped, quickly disappearing down a storm drain. This concrete tube was large enough to admit us and about ten feet in length, sloping down quite steeply. We followed the snake but, thankfully, it was too quick for us and vanished.

We discovered that the inside of this tube was extremely smooth and slippery. A thin but constant trickle of water ran down its centre and we were able to slide on our backs from top to bottom. The inside was so slippery that we could slide from halfway up the side of the tube and zig-zag our way down. My blisters burst but I didn't care. I was having too much fun.

A few weeks later I was sitting in the street with the other children. Behind me a beautiful blonde girl ordered me to sit still. She wanted something to do while she chatted with the other children. She was a lot older and more mature than the rest of us.

She peeled the dead skin from my sunburned back. The blisters had begun to flake and, with infinite finesse, and aided with particularly long nails, she seized a strip and gently tore it away. I was in heaven. I loved my back being tickled and, as far as I was concerned, I would sit there for the rest of my life, if necessary. It ended when a young man in an open-top sports car invited her to ride with him. She accepted and they drove off.

It was while staying with Peter's family that I experienced something I have been informed is impossible.

10

The Supernatural, Fights and a Letter

Everyone insists that it isn't possible, but I know I stood at the end of a rainbow. I was with Peter at the time and clearly remember doing so, enjoying the extraordinary sensation of stepping in and out of the many colours of light.

In yet another strange experience, we were swimming in a circular water tank beneath a windmill. These were a common sight on the dry *highveld* where the water had to be pumped from reservoirs below the ground. The windmill sucked this valuable resource from below and dumped it in the circular corrugated-iron tank.

I remember standing on a platform on the windmill and gazing down into the dark frog-infested water below. None of us objected to their presence, we simply enjoyed the opportunity of a swim.

The tank was perhaps four or five feet deep and I could either jump or dive in. I had still to learn to dive properly and had no intention of doing so then. That could wait until another time but, for the moment, I intended to jump in. For some inexplicable reason I went in head first. I was really surprised that I had, but even more surprised by what I saw below the water.

A tunnel of silver circular rings appeared from nowhere, each hoop parallel to the next, but directed upwards towards the surface. It was almost as if they had been placed there, for me to swim through, guiding me to the surface. They were irresistible and I duly swam through them, finally breaking the surface. Immediately I dunked my head below the surface to see if the magic rings might still be there, but they had disappeared.

I was hugely excited. I had learned to dive and needed to repeat that, but more importantly, I wanted to see the rings again. Try as a might (and I haven't stopped trying even to the present day) I never did see those wonderful circles again.

My final holiday with a family was spent on a farm in Kempton Park. At this time I was about eight years old and now my memories are much clearer.

Kempton Park is not far from the Johannesburg city centre and, at that time, a large power station dominated the surrounding flat terrain. The huge concrete cooling towers were visible for miles around and whenever I saw them again in the future, I was always reminded of my stay with the family that lived nearby.

The family was Afrikaans speaking but that wasn't a difficulty for me.

Ungrateful wretch that I was, I simply didn't want to be there. It was a Christmas holiday and six weeks stretched ahead of me, the time I would be spending with them.

In truth, I was terribly homesick for Johannesburg Children's Home. It says much for an institution that a child should pine when he is away from it, and I did. I loved the place, I loved the boys around me, I loved the staff, I loved everything about it.

On the day before leaving JCH to stay with this family, I and a bunch of girls and boys were looking at a dilapidated but fully-functional bicycle that had appeared in our midst. We were on the road alongside the quad in front of the main entrance.

Most of us had never ridden a bicycle before and were apprehensive. One older girl had ridden before and she demonstrated the fact by riding up and down the road.

"May I have a try?" I asked.

She calmly handed it over to me and within moments I was cycling as if I had done so all my life. It was a joyous feeling and I rode all the way around the main building, thrilled at the wondrous freedom the machine afforded me. I wanted to ride it forever but the other children scolded me for being greedy and I reluctantly handed it to the next child.

It was events and experiences like this that I was leaving behind to live with this strange family in a strange place. On my first night with them, I cried myself to sleep.

They had one son, a little younger than I was, whose name was Jannie (pronounced 'Yahnee' which is 'Johnny' in English). I suspect he was the reason I was invited to be with them during the holidays, a playmate for their lonely child.

I pushed him away when he tried to befriend me and he complained to his mother. She gave me a dark look and tried to reassure him that all would soon be well. But it took me some time to overcome my malaise, during which time I hardly endeared myself to the family.

Eventually Jannie and I became good friends and we romped around the countryside together. Being a little older I tended to be the leader and generally was responsible for our minor mischiefs.

I loved chasing the chickens that wandered freely around, and hearing them squawk when I caught them. The cows in the field stared dolefully at us as we walked past. We gazed up at the massive pylons that carried electrical power from the power station, hearing the cables buzzing above and occasionally spitting sparks that fell harmlessly on the ground around us.

We observed, but were never allowed to participate in any of the farmyard activities. The cows were milked by hand, the warm, white liquid being collected into galvanised buckets. Cream-coloured cotton cloths, wonderfully soft, covered the buckets and were used to catch thick frothy cream when the milk was carefully decanted into special milk containers with metal snap-on lids. The cream was scraped off into another smaller container which I think was used for making butter.

Far more interesting was the slaughter of the chickens. They were chased and caught and then held so that their heads rested on a wooden block. A swift chop with a sharp axe severed the head and the chicken was instantly released. She would run quite some distance, still squawking (which surprised me), before flopping over. The feathers were plucked and the headless bald carcass was hung by its feet from a hook, the blood dripping from the neck onto the ground in the shed. Very gruesome, but for an eight year old boy, fascinating.

Jannie was given boxing lessons. In fact he had been practising even before I arrived. Because of my initial bad temper, I made no attempt to listen to his tales about his boxing lessons and simply thumped him when he feigned a boxing manoeuvre whilst dancing around and jabbing at me. It had the desired effect and sent him crying to his parents. At the time I didn't much care and hoped they would send me back to JCH.

His father, who worked on the farm, kept on encouraging his son, telling him to persevere. Jannie did but inevitably would return crying after I had thumped him again. Then we became friends and my bullying stopped. I began to listen to his boxing stories. I found them very interesting and wanted to try my hand at the art. This was when his father knew I was ripe for the plucking.

He produced an extra set of boxing gloves and set us up against each other in the farmyard. There was a gleam in his father's eye as he fitted the gloves on my totally inexperienced hands. I wasn't concerned. I planned to belt Jannie and show him who was boss, lessons or no boxing lessons.

Jannie was waiting. He easily side-stepped my clumsy approach and landed a beauty on my cheek, eliciting a howl of delight from his dad.

"Didn't I tell you, son? Didn't I say that you could beat him?"

Jannie was in his element. To cut a long story short, he laid me out, a sorry blubbering mess. That day, about halfway through my stay with this wonderful family, the balance of power shifted noticeably in Jannie's favour. I would never again pick a fight with him and he knew it. From now on there was a new sheriff in town.

His dad would sometimes get drunk in the evenings. He wasn't in any way abusive but one evening he picked up a pistol and was firing it randomly at no particular target. I was not in the least concerned but for some reason, Jannie's mother was, and in consequence, inspired a great fear in Jannie.

The lavatory was a wooden outhouse with a hole cut out of a wooden seat and with pieces of newspaper hanging from a hook on the side. Here Jannie's mum hid us while his father continued his shooting spree.

It wasn't long before his father approached the outhouse and levelled the pistol at it. We could see all this through the gaps in the wood. I am not sure if he would have fired at the outhouse but before he could, Jannie burst through the door.

"Don't shoot me! Don't shoot me!" he screamed.

His father could not believe his eyes. His son exploding from the outhouse was clearly the last thing he expected to see.

"I'm not going to shoot you, son," his father said quietly trying to reassure a distraught Jannie, bending down and putting an arm around his shoulders.

I returned to the house but in my heart knew his father would never have done such a thing. I was never afraid at any time and never once thought we were in any danger. Why his mother thought her husband should harm us is still a mystery to me.

* * *

Back at JCH, Uncle Gussy gathered us in the library. In front of each child was a piece of paper and a pencil.

"Now I want you to write a letter of thanks to the people you stayed with," he said.

Try as I might, I was unable to write a single word. I simply couldn't. The other children seemed to be managing quite well but I was a hopeless case. Tears of frustration spilled down my cheeks.

"Joe! Joe! Why are you crying?" he asked, and sat beside me.

"I can't write," I blubbered.

"Oh, don't let that bother you, child," he gently chided. "Now, let's see."

He took the tear-stained paper from me and, taking up the pencil, he began to write.

"It was Mr and Mrs van der Merwe that you stayed with?"

I nodded.

"And you had a good time?"

"Yes."

"Then we will say that. And of course we want to say thank you, don't we?"

Another nod.

I would like to offer my most heartfelt thanks to all the wonderful people who so kindly accepted me into their homes. I know I am very late in doing so but it is all I have to offer.

"Right," said Uncle Gussy, "all that's left is for you to write your name. You can do that, can't you?"

Yes, I could, and I did, albeit clumsily.

This was yet another example of Uncle Gussy's sensitive handling of a delicate situation. He loved children and knew how to speak to them at their level.

11

The Sea and Games

"**Y**ou're going to the seaside," Uncle Gussy told us one day.

I had already seen the vast ocean when I was with Ma and Lizzy but I was still excited about seeing it again. I also appreciated that it was a long way away and would require an exciting train journey to get there.

It was all sponsored by the Star newspaper. The Star was a popular English language daily that was regularly at variance with the Afrikaner Nationalist government. For one reason or another, the government often shut it down, although I only became aware of this much later when I was older.

For the moment, all that concerned me was that this newspaper was paying for us to enjoy a week at the seaside in Durban. The charity was called The Star Seaside Fund and was for disadvantaged children, not just those from JCH. About eight of us from JCH, all boys, were selected to go.

Off we went, enjoying a long train journey through the night, down to Durban on the south coast. It took about eleven hours on the slow-moving train and we slept on bunks, six to a compartment.

Once in Durban, we were shown into a big building with a vast open plan dormitory. A hundred or more beds were neatly arranged to receive children between the ages of eight and fourteen. We ate our meals in a large dining hall and during the day we invaded the public beach which was walking distance away.

Apart from swimming in the sea, we investigated the many rock pools and on one occasion we found a tiny crab. One of the older boys, about fourteen, picked up the crab and stared at it. Then he put it back in the water.

"Just leave it alone. Don't touch it," he told the rest of us and left.

I couldn't resist and crouching down, picked it up. From out of nowhere the boy appeared above me.

"I thought I told you to leave it alone," he said and struck me in the mouth with the back of his hand.

The blow caused my eyes to water and I quickly returned the creature to the water. Only in the Afrikaans Place had I experienced such violence. There, I was taught that the avoidance of pain was a mighty incentive for following rules and regulations. Clearly, I hadn't learned my lesson and I never did.

In the open plan dormitory I was alongside another boy, about my age, but not from JCH. Like me, the JCH boys were scattered about amongst the other boys. The girls occupied a similar dormitory on a floor above us.

The boy next to me clenched his fist at me. I had done nothing to invite this behaviour but remembered the blow to my mouth on the beach. I hunkered down on my bed, protecting my head with my arms and whimpered like a baby. When nothing happened I glanced up and saw him still in the same pose above me. I repeated my action and so it carried on until he got bored and walked away.

Coward that I was, my reaction had saved me from a beating and I would repeat it every time he came near me.

"Look at this," he said to one of his friends, and he lifted his fist to hit me.

I duly responded as I always had and the two boys laughed and walked away. As far as I was concerned, my behaviour had protected me and I was content to repeat it until doomsday if necessary.

Unbeknown to me, the other JCH boys had been observing me all this time.

"Joe, you big baby, what's the matter with you? The next time he does that, stand up to him!" one of them said to me.

In a flash I saw the light. I am naturally a coward but there are times that one should stand up for oneself and clearly this was one of them.

I returned to my bed waiting for the boy to turn up. He did and immediately threatened me again. I stood up, and stared boldly into his eyes. Fear flickered in them and I saw him glance over my shoulder. I turned around and all the JCH boys were standing quietly behind me. He fled and we gave chase but we didn't catch him. He never troubled me again.

* * *

Back in JCH, Uncle Gussy had enrolled us in the Sea Scouts.

We got to wear neat round sailors hats with the words *Sea Scouts* embroidered in gold around the rim.

One might think that joining the Sea Scouts had something to do with sailing and water. However, in our case, we didn't even see a boat, let alone any water. We never learned to tie knots or indeed to do anything scouty.

No, the real reason for enrolling us in the Sea Scouts was far more subtle and one that we boys greatly applauded and approved of. Yet again, Uncle Gussy had spotted an opportunity for us to have a great time and had seized it with both hands.

The reason was football. We loved playing soccer on the playing field and Uncle Gussy knew this. By enrolling us in the Sea Scouts, we would automatically be included in a league and play against Scout troops from other parts of Johannesburg. It was perfect.

The footwear and kit appeared and we were ready to take on all comers. Uncle Gussy drove us in the home's bus to our first venue, a full-sized football pitch, somewhere in the city, and we all gasped.

It was at least four times the size of our playing field but the greatest shock was seeing the goal posts. Ours at JCH were two metal posts painted white and no higher than the tallest of us and about four feet apart. The regulation set, now before us, was positively cavernous by comparison. It dwarfed Joss, our goalkeeper, whom we thought nobody could get a ball past. At JCH we considered him the greatest goalkeeper in the world. What was more, this goal had a cross bar and an attached net, neither of which we had seen before.

When the opposing team exited their changing room, it was clear that each player was at least two years older than any of us. We were in for a thrashing. By the end of the game, Joss was the only one of us that actually had an opportunity to touch the ball. He spent most of the time retrieving it from the back of his net. The rest of us simply chased after shadows as the opposing team ran circles around us. They openly laughed at us and after deciding that twelve goals were enough, they simply passed the ball to one another, making us run after it. It was embarrassing.

Uncle Gussy didn't mind. It was the beginning of a steep learning curve and we had played our first official match. Experience counted for everything.

He then arranged for us to see a match, with professional footballers, taking place in an all-seated stadium. I was greatly impressed and marvelled at the efficient use of the ball as the players accurately passed to one another. This, I believed, was more important than the dribbling skills of individual players.

Sadly our losing streak never deserted us. We never won a single game and we comfortably lounged at the bottom of the league table. But the pleasure we derived from these games was immeasurable.

* * *

Sometimes Uncle Gussy allowed some of us to accompany him to a huge open air market, somewhere in Johannesburg. Here he bought the vast amount of fruit and vegetables the home would consume in a month.

He knew we loved to go because of the freely available delights that fell from the stalls. We feasted like there was no tomorrow, guzzling on a variety of fruits. Peaches, pears, plums and apricots were amongst a variety that littered the smooth stone floor. We had no scruples about retrieving and eating unwashed fruit from the ground.

"Joe? How is the writing going? I haven't seen you doing any for ages. Every time I see you on the computer, you're playing that silly game."

No answer.

"Joe? Did you hear me?"

"Ssh, I have to discover this secret. And shoot the monsters trying to stop me."

"How far have you got with your book?"

Joe sighed and turned away from the flashing monitor. Behind him an armed pig, dressed in uniform, leaped out from its hiding place in a cave, levelled its weapon and fired.

"That's the trouble, Vicky. I've got to the part where I leave JCH and it's really hard to write about."

"Ah, when you were nine years old."

"That's right. I will carry on, but I just want to kill a few pigs and monsters first."

* * *

I was now reaching the age of nine, and the time approached when I had to leave that children's haven. Rumours reached us that the next institution, Johannesburg Home for Boys, or JHB was not as pleasant an experience as Johannesburg Children's Home. Martin, Kevin, John and Karly had already spent a year in The Boys' Home and we were about to follow them there.

Karly paid us an unexpected visit.

"It's tough, Joe," he said. "For a start, you have to make your own bed every day. You're also given lots of jobs to do, like sweeping the dormitory floors and cleaning the toilets."

"No!"

At my beloved JCH we never did any chores. Everything was done for us by the staff and African servants. I would soon learn that we had enjoyed a very spoiled existence indeed.

At the beginning of 1961, Les, Joss and I, and a few other boys, were driven by Uncle Gussy in the Home bus, passing through the main entrance for the last time. Not a word was spoken as we began the half-hour journey to The Boys' Home.

The atmosphere was thick with the grief that we felt at having to leave. Somebody sobbed, I don't know who, but it was the catalyst for a general quiet weeping by a number of others. I gritted my teeth, successfully fighting the urge to weep with the rest. Uncle Gussy remained impassive but I think that he, too, was affected by the atmosphere and was sorry to see us go.

Soon we arrived at the place that was to be my home for the next nine years. We climbed out of the bus and I was delighted when the first person I saw was Karly.

"Come on, Joe, I'll show you around!" he said.

But first I wanted to say goodbye to Uncle Gussy. It had not taken us long to disembark and, having greeted Karly, I turned back to the bus and was very surprised to find that it had gone. I imagined Uncle Gussy wasn't the type for fond farewells and had departed as speedily as possible. Either that or he felt the pang of our separation as keenly as we did. Whatever the reason, I greatly regretted not saying my last goodbye to a man that was the closest to a father that I could have wished for.

Rumours later reached us that he had behaved inappropriately with one of the older girls and had been asked to leave. I refused to believe the talk and still don't.

* * *

In March, 1974, when I was twenty-two years old, I left South Africa and didn't return until November 1994, two decades later. I had become a citizen of the United Kingdom and, for a brief two week holiday, was returning to the land of my birth.

South Africa had recently undergone a bloodless revolution in which power was handed over from the white Nationalist government to the predominantly black African Nationalists.

All this I found very interesting but I had an overwhelming desire to visit JCH and see how it might have changed during my prolonged absence.

I passed through the familiar front gates, travelled up the tarred road and was soon standing in front of the familiar main building. No change there. Behind me, the grassy area was the same but, understandably, the fir trees were somewhat taller.

I didn't bother to enter the main building but walked around to the path that led down to the playing field. It hadn't changed much but I could see that radical changes had occurred on the playing field below.

Bungalows had sprouted up where we had once played soccer. The tennis courts and other buildings had disappeared but the swimming pool was still there. To my left, the path leading diagonally down through the rockery had not seen much change either.

Down I went for a closer inspection of the bungalows. I approached the nearest one and was about to shade my eyes to peer through the small-paned windows when I noticed that one of the panes was missing. More astonishingly, a five year old boy with blonde hair and blue eyes was staring solemnly back at me. It was 4.30 in the afternoon but he was dressed in pyjamas and sitting on one of the familiar high metal beds we had slept in.

Immediately I understood that nothing really had changed. The facilities, previously available in the main building, had simply been transferred to these bungalows. The dormitories might be much smaller now, but the beds were still the same.

"Did you do that?" I gently asked him, pointing at the empty space where the pane should have been.

He gave me a solemn nod.

"And that's why you are in your pyjamas so early?"

Again the solemn nod.

I might have been gazing at a reflection of myself forty years ago.

Part Three

The Boys' Home

12

How it all Worked

"Keep it simple, Joe," I said, reading over his shoulder.
"What do you mean?"
"You have a tendency to over-describe. Just keep it simple."
"Noted," said Joe.
"No, I don't think you're listening. Ask yourself, do your readers really want to know every detail of the architecture of the place?"
"Some will."
"Most won't."
"Well, they can skip over this bit then, can't they?"
I sighed as Joe carried on typing.

* * *

In 1915, during World War One, the Reverend Noel Aldridge, an Anglican priest, decided to create a refuge for boys in Johannesburg. It would be called The Johannesburg Home for Boys (JHB) and was primarily aimed at those boys whose fathers had been killed during the Great War and who now had nowhere to live and were unable to support themselves.

Reverend Aldridge, cap in hand, approached several corporations controlling the gold mines that proliferated in and around Johannesburg. These generously donated both funds and lands and a fifty-five acre (twenty-two hectare) plot was acquired on the east side of the city.

The land, essentially in the middle of nowhere at that time, sloped gently downwards from a public road. The services of Sir Herbert Baker, then a famous architect, were secured. His penchant for rough stone, prominent in all his designs, was especially obvious at the Home.

The main complex comprised three single-level structures in the shape of the Greek letter π. The upper limb, which was the longest and ran parallel to the public road, was to be the administrative block, containing the offices of the Headmaster and his deputy, separated by another for their shared secretary. Also included were classrooms, a tailor's room, a linen room, the quarters for a resident Anglican priest, and a staff meeting room.

The other limbs in the π shape were to be a Chapel on the left and a dining hall on the right. The three structures enclosed a large paved square, destined to be the Parade Ground. Because of the slope of land, the lower end of the Parade Ground had to be raised and access was via three sets of stone steps: one at the dining Hall end, one at the Chapel end, and one in the middle.

An external corridor was the single unifying feature of the main complex. Paved with a smooth grey-black slate, it was bounded by the buildings on one side and the Parade Ground on the other. It ran the full length of the administrative block, seamlessly joining those belonging to the Chapel and dining Hall. The corridor overlooked the Parade Ground through multiple stone arches from a height of a few feet. Viewed from the Parade Ground, the arches resembled the cloisters in a monastery.

In the centre of the long administrative building, a square tower rose to twice the height of the building on either side. It would serve several purposes but primarily it was to be the living quarters of a resident Anglican priest. It was also the main entrance to the Home.

Its outer façade was formidable. Long arrow-slits on either side of a large entrance arch, with heavy wooden doors covered in black metal studs and substantial black metal handles, might leave visitors with the impression that they were entering a fortress. The doors opened into a darkened area, reinforcing the impression. Opposite the entrance arch was another that framed a view of the Parade Ground beyond.

Access to the rooms in the Tower was via a flight of stairs that led from an arched opening in a corner of the darkened entrance. At the top of these stairs was a door that led to the resident priest's living quarters. His rooms were divided into two levels. The first was a reception area with a covered balcony. The balcony overlooked the Parade Ground from a rough-stone archway. Above his reception rooms were his bathing and sleeping quarters.

One final feature of the Tower was the Chapel bell. This hung beneath a simple rough-stone structure on the roof above the balcony. A long thin rope linked the bell's clapper to a sturdy wooden bell-pull in the corridor below. A tug on the bell-pull elicited a single gong from its medium-sized housing.

The roofs of all the buildings in the main complex, including the Tower, were crowned with the same reddish-brown terra-cotta tiles. Atop the pinnacle of the Tower roof was a cruciform that served a dual purpose. The first was religious but the second was more practical. A lightning conductor provided the cross with a solid support as well as diverting the all-too frequent lightning strikes from the highest point in the entire complex. Surrounding the complex was a generous thoroughfare that branched off to the other structures within the extensive grounds.

In November, 1921, some six years after the first stone was laid, the complex was opened by no less a personage than His Royal Highness Prince Arthur of Connaught, the Governor-General of the Union of South Africa and a grandson of Queen Victoria.

Access to the property was via three entrances that faced onto the public road. These, like those at JCH, were un-gated and unguarded. The middle entrance was opposite the arched doorway of the Tower and, from the Parade Ground, one had a clear view of it through the two arches at the front and back of the Tower. Finally, a low barbed wire fence surrounded the entire property.

* * *

"You didn't listen to a word I said, did you?" I said, exasperated. "Honestly! 'A lightning conductor provided the cross with a solid support as well as...' blah blah blah. Do you really think that's important to your story?"

"What do you mean?"

"I told you not to add too much detail!"

"Well, I have to explain what the place looked like, and how it all worked. Anyway, like I said before, readers can skip this bit if they want."

"You mean there's more?"

"Well, yes."

"Oh, for goodness sake!"

* * *

As the years passed, the roads were tarred and additional buildings were added. Four two-level Houses, each accommodating forty boys as well as a Housemaster and his assistant, were erected near the main complex. They were named after benefactors who had willed the Home substantial amounts of money.

Two Senior Houses, Spackman House and Taylor House, were for boys aged between fifteen and eighteen. They were located closest to the main complex with Spackman near the dining hall and Taylor near the chapel.

The thoroughfare surrounding the main complex was extended to bypass Spackman House and reach down to two Junior Houses, Simpson and Beaton, with Simpson House being the furthest. The Junior Houses were for boys aged between nine and fourteen.

Although the road ended at Simpson House, it continued as a narrow well-maintained path around the House, passing a square single-level fenced-in building on its left. This was the Home's laundry.

The path continued downwards for another thirty yards, ending in yet another single-level square building, the living quarters for the male African staff. It was poorly lit and poorly furnished and was called the *Kaiya*, the Zulu word for 'home'. These men were expected to perform menial tasks throughout the Home. Some worked in the kitchen, some maintained the extensive grounds, some were needed in the workshop, and some worked as cleaners or were called upon to perform any labouring duties as required.

Opposite the chapel was a set of open-fronted garages that housed the Home vehicles. These were alongside a gated and walled-in workshop, where tools and machines were stored. A full-time white workshop manager ensured the machinery was always in proper working order.

The workshop also accommodated a part-time cobbler who repaired the boys' shoes and was the venue, too, for a visiting barber.

Mention should be made of the kitchen. This was L-shaped and bolted onto the dining hall. Apart from a single doorway that separated it from the dining hall, a large hatchway provided access for food and crockery to be efficiently passed to the boys at meal times.

A sanatorium, known as Surgery, a single-level building, was located near Spackman House and the kitchen.

Finally, the Headmaster and his family were housed in a comfortable single-level bungalow just below Taylor House. The Deputy Head and his family lived in a similar bungalow between Simpson and Beaton Houses.

* * *

"Joe, have you quite finished?"

"No, not really. I want to tell them about the sports facilities."

"I guess there's no point in saying that you've described enough?"

"No point at all."

"Well, don't blame me if your readers throw the book across the room in frustration."

"I won't."

"Mind you, I still can't believe what facilities you had! I went to an expensive girls' private school in England, and we didn't have a fraction of the stuff you had at the Boys' Home. I can't believe you were allowed pets. You could ride horses, go swimming, and you had fantastic cameras and a dark room for developing your own photos…"

"Are you jealous?"

"Yes, a bit."

"Don't be. I'd have given all that up to have a normal family life with ordinary parents."

* * *

The sports facilities at the Home were, quite simply, second to none. A narrow path, about a hundred metres long, led directly from the back entrance of Spackman House, passing Beaton House on its left and ended in a flight of rough-stone steps that led down to the sports fields. These accommodated two full-sized soccer pitches.

The broad tarred thoroughfare that surrounded the main complex, apart from being extended to reach the Junior Houses, also made its way past Taylor House to the Headmaster's bungalow. It did not end there but continued, un-tarred and stony, past a horse paddock on the right, the sports fields on the left, past two all-weather tennis courts below the paddock, and ended in two additional sand-covered full-sized soccer pitches called the Old Boys' Fields, These were located at the lowest point of the property and formed its lower boundary.

As if the facilities for soccer, cricket, athletics, tennis and horse riding were not enough, the Home provided an additional gem. This was a swimming pool, thirty metres long by ten metres wide, the venue for recreational swimming and the Home's annual swimming gala. Situated near the Surgery and above the Junior Houses, it even boasted a high ceilinged gymnasium alongside. The gym was well equipped with all the latest apparatus and was also the venue for a visiting boxing instructor who imparted his knowledge and skills to boys wishing to learn the art.

* * *

"Finished with all the descriptions?"

"Yes."

"Thank goodness. But I have a nasty feeling you're going to start pontificating on the subject of discipline."

"You know me too well," sighed Joe. *"Yes. It has to be said."*

It was my turn to sigh.

"Listen, Joe, I'm sure it was no worse than expensive boys' boarding schools in England at the same time. Corporal punishment was the norm everywhere in those days."

"I know, but that doesn't make it right."

"No, of course not. Thank goodness it isn't allowed anymore. But don't dwell on the cruel, dark stuff. There were lots of things about the Boys' Home you loved, too. Never forget that."

"I'll try not to."

* * *

Somebody once accurately described the Johannesburg Home for Boys as 'a place of militaristic piety'. The religious nature of the Home was obvious: it was an Anglican establishment and attendance in Chapel was compulsory. The source of its martial nature, however, was not so apparent.

Reverend Aldridge probably approached the South African Army for financial support. What is certain is that a cadet force was established and the boys were given the rudiments of a military training. This included marching and shooting and a firing range was constructed in a corner of the Sports Fields. Weapons (Lee-Enfield .303 bolt-action rifles) were provided and stored in a locked armoury, below the Chapel, at the stone steps leading to the Parade Ground above.

At some time in the 1940s or 50s, the weapons were returned to the Army and the shooting was discontinued. Cadets continued, however, and were supported by a fully provisioned marching military band. Instruments included drums, cymbals, bugles and trumpets. No doubt the Army warmly rubbed its hands, knowing it had a rich vein of military personnel to draw upon in times of conflict.

Obedience and discipline, one might argue, are necessary attributes within any military environment. Failure in either could lead to a catastrophe and offenders are likely to be penalised. In the military, these punishments are meted out by court martial but what disciplinary measures might one apply to personnel within a *schoolboy* cadet force?

The answer to this question, I believe, led to a system of bullying and punishment that began with the cadets and then spread throughout the Home. The Deputy Headmaster, Housemasters, and Assistant Housemasters liberally brandished thin, hooked, bamboo canes, whipping a miscreant's behind until it bled. 'Cuts' was an apt description for these lashings.

"Hey, Twead, those cuts you had today made your backside bleed!"

I hadn't been in the Home very long and the comment was from another boy in the communal shower with me. Surprised, I swung my head around and saw the flecks of blood above and below the weals where the cane had landed. These weals, initially pallid and swollen, would bruise and discolour, eventually changing into every hue of the rainbow before disappearing. Unfortunately they never did because a new set would soon replace them.

One day we gently chided Adrian who refused to sit still at the dining room table.

"I can't!" he wailed, "I was given cuts twice today and my backside is too sore to sit down!"

We understood and laughed but that evening Adie ate his dinner standing.

The punishment wasn't limited to the use of a cane. I was slapped, kicked, and even my nose was punched, and that was just by the Housemasters. These slaps, kicks and punches were more common amongst the boys and bullying was rife. Housemasters rarely heeded the boys' complaints, preferring to endorse a policy that frankly made their jobs easier.

One should not be disheartened by such tales of woe. In spite of them, I would enjoy some of the most wondrous experiences of my life. At least the punishments were predictable (some might say deserved), unlike those at the Afrikaans Place where they were unexpected and administered for no apparent reason. At the Boys' Home I knew what was coming and the reasons why.

The Children's Home was a loving parent that gently guided me through the rights and wrongs that any normal parent might wish to teach its child. The Boys' Home was a harsher, more brutal place where, without any guidance whatever, I would teach myself the rudiments of adulthood. How successful I was, I have never been able to judge.

All I can say is that, in time, I grew to both love and hate the place in equal measure. It left me with indelible memories that I have never been able to shake off.

* * *

"Okay, can we get on with the story now? Have you got all that stuff out of your system?"

"Yes, Miss."

"Thank goodness."

* * *

13

Cuts and Dorms

Johannesburg, January 1961

When we arrived, the first person I met at the Home was Karly.

"Hey, Joe, I'll show you around the place," he said in greeting.

It was good to see a familiar face.

* * *

"You already said you met Karly in an earlier chapter," I said. "Why are you repeating yourself?"

"I'm just reminding the reader that I had arrived in the Boys' Home. You used the same technique in 'Chickens' in the first paragraph of the book. I quite liked it so I thought I'd use it too."

"Oh, okay," I said, walking away. "Copycat."

* * *

JCH was not the only children's home to send its nine year olds to the Boys' Home. Several other homes were sprinkled among the suburbs of Johannesburg.

I therefore recognised none of the other new arrivals when we were eventually shown into the Housemaster's flat in Simpson House. I was bitterly disappointed that Les and Joss were not with me. They had been allocated to Beaton House.

It was early January, 1961, a little less than forty years after the main complex was opened. I was nine years old and Simpson House was to be my home for the next five years. It made the greatest impact on me during my stay in the Home, and the memories of it are still etched deeply into my psyche.

"My name is Mr Brian," said the Housemaster, "but you will address me as *sir*, do you understand?"

"Yes, sir," we dutifully replied.

Mr Brian was quietly spoken and never raised his voice. He was handsome with dark hair, blue eyes and a pale complexion. He was young, tall, and somewhat effeminate. He seldom wore a tie, preferring a cravat, but was always immaculately turned out. He was a fastidious man, cultured and intelligent, whose interests were non-sporty, mainly musical, a talent he exploited in his capacity as choir master. He was the Chapel organist but also enjoyed thumping out tunes on a piano in his flat. We were led to believe that he won the piano in an essay-writing competition at some unknown university. He owned a dog, a cocker spaniel called Barry. He would be my Housemaster for the next three years.

Mr Brian's flat was located above Simpson House's ablutions. It comprised a bedroom, a small bathroom and an even smaller kitchen. But the central room, the one we all stood in now, the first room a boy saw when entering his flat, the room wherein he kept his piano and the gramophone player from which music was piped into the dormitories, the room where comfortable sitting chairs were juxtaposed between musical and personal paraphernalia, the room that prominently displayed a thin bamboo cane on a wall, delicately balanced on two supports, the room where we boys would be regularly beaten, was this room, his sitting room.

The canings didn't begin immediately. A month elapsed during which we were lulled into a false sense of security. Then one day Mr Brian announced that he was tired of seeing how untidy our lockers were and that future transgressors would be punished. The punishments followed almost immediately and it would soon be a common sight to see a line of offenders on the landing outside his flat. From within the swish and thwack of a cane being applied to young behinds could be heard. The door would open and a teary, red-faced boy would emerge only to be replaced by the next in line.

"What are you here for?" somebody would whisper in the queue.

"Untidy locker."

"How many cuts?"

"Three."

Having a very low pain threshold, I detested these beatings. I am not sure if Mr Brian enjoyed administering them but certainly they did nothing to deter me from any mischief I might have been planning.

Mr Brian's routine was always the same. He would briefly but quietly explain to a boy why he was being caned and then tap the floor with the tip of the cane. He was marking the spot where the boy was expected to stand before bending down to touch his toes while keeping his legs straight. The boy might complain that he was undeserving of the punishment and Mr Brian would answer the plea with another tap. Persistent pleas were met with persistent taps and eventually the boy was forced to bend down. Depending on the length of the delay, additional strokes were added. Then the cane would literally whistle before landing loudly on a soft behind. Only the toughest boys accepted the punishment without flinching. It ended when Mr

Brian stopped tapping the floor. Rarely was it just one stroke and the average was three.

Mr Brian usually closed his door but one day I inadvertently witnessed him beating a boy. I was surprised to see that both his feet actually left the ground when he delivered the blow. At this time I did not wear underpants and the thin material of my shorts/pyjamas was all that protected me from that malignant stick. I am therefore not surprised that the cuts I received drew blood.

The canings now became a daily occurrence and I regarded Mr Brian's three-year tenure as nothing short of a reign of terror. Thankfully, there were hiatus periods, when the punishments were put on hold, but these were all too brief.

The caning didn't stop at the Home either. School teachers inflicted beatings on top of those already received and, like Adie, we found it difficult to sit without wincing.

* * *

Simpson House was identical to Beaton and Taylor Houses. Its simple rectangular shape was spoiled by the addition of an ablution block, above which was the Housemaster's flat.

A single narrow doorway on the corner of the ground floor served as the House entrance. Inside, one had three choices: ascend a flight of stairs leading to the floor above, walk down a narrow passageway leading to half the ablutions and beyond, or enter a doorway leading to a common room and one of the dormitories. Walking down the narrow passage, one arrived at another, less used, entrance.

It was, however, identical to the main entrance, giving access to the other half of the ablutions, an identical flight of stairs leading to the floor above, and a doorway to another common room and dormitory. The two staircases met at the infamous common landing outside the Housemaster's flat.

Here the stairs parted in opposite directions leading to the upper dormitories. Next to these dormitories were, on one side, the Headboy's rooms, and on the other, the Assistant Housemaster's room. The House was perfectly symmetrical, both halves having two dormitories, a common room, a small flat and ablutions. The only exception was the Housemaster's flat which was spread above the ablutions.

***

"Joe! You're doing it again!" I exclaimed.
"Doing what?"
"Describing stuff too much!"

76

"Whose book is this?"

"Yours..."

"Well, stop pouting. I need to explain how the Home worked."

Joe turned his back on me and carried on tapping at the keyboard.

***

In the middle of the narrow passage and located in a sizeable rectangular niche beneath the stairs, was a bain-marie (we always pronounced it as the 'bay-meray'). The evening meals were prepared in the kitchen in the main complex, then carted down to the Junior Houses to be kept warm in the bain-maries. One of the common rooms was converted into a dining room having a suitable number of benches, tables and chairs.

I, along with the other new boys, were allocated Dorm 4, which was on the ground floor and opposite the outside laundry. There were ten of us plus the Patrol Leader, who was in charge, and his deputy who was called the Corporal. These were much older boys, fourteen years old, and therefore giants compared to us nine year olds. They did not hesitate to punch, slap or kick us should we annoy them in any way and initially even had the power to cane us. This practice thankfully ended and became the sole domain of the Housemasters.

The dormitories were graded according to age, with Dorm 1 housing the oldest boys. Patrol Leaders and Corporals were put in charge of each dormitory and overseeing it all was the Headboy of the House.

Each dormitory had twelve simple, metal beds, each with a small metal locker alongside. These were lockable but only if a boy had a lock with which to keep it secure. Most did not bother and theft of anyone's personal items was greatly frowned upon. Thieves, if discovered, were beaten (by both the boys and Masters) and ostracised. Theft was rare but nonetheless it did occur.

On each bed was a mattress, two white sheets, a pillow with white pillow-slip, two blankets and, for the few bed-wetters, a red rubber under-sheet to protect the mattress. Fortunately, I was not one but I silently sympathised with those that were. Some boys were intolerant, accusing bed-wetters of being lazy during the night.

"Get up and go to the ---- toilet, you lazy ----!" the Patrol Leader would snarl.

It made no difference because the next morning their beds were wet again.

Apart from the small metal lockers alongside every bed, separate tall metal lockers were provided for school and Home blazers. These lockers were stacked in a row at the end of the dormitory.

Each boy was issued with a towel, white and khaki shirts, school and Home neckties, grey or black socks, a pair of black shoes, grey shorts for school and Home wear, and pyjamas. The clothing, towels and bedding were not new, inherited from previous generations of boys who had passed through the Home, replaced only when they became too worn.

We had three meals a day, attended local schools, a barber cut our hair and a cobbler tended to our footwear. In short, apart from simple homely affection, we were given absolutely everything we possibly needed.

14

Injustice

Every morning, except at weekends, a bugler sounded reveille at 6.00 am. At weekends it was 7.00 am. He was a member of the Home military band and he always performed the task from the road alongside the Dining Hall. Thereafter, the routine for each House was dictated by its own electric bell which was operated from a switch in the Housemaster's flat. These bells ruled the boys' lives, calling them to various activities throughout a day. It was shrill and boys ignored it at their peril. The routine for a typical weekday was as follows:

- Bugler sounds reveille at 6:00am
- Showers and get dressed for school by 6:30am
- House chores until 7.00am
- Breakfast attended and completed by 7:30am
- Get to school for 8:00am start
- School-day ends at 2.00pm
- Lunch shortly thereafter
- Free (unless gardening or cadets) until 5.00pm
- Showers and dressing for evening meal at 6:30pm
- Prep from 7.00pm until 8.00pm
- Free until 9.00pm
- House lights turned off for bedtime at 9.00pm
- Bugler sounds last post at 9.00pm

The free times were invariably spoiled by House Meetings. The bell would ring continuously, calling all boys to assemble in the common room. The members of each dorm would line up along one of the walls of the square room with the Housemaster addressing the boys from the middle. The state of our lockers was responsible for one of the first we had.

"I've called this meeting," said Mr Brian, "because I am not happy with the conditions of the lockers. I took the liberty of inspecting a few while you were at school and the ones I looked at were extremely untidy. In future, if I find an untidy locker, the boy responsible will be punished. Do I make myself clear?"

"Yes, sir," we mumbled, and were dismissed.

What I didn't realise was that the inspections would begin immediately because shortly afterwards I and a number of others were called to his flat where we received the first of many canings. No doubt this initial one was to make an example of us and designed to teach the others a lesson. Unfortunately, it wasn't learned and the beatings persisted.

To aggravate matters, the Patrol Leaders, no longer having the power to cane boys, were invited to send offenders to the Housemaster who was only too pleased to carry out the task for them.

"My Patrol Leader sent me because I was late for showers," I said to Mr Brian.

Without a word he closed the door to his flat and removed the cane from its pride of place on the wall. He tapped a spot on the floor with the tip. By now I knew the drill and, other than jerking up when the blows landed, tried to be as stoic as possible. I failed miserably and bawled like a baby.

Sometimes the injustice was so great that I did not mind the caning. Our dorm members were in the common room and we were being addressed by our Patrol Leader.

"I'm tired of you lot not listening to me," he began and we stared at him. "If I tell you do something, you just ignore me and I'm getting sick of it."

There was nothing unusual in this, we had heard it all before and didn't pay much mind to his words. It was bed time and we simply wanted to go to sleep.

"You laugh when I tell you anything…"

At this point he paused and carefully looked at us. We, just as carefully, stared back at him. Then from nowhere he released a thunderous fart which he followed immediately with, "Pop goes the weasel!"

For us nine year olds, this was sublime humour and, of course, we laughed. Even today I laugh thinking about it.

"You, you, you, up to Mr Brian!" said the Patrol Leader, selecting those that were laughing the hardest.

"What for?" we complained.

"For laughing, of course!"

I laughed all the way up the stairs. To me, the injustice of it was wonderful. My mirth, however, was somewhat subdued by the caning.

* * *

"Joe, I can definitely understand why you laughed when he said 'Pop goes the weasel' but I can't understand why you thought the injustice was 'wonderful,'" I said, puzzled.

"Don't you think it was exquisitely outrageous and unfair?"

"Yes, it was hugely unfair! But that would make me cross, not make me

laugh."

"Well, we must have very different senses of humour."

* * *

It was not the last time that I would laugh having been unjustly punished. Several times in the future, a good friend would report me to a school teacher, accusing me of doing something of which I was totally innocent. The friend knew I delighted in anything ridiculous and that I would be unable to refrain from laughing at the injustice of it.

One such was Eugene Tait who could make me laugh with just a look or a word. He was forever deliberately getting me into the kind of trouble that ended in me being caned.

For example, without my knowledge, he would hide pieces of expensive school equipment in my school bag (we had rucksacks in which to carry our books) then, ensuring I was within hearing, report me to the teacher.

"Sir," he would say, "I saw Twead putting something in his bag. I think it was a bunsen burner. Should he be doing that, sir?"

Naturally he would accompany the statement with a look at me and I would begin to smell a rat. Unfortunately the hint of smile would appear on my lips and the teacher would smell a rat too, but not the same one that I did.

"Well, Twead, did you?" the teacher asked.

"Sir, I did not! I haven't been near my bag."

"I don't believe him, sir," Eugene would say and I would begin to laugh, another fatal error.

"Now, boy!" the teacher thundered, "open your bag and show me what you have inside!"

"Sir," I said, by now knowing full well that the bunsen would be inside, "if there is a bunsen burner in my bag, Tait put it there."

"Did you, Tait? Did you put a bunsen burner in his bag?" the teacher asked doubtfully.

"All I can say, sir," said Eugene, "like George Washington," here he would glance at me, "I cannot tell a lie. I saw him put one in his bag."

We had recently learned about America's first President purportedly being unable to lie, and since then had adapted the phrase to suit his rascally purposes. It now became commonplace to hear him accuse a classmate (who was innocent) when a teacher loudly demanded the name of a culprit who had perpetrated some misdemeanour. Paper aeroplanes, for example, sometimes appeared in the air when a teacher's back was turned.

"Who was that?" the teacher wanted to know.

"Sir, I cannot tell a lie," Eugene would say, "but I saw X throw it."

X, of course, justifiably denied the preposterous charge.

I, on the other hand, could not help but laugh if I had the misfortune to be his target. He knew that such outrageous injustice always made me laugh.

Despite my protests of innocence, the teacher always construed my laughter as disrespectful and a sure sign of guilt. Eugene would stand behind the teacher, with a squint in one eye, and a stupidly surprised expression on his face, making sure I could see him. That made me laugh even more and, as Eugene well knew, would be the final straw that broke the teacher's patience.

I would be caned.

"Ooooooo, Joe!" Eugene would say, after I had been caned by the Headmaster, "was it *very* painful?"

How could I not laugh?

"I'll get you back, Eugene!" I threatened.

"Yeah, Joe, right," he would say.

I never did.

That is not to say that I laugh at all injustice. The gross injustices perpetrated by the white minority upon the huge black majority was anything but a laughing matter. Despite my circumstances, I was given every opportunity to excel in whatever field of endeavour I chose, simply because of my European blood. No black child, whatever his or her situation, was afforded any such opportunities.

As a result, huge gaps in the black population's education were created. Later, when power was handed over to the blacks, the new government allocated jobs to many black people who possessed neither the knowledge nor skills to perform their tasks.

During the early 70s, a few years after I had left school, I worked for a large company as a store man. I was one of a team of eight white men who had charge of one hundred male Africans. My section was small, selling plastics and plastic tubing to builders' merchants, and I had three Africans working with me.

The African work force was paid weekly, at the close of work on Fridays, and they waited in a line outside a glass office, impatient to be away for the weekend. Usually the store manager issued their wages, in cash, and in small brown envelopes. I, too, was impatient to be away at weekends so never witnessed the event. Then one Friday I was asked to do the job.

"Me, Fred? I wouldn't know what to do," I said to the store manager.

"Nothing to it, Joe," he said placatingly. "All you have to do is give them their pay. They sign for it, one at a time, mind, and that's that."

I only wish it had been as simple as that. That Friday, I sat nervously in the glass office, awaiting the arrival of the small box containing the workmen's wages. It duly appeared, along with a register listing the payees. Alongside each name was a box for the recipient's signature. A pen was provided as well as an ink pad.

"What's the ink pad for?" I asked.

"You haven't done this before, have you?" said the lady who brought the box, and left before I could answer.

I would soon learn the reason for her hasty departure and purpose of the ink pad.

Within moments of the money appearing, a line had formed outside the office and impatient knuckles rapped the glass. I called out the first name and he fairly ran into the room, gathered up his envelope and then slapped my hand away when I offered him the pen to sign for his money. He quickly opened the ink pad, placed his thumb on the pad, leaving his thumbprint in the box alongside his name before departing. From beginning to end it took less than ten seconds.

I was thunderstruck. It never occurred to me that the man could not write. I was so shocked that I hardly noticed the next in line had entered, uninvited, and followed the same procedure as the first. Before I could react the line had spilled into the room and I had become a helpless, ineffectual bystander. Nobody pushed or shoved. The first in line helped himself to the leading envelope in the box and left his thumb print next to his name.

Surely they could read, I reasoned, *how else did they recognise their names on the list? And were they leaving with the correct envelopes?*

The answer was simple. They knew exactly their place in the line and that, every week, the envelopes and names on the list were always in the same order. The important thing was speed: the faster they were paid the sooner they could be away for the weekend.

Of the hundred workers, only one signed for his money and he took a full minute to proudly write his name. He even expected some form of commendation from me but I did not have the heart to stoop to such patronisation. One congratulated infants and dogs for performing simple tasks, not grown men. I simply thanked him and was left with ninety-nine thumb prints and one clumsy signature.

It was that level of illiteracy that the African National Congress inherited from the white Apartheid government. Now, in 2016, more than twenty years after the handover of power, many whites have left the country, alarmed at the ineptitude and corruption prevailing in their homeland.

I, however, am optimistic. I believe that the present problems will eventually be resolved, albeit within the timespan of several generations.

But back to the Home. It was January, 1961 and I was in the Junior dormitory of a Junior House, with a tyrant for a Patrol Leader, and sharing the experience with nine other nine year olds.

15

Weakness and Strength

The first boys I saw in Dorm 4 of Simpson House were Benny and Richard. Benny was a fair-haired, blue-eyed boy, much like myself, but a few inches shorter and more thick-set. Richard was a good deal shorter, thin and extremely dark.

"Agh, I think he will be easy," Benny said to Richard, when I walked into the dormitory.

Richard said nothing and both boys stared at me. At the time I had no idea what Benny meant but would later learn that he thought me easy prey in a fight. Ignoring them, I placed the clothes and shoes I had been issued with into the grey metal locker alongside my bed.

As with any group of people that live together for any length of time, those with the strongest characters inevitably emerge as leaders.

Richard was one of a kind. His company and approval were sought by us all but only a few were welcomed into his inner circle. Unfortunately, I wasn't one of them but I enjoyed the rare times I did spend with him.

His favoured few were Macky and Ticky and these three spent much time together. Just outside this inner circle were Jogs and Bossy who were often included or interchangeable with Macky and Ticky. All these boys were natural leaders and would eventually become Headboys, Patrol Leaders and Corporals. But always at the centre, and the ringleader, was Richard.

Richard excelled at the sports that mattered, soccer and boxing, and in the latter he was formidable. Although slight of stature, his hand-speed and hard little fists were potent weapons that nobody wanted to be on the receiving end of. He also possessed a sharp wit. If his tongue did not subdue an opponent, he could always depend on his quick fists to drive a point home.

I always regarded him as being very clever. He seemed to know things that none of us had heard of before.

"It's an hotel, not a hotel," he informed us shortly after our arrival and apropos nothing in particular. "You use 'an' before words beginning with vowels and 'a' before words beginning with a consonant."

"What are you talking about?" somebody wanted to know.

"You okes are really dumb, you know that?"

'Oke' was our word for 'person', just one of many slang words commonly used by us.

"The alphabet has 26 letters and a, e, i, o, u are vowels," he explained, "the rest are consonants. You use *an* before a word beginning with a vowel and *a* before one beginning with a consonant. So it's *an* egg and *a* ball. But hotel is an exception: it's *an* hotel."

On another occasion he surprised us all by stating that America had a bomb that could blow up a city bigger than Johannesburg.

"No! A single bomb?"

"Yes. It's called an atom bomb."

Although I was his age, I wasn't in his class at school. My birthday fell in the latter half of the year making me younger by just a few months. This small discrepancy resulted in me being placed in a class a year behind him and his friends and was enough to distance me even further from them.

Academic ability was the last thing on any boy's mind in the Home. The Headmaster made every attempt to instill its importance into us but to little effect. A message was circulated that the Beak (our nickname for the Headmaster) would celebrate the Home's end-of-year school results by smoking a cigar. The size of the cigar reflected the quality of results. A small cigar indicated that only a few boys had passed their school exams, a medium one meant that a little more than half had passed, and a large one represented a seventy-five percent plus pass rate.

Usually the cigars were medium sized but one year he entered the dining hall smoking a whopper. It must have been a foot long.

"School results were good then, Father?"

The Headmaster, invariably an Anglican priest, was addressed as Father.

"They were excellent!" he beamed. "More than ninety percent this time!"

But these gentle nudges to do well at school did not wash with the boys. A boy either did well at school, in which case he was called 'a swot', or he did not. If he was *not* a swot he was considered normal. Being a swot was not necessarily a favourable trait amongst the boys.

Popular traits included doing well at sport, being handy with one's fists, being a regular trouble-maker, and not being a squealer (our slang for a telltale). Simply being a swot was not enough: one had to combine it with one of the popular traits.

Jogs was a case in point. He was, in fact, a major swot. Academically, he was peerless. He won prize after prize as the best student in every year at school. His heart was in the sciences but he excelled in all subjects, passing them all with near perfect results. Being a phenomenon, his type of swottishness was acceptable. But he also combined it with being a good swimmer and nobody dared take him on in a fight. Consequently, he did well in the Home.

Dirk, on the other hand, was the exact opposite. He wet his bed every night, constantly whined, was un-sporty, and physically weak. In short, he possessed every trait guaranteed to make him unpopular. From reveille in the morning, until last post and lights out at night, he could be found crying his eyes out. He was regularly caned, bullied and beaten, far more often than any other boy, and miserable indeed must have been his existence.

On one occasion, Dirk had the misfortune to be on trial for theft. The Deputy Housemaster, Mr Derek, decided to use the occasion to demonstrate trial procedure in a typical criminal court. A judge was appointed, a jury selected and sworn in, counsel for the prosecution and defence were chosen, all under the supervision of Mr Derek. A makeshift court room was constructed using the tables and chairs in the common room. I arrived ten minutes after proceedings had begun and saw Karly waiting in a queue in the corridor outside the common room.

"What's going on, Karly?"

"Joe!" he said excitedly, "Dirk's on trial for stealing! I'm a witness!"

"What did he steal?"

" For ------ sake, Joe, how do I know?"

"How can you be a witness if you don't know what he stole?"

"Wake up, Joe, it's all make-believe! I'll just make it up as I go along."

It might have been make-believe for Karly but not for Dirk. Despite being innocent, he was found guilty and sentenced to be caned. In my mind's eye I can still see Dirk standing in the 'dock', looking bewildered and frightened, as witness after witness swore to have seen him steal whatever he was accused of stealing.

On another occasion we had to practise using the fire escape. The fire escape was simply a galvanised pole down which the boys had to slide in the event of a fire. It was located externally at a corner of the building and accessed by climbing through the double window at the end of an upper dormitory. We had to sit on the window sill and then reach for the pole with an outstretched hand. Any mistake and the plunge to the ground below could prove fatal. It was a tricky manoeuvre and, because of the obvious danger, only attempted by the most athletic among us.

During the exercise, overseen by the Housemaster, each of us slid down the pole, grateful when we arrived safely on the ground. Then it was Dirk's turn. In hindsight we should have known it was beyond his capabilities but we were more concerned for our own skins to be bothered about his.

He tentatively stretched out his hand and grabbed the pole. But it was the next step, simultaneously stepping off the window sill and grabbing the pole with the other hand that was the most difficult. Once both hands had hold of the pole, the legs would automatically follow suit and it was then safe to slide down. All this was beyond Dirk's abilities and understanding. He did clasp the pole with one hand but stepped off the sill before grabbing the pole with the other.

Faces crowded the dorm window, watching Dirk fall. He hit the ground, flat on his back, and lay there quite still, turning a ghastly shade of grey. How long he lay there is uncertain.

"He's gotta be dead," somebody whispered.

Then suddenly colour returned to his face, a deep pink, and he let rip with his trademark Dirk howl. Everyone breathed a huge sigh of relief. Strangely, other than being winded, he suffered no injuries.

Dirk was an outcast and befriended by nobody. Should any boy show him the least kindness, he would become maudlin and tearfully ask the boy if he would be his friend. It was a sickly request, delivered by a sickly boy, and it was inevitably declined with either a push, a curse, and often both.

The characters of the rest of the boys ranged between these extremes: none was more popular than Richard and none less so than poor Dirk. Since those momentous times, I have often wondered (but never discovered) what became of Dirk. Exactly when and why he disappeared from the Home is a mystery but I do know that he was with me in Simpson House for the first five years.

* * *

"Poor Dirk, he had a rotten time at the Home, didn't he?"

"Yes. I feel very guilty about it now. Kids are so cruel." Joe stared into the distance, clearly reliving a kaleidoscope of painful childhood moments.

"What about Richard? Do you know what happened to him?" I asked, attempting to change the subject.

"Richard? He died young, I think."

"Oh, I'm sorry."

* * *

One morning before breakfast, a few months after my arrival at the Home, I was doing housework. Each boy was allocated a weekly task and mine was sweeping the dormitory floor. I momentarily laid the broom to one side and when I looked again it was gone. A quick investigation revealed that Benny, the boy who claimed that I would 'be easy', had taken it. He needed it to sweep the common room, which was his weekly chore. Each dorm had one broom that had to be shared.

"Benny, I had the broom first," I complained.

Benny said nothing and carried on sweeping.

"Are you deaf, Benny? I had the broom first. Give it back."

Benny still ignored me, so I decided that there was nothing else for it but to take it by force. I grabbed hold of the broom and tried to wrench it from him but he staunchly held onto it. Neither of us seemed to be making much progress and by now the rest of the boys had gathered to watch the entertainment. Then I did something that I greatly regretted. I let go of the broom and punched him on the jaw.

Benny's reaction was immediate. He also let go of the broom and came at me, his head down, blindly swinging his fists. I easily parried them and socked him again. By now the Patrol Leader had been alerted and stepped in.

"What's going on here? Are you two having a fight?"

Benny and I simply glowered at one another. We expected him to stop the fight, but he didn't.

"It has to be a fair fight," he began, but I didn't wait to hear the rest of the rules.

My blood was boiling and I stepped forward and punched Benny several times before being pulled off. Unhappily, I earned an undeserved reputation of being someone not to be trifled with. I am, in fact, a coward and will only willingly enter a fight when my temper is lost and I am bereft of reason. Many times in the future I would demonstrate a yellow streak, belying my reputation.

Nevertheless, rightly or wrongly, my reputation was established and, like the gunfighters of the American wild west, challengers would soon come looking for me. I did not have long to wait.

"Do you want to have it out?"

The words were quietly spoken and came from behind. I turned around and looked into a pair of eyes that were flat and without expression. One sees them in snakes and on rare occasions, humans. It was Raymond. Why he wanted to fight me, I didn't know, but I would later learn that he simply disliked me. From that moment he would become one of my very few mortal enemies in the Home.

The challenge may have been quietly spoken but it was loud enough to be heard by others. Refusal to accept would be interpreted as cowardice. In truth I had no desire to fight. I hadn't spoken two words to Raymond since arriving in the Home but I had little choice but to accept the challenge.

I have an impatient, impetuous nature, keen to do things immediately. I always believed (and, to an extent, still do) that iron is best struck when molten. On several occasions in the future I would be forced to wait before having a fight. When challenged during a meal, for example, I was compelled to wait until it was over before going into battle. Then I had time enough to ponder the potential consequences. The bloody nose and blackened eyes, inevitable end products of any fist fight.

So instead of waiting until supper was over, I threw a fist at his face but missed. He retaliated with one that connected. Infuriated, I returned the favour and before ten seconds had elapsed, a swathe was cut through the boys surrounding us. It was fast and furious, our punches landing but seemingly without effect. Actually, Raymond was much stronger and it didn't take me long to appreciate the fact. At the end of a minute we were pulled apart, fortunately by the Headboy and not the Housemaster, who undoubtedly would have caned us.

I did not accept Raymond's subsequent challenge, to continue the fight after supper, and it was tacitly understood that I had been bested. However, I didn't lose too much face with the other boys and would later discover that Raymond was a year older. At that age, it was a significant advantage.

I rarely, if ever, fought with any of the boys I liked. I actually liked Benny but would fight him one last time a few months later. Strangely it was for the same reason, and with the same outcome. Richard, Ticky, Jogs and Bossy were unassailable, much tougher than I was, and I was prepared to bow my head should they ever threaten me. Apart from Richard, they never did. Richard regularly told me to wind in my neck and I always obeyed.

Macky once threw a punch at me that landed on my jaw, barely making my head move.

"Okay, Joe, let's forget I did that!" he said hastily as I glared at him.

I was only too happy to oblige and the incident passed as if it had never happened. Apart from one occasion, I never fought with any of my friends.

One day, when I was twelve and had been in the Home for three years, I was looking for Joss or Les in Beaton House. Boys from Beaton House often visited us in Simpson and vice versa. However, the Senior Houses were out of bounds and we Juniors rarely visited them.

I found neither of my friends but spotted a Superman comic on one of the beds. Without a thought I lay on the bed and began reading it. Other boys were in the dormitory but they were busily engaged in their own affairs and paid me no heed. Sharing comics was a common practice and nobody raised any queries or concerns about my presence in the dorm.

"Hey, Twead, do you want to have it out?"

My blood went cold and I looked up to see Martin and Derek staring at me. Two more lethal boys could not be found in either of the Junior Houses and I had no notion why they wanted to fight with me. Martin, in fact, was Les's brother, and we had been in the Children's Home together.

"Yes, why not," I said.

I was taking on two older boys, not separately, but at the same time, and I still don't know why I was so stupid to accept such a challenge. Within five minutes I was left a bloody mess and bawling my eyes out on the dormitory floor. Through my tears I saw them walk away, an arm around the other's shoulder, laughing and joking about having dispatched me so effortlessly.

The occasion I did fight with a friend was with Anamond. I was fifteen and in my first year as a senior in Spackman House. By then I was well past the age of having to prove myself physically. Anamond was my age and one of four brothers, the others being younger than we were. I liked them all but Anamond particularly.

We were play-wrestling and for some inexplicable reason it got out of hand. I lost my temper and challenged him to a fight. He accepted and we began trading punches.

Of all the fights I had in the Home, I regretted this one the most. At the age of fifteen I had become a very angry young man and unfortunately the focus of my anger at that moment was centred on Anamond. To this day I wish it had been an enemy and not Anamond.

The fight lasted about ten minutes and, although I was keenly conscious of the painful blows I felt striking my face, I returned them with interest. He never flinched or uttered a sound, doubling my anger and the number of punches I threw. At the end of the ten minutes we were pulled apart and silently glared at each other, neither of us having gained any advantage or superiority. Or so I thought.

My Patrol Leader approached me half an hour later.

"Twead, you ----- animal," he said angrily, "what's the matter with you?"

"What do you mean?"

My response was sullen but also respectful. The consequences of being disrespectful, I knew, were dire. He was a big boy, older, and would have little scruple beating me to a pulp should I step out of line. On a previous occasion he had socked me on the jaw and the memory of it lingered. I had just been in a fight with Anamond and didn't relish nursing additional wounds from my Patrol Leader.

"Have you seen what you did to Anamond?" he said angrily.

"Nothing. We just had a fight. The last time I saw him he was okay."

"You ---- idiot! He has just been taken to hospital!"

My jaw dropped. In a flash I realised that the angry blows I had rained upon Anamond's face and head, although the effects were not immediately visible, were severe enough to hospitalise him. I had felt my fists land, had felt the juddering up my arms when they landed, but was amazed when he appeared to be impervious to them. This merely enraged me, making me redouble my efforts.

My Patrol Leader turned away in disgust, cursing me again for being an animal.

"I'm really sorry, Anamond," I said when I saw him a week later.

"That's okay, Joe, forget about it," he said quietly.

We never spoke again and, shortly after that, Anamond left the Home and I never saw him again.

* * *

"Did that happen a lot?" I asked. "I mean boys just leaving?"

"Yes. Especially the older ones. In those days you could leave school at fifteen and if you were white, jobs were easy to find. Boys just walked out and we never saw them again."

"Talking of disappearing, what about your mother? Did she ever appear again?"

"Yes, she did. I was just about to write about that."

16

Family

About two months after I arrived at the Boys' Home, Ma appeared. It was at night and the House was preparing for bed.

"Twead, your mother's here!" a voice shouted into our dormitory.

I dashed out to the entrance and there she was. Without a word, I flung my arms around her waist and clung to her for dear life.

"Hi, Ma."

"Hello, Boy."

While I clung to her, she placed a hand on the top of my head, and we remained like that for a full minute. Ma was never one for caresses or demonstrative affection.

"Come sit down here," she said, unclasping my hands from behind her.

We sat on the low wall that ran along the front of the House. I babbled away while she smoked a cigarette, apparently listening. Whether she was or not, I didn't care, I was just too pleased to see her again. The 'reign of terror' had begun and I was feeling terribly vulnerable.

The situation was like seeing Lizzy's face at the Afrikaans Place. Her little face had lit up and her smile had enchanted me. She had been my salvation during those dark times. Ma, however, never smiled but her presence was enough. At least one other person, I knew, cared about me.

Unconditional adult affection was a very rare commodity in any of the Homes in which I was raised. Uncle Gussy never showed any favouritism but his affection for children was apparent. Although I wasn't aware of it, I craved adult intimacy, being held tight, embraced, cuddled. I would learn this fact shortly before Ma's visit.

I had wandered into Beaton House. I was curious about how their system compared with ours in Simpson. I would have been delighted to see Joss or Les but I didn't. I wasn't looking for anybody particularly and the visit was purely exploratory. Curiosity directed my steps there.

I heard a ruckus coming from upstairs and, because it included laughter and music, I sought out the source. The Housemaster's flat. I was amazed by what I saw inside. The door was wide open and boys my age were actually playing inside. Nobody entered Mr Brian's flat without permission, but Mr Piet, the Beaton Housemaster, appeared to have no such scruples.

Boys were running in and out, chatting and sitting on the floor, seemingly free to do as they pleased. What was more surprising was that Mr Piet actually had a boy on his lap. I couldn't believe my eyes and shyly entered the flat. Mr Piet saw me, smiled, set the other boy down (who, unconcerned, ran off) and before I knew it, I was on his lap with his arms around me.

I basked in the comfort and security of those powerful arms. It was the first time in my life that any adult had shown me such physical affection, and I loved it. I looked at the other boys but saw and heard nothing untoward.

Every now and again Mr Piet would set me on the floor to disappear behind a closed door that led, I presumed, to his inner sanctum, his bedroom, bathroom and kitchen. I had briefly seen similar modest facilities in Mr Brian's rooms in Simpson House.

A minute or two later he would reappear and sweep me back into his arms as he sat down. I never begged to be treated so and there was no competition from the other boys for his attentions. I simply stood close to the chair, hoping he would favour me, and I wasn't disappointed.

How long I enjoyed that blissful attention, I cannot remember, but I do recall wishing I'd been a member of Beaton House instead of Simpson. Then a movement in the doorway caught my eye.

Two older boys were standing there, silently staring at me. I had seen them earlier but had paid them no mind. I didn't care that, unlike the other boys in the room, they apparently were not enjoying themselves. When Mr Piet had put me down a third time, they approached me.

"What the ---- do you think you're doing?" one of them demanded.

I was shocked and it occurred to me that they might be jealous of the attention that I, a Simpson House boy, was being shown by their Housemaster.

"Nothing," I answered tentatively, "I was just sitting on his lap. What's wrong with that?"

"What's wrong with that? Are you dense, you stupid ----? What do you think he's doing behind that door?"

"I don't know. Using the toilet?"

"No, you ---- idiot, he's having a drink! And why do you think he's got you on his lap?"

I needed to hear nothing more. In a flash I absorbed and understood what I was being told. I might have been mistaken but I was taking no chances. I perfectly understood the implications and needed no additional explanation. Without a word I walked past them and out of Beaton House.

From that moment on I would never trust another male adult. I had thoroughly enjoyed the all too brief moment of physical affection but realised that, with strangers, it would always be conditional. The attached strings could be anchored in something despicable.

Ma's affection, although limited, was unconditional and as things then stood, she was my only friend in the world. We arranged to go out together on Sundays, when boys were allowed to visit whatever relatives they had. Aunts, uncles, mothers, fathers, grandfathers and grandmothers were all visited every second Sunday and during holiday periods. Boys who had no relatives were provided with hosts, kindly strangers who accepted boys into their homes.

Ma soon left and I watched her walk slowly away into the darkness, along the road past Beaton House. I would see her again that Sunday and on the subsequent Sundays that we were allowed out. She and I would go into the city and sit on a bench in one of the parks or in a café, eating modestly. She was forever asking me about my sister.

"Are you sure you don't know where your sister is?" was her constant refrain and I would always give her the same answer: I did not know.

"I'm having you for the holiday," she told me one Sunday.

Easter was approaching and the Easter holiday was a valuable week away from the Home. I was excited by the prospect.

"Where will we stay?"

"I've got a room not far away. I'll come and get you."

During that week, in which I spent most of my time wandering through the surrounding streets and visiting the local cinema, I was surprised when Ma told me I would be spending a few days with a cousin. Apart from my sister, I wasn't aware of any other relatives.

My cousin's name was Stephanie and she had recently married Tony. They lived near Ma's lodgings and I stayed a night with them, sleeping on the floor with a blanket as a mattress and another to cover me. Besides Steph and Tony, I shared the house with their three pets: a crow, a dog, and a cat.

I found it fascinating that these three creatures lived in seeming harmony with one another. Unfortunately the crow had a nasty habit of pecking the dog's tail, especially when the dog was dozing. The dog would angrily snap at the crow which then sought refuge on a curtain pelmet or the top of a cupboard.

On another occasion Tony amused me by gently spinning the cat on its back. The wooden floor was smooth and, when released, the cat would stand, greatly disorientated, then topple over. It may have been cruel but for a ten year old boy it was hilarious. I laughed so much I could hardly breathe.

"We can't look after you," Tony informed me, at the end of my stay.

They were a young couple, recently married and embarking on their own lives together. They could ill afford the additional incumbrance of a ten year old relative. Financially, too, it was impossible for them, as evidenced by the obvious lack of house furnishings.

I loved the all-too-brief time I spent with them and remember wishing I could do so forever. Tony was wonderful and I thought Steph the most beautiful woman I had ever seen. She hardly said a word to me but Tony more than made up for her silence.

Back with Ma, in her rented room in a residential house in the suburb near the Home, my time this holiday was drawing to an end. I had enjoyed the return to my former freedom, when I could do as I pleased, and being away from the harsh strictures imposed by the Home. Then Ma sprung a surprise on me.

"You're not going back. You are staying here."

"Ma, they'll hit me if I don't go back! I must go!"

"No," she said quietly, "you're staying here."

In the face of such finality I relented and awaited my fate.

Mr Brian, accompanied by his assistant, Mr Derek, duly appeared and quietly demanded my return. Ma put up no resistance and I was taken away. There were no fond farewells and Ma, languidly smoking, simply turned her back on us as we walked out.

Neither Housemaster said a word to me, choosing instead to talk jovially to one another as we returned to the Home in Mr Derek's car. Their voices were too low for me to hear what they were talking about but they seemed cheerful and unconcerned about having to retrieve a boy from his parent. Nevertheless, I feared the consequences of Ma's unilateral decision. At the least I expected a whipping.

Arriving back, Mr Brian ordered me to go to my dorm and get ready for bed. Other than that, nothing more was said or done. I was grateful to have escaped a beating.

My week-long holidays with Ma were similar to that described above, but without meeting other relatives or being forbidden to return to the Home. They all occurred during the first two years I spent at the Home. The rooms she rented were varied, sometimes in a residential house and at other times in a low-cost high-rise building in the heart of the city.

What surprised me was that she was permitted to have me at all, especially after her earlier behaviour. Even more surprising was that she was allowed to have another boy accompany me during one holiday. It was John, already familiar to me from our time together at the Children's Home. John was a year older but a good friend.

During that holiday he and I romped together, frequenting the local cinema and feasting on fish and chips. In fact, it always was fish and chips with Ma. She would place a few coins in my hand and tell me to go and get some fish and chips and then turn away to puff on a cigarette.

I didn't mind because I loved fish and chips. Never once do I recall she and I sitting down to a proper meal at a table. It was always fish and chips, eaten with our hands, from the folds of a greasy newspaper.

* * *

"You will be staying with Ouma this Christmas," Ma told me one Sunday.

I was aged ten at the time and I knew about Ouma, having briefly seen her before, but never truly appreciated her significance. I certainly didn't think she was related to me. Ouma (pronounced oh-mah) was the Afrikaans word for grandmother and the term South Africans used for all elderly women, whether related to them or not. It never occurred to me that the lady I knew as Ouma was in fact my own grandmother.

The difficulty is that I never saw Ma talk to Ouma. Had she addressed her, in my presence, as mother or mom, I am certain I would have recognised her as my grandmother. But Ma didn't interact with a single other relative, at least not in my presence, and so my confusion was understandable.

She was an elderly one-legged woman who got about on a set of wooden crutches. Her black hair was always drawn severely back and tied in a bun at the back of her head. Her features were regular but her eyes were startlingly blue and exceedingly cold. She rarely smiled and when she did, a set of brilliantly white false teeth were revealed. She was a rotund lady and not particularly tall. She always wore black, was exceedingly religious, and I never did discover how she lost her leg.

I spent the Christmas holiday with her in a house owned by an Afrikaans family with whom she boarded. They had a son, Pieter, who was my age and I suspect the reason I was allowed to stay. Piet and I got on very well and spent most of our time with his friends at the nearby outdoor public pool or at the local cinema.

Being out every day, I rarely saw Ouma. When I did, she ordered me about, using her crutch to point out objects she wanted me to get for her. I was always happy to oblige. At night, as I lay in bed in the room I shared with her, I could hear her whispering Afrikaans verses from a large Bible that lay open on her bed. She would then remove her teeth and cover her hair with a flimsy net before turning in for the night. She always left the small bedside lamp burning.

During this holiday, I was reacquainted with Steph. She had dropped in to visit Ouma and I was delighted to see her again. In my enthusiasm, I wrapped my arms around her waist, just as I had when seeing Ma after a long absence. I was shocked when Steph giggled nervously, clearly uncomfortable with the situation. I snatched my arms away and, embarrassed, ran into the house. I remember Ma having told me she was family and I couldn't understand her strange reaction.

Several decades later Stephanie and Tony were attacked in their home by an intruder. Tony survived but Steph was killed. Tony would never remarry. I don't know if they had any children.

At the end of the six weeks with Ouma, we parted company and I never saw her again. I still wasn't sure why Ma wanted me to spend time with a strange old lady and even after Steph's visit I still didn't appreciate Ouma's significance. This only came to light a few years later.

I was walking back to Simpson House one Friday evening, after seeing a movie in the Dining Hall. Neville, a younger boy, came running up to me.

"Joe," he said, "your grandmother died."

He stared into my face, hoping I would tearfully bewail her loss. He was disappointed. I simply thanked him and turned away to ponder the information. It dawned on me that I had just been informed of the death of Ouma who, after all, must have been my grandmother.

Why did Neville inform me of my grandmother's death and not a member of staff? How had Neville been made privy to such personal information? These questions only occurred to me when, unfortunately, it was too late to get any answers.

17

Lost

Ma moved to a decrepit room in a building that should have been demolished decades earlier. I was ten and a half years old and, as always, we shared a dingy bed and I would fall asleep to her mirthless laughter. No doubt she was recalling some distant incident that had amused her. I remember that and the glowing end of the cigarette she was smoking in the dark.

The building was located near the Cinerama cinema in Johannesburg which, at the time, was something of a novelty. The wide, curved screen and comfortable seats was a departure from the narrow screens and uncomfortable seats of other cinemas. *How The West Was Won* was showing and I sat in the front row. Ma rarely accompanied me and I was sandwiched between well to-do patrons.

I was dressed in my Home uniform: a Home blazer with the Home badge on its breast pocket, a white shirt and Home tie, grey shorts, long grey socks and black polished shoes. This would always be my 'Sunday Best', the smart attire all boys were expected to wear when attending Chapel or when out in public. So I didn't feel too out of place amongst the surrounding finery.

Throughout this wonderful film, my head swivelled back and forth as my brain attempted to absorb the storyline and gorgeous scenery depicted on the vast, curved screen. Even at the age of ten, I recognised it as a masterpiece and thought Carol Baker one of the most beautiful women I had ever seen.

The lady to my left offered me a chocolate from a box brim-full of them. With a shake of my head I declined the offer but she insisted. Again I refused with a shake of my head. In truth I wanted the chocolate but was canny enough to realise it probably came with strings attached. Had I accepted, she may have asked questions I would have been unwilling to answer. At worst it would have spoiled my enjoyment of the movie and I wasn't having that. When the film ended, I was one of the first to shoot away.

One day, during that holiday, Ma took me clothes shopping. I was suddenly the proud owner of several casual shirts and shorts that would supplement the standard Home issue of khaki shorts and shirts. It was the first time she had bought me clothes and it surprised me.

Ma never had much money, I knew that. This was a generous gesture that I did appreciate but I never showed my gratitude in either word or gesture. Indeed I knew not how and I doubt she would have responded with anything more than surprise had I done so. But Ma was generous and had a generous nature.

Whenever we passed a beggar in the street, and in Johannesburg, sadly, there were all too many, we would pass, then stop. She would then put a coin in my hand and tell me to give it to the person who was seated on the pavement.

When the holiday ended, I returned to the Home, knowing I would see her the first Sunday we were allowed out. The Sunday duly arrived and I made my way to the dingy building near the Cinerama. I rarely had enough money to ride on the public transport but never minded the five mile walk. The route was flat and there was always much to see along the way.

Arriving at the familiar building, I climbed the familiar stairs to the first floor and walked along the familiar dark corridor to her room. The door was locked. I knocked and waited.

Nothing.

"Ma!" I said quietly, but loud enough for her to hear.

Nothing.

"Ma!" This time a little louder.

"What the ---- do you want?"

It was a man's voice and it came from a room further along the corridor.

"I'm looking for my ma," I said, "she lives here."

"listen you ----- little ----, your ---- mother is not here. so get the ---- out before I ----"

I didn't wait to hear more. I fled the building and stood outside in the bright sunshine. I wasn't surprised that Ma wasn't 'at home'. By now I was well accustomed to her erratic behaviour. I would have been more surprised had she behaved normally. Had Ma been in, we would have walked together into the city centre and sat in a park or café.

I was now in a bit of a quandary. It was 11.00 am and I needed to kill time before 5.00 pm, the time when all boys were expected back at the Home. I had no desire to return early but neither did I feel like walking aimlessly through the streets of the city.

I was already familiar with the long main street that linked the Home to the city. It did not deviate by so much as an inch from its east-west direction. Car sales, garages, shops, cinemas, houses, all lined this wide avenue with its pedestrian walkways on either side.

For a change, I chose to return to the Home via the most circuitous route available. I prided myself on my sense of direction and knew the Home was due east from where I stood. I intended to walk back along streets that were unknown to me, hoping to see and explore different areas of the city.

My plan was to initially head south, then turn east, and finally to head north. That way I would be in the right ball-park at the journey's end. At worst I might get lost but trusted that eventually I would recognise a familiar landmark to help me find my way back. Of this I was fully confident and, without a care or a penny, I set off on my great adventure.

An hour later I was hopelessly lost and had lost all sense of direction. I was unconcerned. A scan of the horizon from some high ground, should reveal a landmark, perhaps a familiar water-tower, or a high-rise building, and I would be on my way again. The trouble was there was no high ground and the territory I found myself in was as familiar to me as the far side of the moon.

Two hours later and now I did worry, not because I was lost, but because of the consequences of reporting back late at the Home. A beating was inevitable.

Then a family in a car stopped alongside me.

"Are you lost?" the driver asked me.

"No," I said.

"Do you live around here?"

"Yes."

"Really? Are you sure? In a township?"

I had no idea what a township was. I would later learn that the non-white populace was forced to live in these undeveloped 'townships' on the outskirts of cities. They were part of the government's policy to separate whites and blacks and provided the cheap labour on which the South African economy thrived.

I was a young boy, dressed in his Home uniform, blissfully unaware of all this. In hindsight I must have looked very odd as I made my way through the township.

"What's a township?" I asked, and before the words had barely left my lips the driver had pulled me into his car and I found myself squashed in the back with the rest of his children.

Now It was the wife's turn to assume the role of inquisitor.

"Don't you know it's dangerous to walk alone around here? Where are your parents?"

Where indeed?

"They're...at home," I said.

It was an Afrikaans family and, following a whispered consultation between husband and wife, in which I heard the word 'police' frequently spoken, I soon found myself in a nearby police station. I knew that I was in serious trouble at the Home, especially now that the police were involved, and anticipated a death sentence at the very least.

I informed the policeman behind the counter that I was from the Boys'

Home.

"Where's that?"

I felt insulted. It amazed me that the police hadn't heard of the place. I imagined every member of Johannesburg society had heard of it. But, for the life of me, I could not tell them where it was.

They decided to search for it in a telephone directory. A telephonic conversation ensued, following which I was placed in a police car and delivered to the Home. There, the Beak, Father Eric, was waiting for me at the side entrance to the Chapel.

Father Eric, of all the Masters at the Home, was by far the gentlest. That is not to say that he was a push-over. Once he had made up his mind about anything, nothing changed it, no matter how unpopular the decision might be. But he never raised his hand or voice in anger.

On one occasion, I was shown into his office for a caning. I had perpetrated some misdemeanour that warranted chastisement from the Headmaster. I had already experienced the ferocious beatings meted out by my Housemaster, Mr Brian, his assistant, Mr Derek, the Deputy Headmaster, Mr Ken, and now it was the turn of the Headmaster, Father Eric. I anticipated a thrashing.

I was in for a surprise. He looked fearfully at me and then at the cane in his hand. With a tremulous voice he ordered me to bend over and I obeyed. I gripped my ankles and clenched my teeth. This I found helped during the torture. Not much, but every little was welcome. I waited and nothing happened. Perhaps it was a test, I thought. Messers Brian and Ken were inclined to reward a boy with additional cuts if he so much as moved during a caning.

Father Eric's cane did fall but so lightly that I genuinely thought he was measuring out a spot on my behind, taking aim so as to speak, before landing a far heavier blow.

"Let that be a lesson to you!" he said, and I immediately recalled Uncle Gussy.

I stood up to face him and to my astonishment discovered he had tears in his eyes. If having to cane a boy reduced this gentle man to tears, then I was a fan, and from that moment my respect and admiration for him never diminished.

Father Eric it was who awaited my return from the police station. Dressed in his black cassock and standing alongside the Chapel, smoke billowed from his pipe as he looked down at me. It was late afternoon.

"I'm sorry, Father," I began but he cut me short.

"That's alright, um, Peter," he said.

"It's Joe, Father."

He had a tendency to absent-mindedness.

"Ah, yes, Joe. Off you go then," was all he said.

My fears of being punished were unfounded and I heard no more regarding these events.

I was not concerned about Ma's disappearance. At the age of ten and a half, I never doubted that I would see her again.

But I was mistaken and I never did. Ma disappeared altogether from my life and many years later I learned that she had moved down to the Durban area and had died there in 1989. Her ashes, I was told, were scattered on the waters of the Indian Ocean. The clothes she had bought me must have been her parting gift, a kind of severance payment as it were.

I would also learn that, when I was born, we parted ways, she to a psychiatric unit in Johannesburg called Westkoppies, and I to Grantley's Baby Home. I don't know how long we were apart and it wasn't the last time either. Apparently I was also an incumbent in the Charlotte Theron Kinderhuis in Bethlehem, Orange Free State. I have no memories of either of these establishments.

I missed her. I have no idea why she decided to turn her back on me. I guess I must have been a severe drain on her limited resources. I only wish we had had a normal existence, one that most families take for granted, but it was not to be. No doubt there were good reasons that absolved her from being a typical mother and parent, and I imagine her mental illness was a factor.

I was too young to understand her abnormalities and simply accepted them as the norm. When I was with her, I enjoyed my many freedoms, doing as I pleased and seemingly without a care in the world. But Authority decided that was unsatisfactory. It is true that JCH was a wonderful place, an excellent substitute, but JCH was not Ma.

The Boys' Home was now my mother. It may not have been ideal but it did provide me with everything I needed. However, I had to tread warily to avoid the many pitfalls, from both boys and Masters. But I wanted for nothing and I was content to explore my horizons, taking advantage of everything that fell within my reach.

And very soon an opportunity did avail itself. I was about to embark on another adventure which eventually had a bitter-sweet outcome.

* * *

"It's hard to believe your mother simply moved away and you never saw her again," I said.

"Well, it's true," answered Joe, sighing. "Yes, it's sad, but I wasn't the only child she left behind. There was Lizzy, and at least four other older ones *that I didn't know. And who knows, perhaps she had more later."*

"When you look at the Spanish families here in the village..."

"I know."

"It's such a contrast! The Ufartes next door have six children, with probably more on the way. There isn't much space for them in that little house, but they all care for each other, and the grandmother. It just seems so unfair that you were dealt those cards."

"I was lucky really. I could have been born black, for instance. And I'm sure some of the other boys at the Home had worse backgrounds than I had."

"Well, it's all history, I suppose. At least we have our own family now, and grandchildren to adore. None of our family will ever suffer like you did."

"Amen to that," said Joe, reaching for my hand and enveloping it in both his. "Amen to that."

18

Fun

Not long after being brought back to the Home by the police, Mr Brian called me into his flat. For once I was not to be caned and it was one of the rare moments that he smiled rather than scowled at me.

"Sit down, Joe."

More surprises. Not only was he addressing me by my first name, he was also inviting me to sit down. A day of firsts.

"You and Billy M will be staying with hosts this Christmas. They are very wealthy. I think you will enjoy yourselves."

I said nothing. Mr Brian studied my face.

"You don't look very excited, why not?"

"Sir, I'd rather be with my mother."

"Joe," he said, "we've been unable to contact your mother and we have no choice but to send you to hosts. You and Billy are very lucky to have been selected, you know."

I should have felt honoured, especially as he had chosen me instead of one of his favourites. It was common knowledge that he had favourites, boys who enjoyed privileges that the rest of us could only envy. Just as Richard and his select circle of friends were the most popular amongst us boys, they were also Mr Brian's favourites.

Sometimes he and his favourites would slip away in his car to a nearby popular fast-food outlet. There he regaled them with the delights of the establishment and we would hear an account of what they enjoyed when they returned. I was always most envious.

Some of the more senior boys in the House were included in the fortunate few. One in particular, Richard's older brother, Freddy, was Mr Brian's top favourite.

Freddy, like Richard, was dark-complexioned but unlike Richard, he was an Adonis. His eyes were startlingly blue, contrasting vividly with his dark skin. They would fix themselves on whomever he was addressing and, if amused, they gleamed when he smiled. His smile was not dissimilar to that of Elvis Presley with his full lips curling off perfect white teeth. His dark hair was short and naturally curly, much like those shown on the busts of young men in Greek or Roman antiquity.

Like Richard, he had a formidable personalty and both boys were utterly fearless. Richard always tried to best his older brother and on one occasion I gaped at the apparent disregard they had for their own safety.

They were on bicycles and Freddy challenged Richard to a game of 'follow my lead'. Richard was to keep his front wheel as close to the rear of Freddy's as possible as they cycled at speed through the streets of the local suburb. Traffic, although not heavy, posed a potential danger as did the terrain. The roads were not flat with cars parked along the kerbs. For both boys it was hazardous, to say the least, and certainly not to be attempted by the faint hearted.

I watched as Freddy and Richard zigzagged in and out of the parked cars at a breathtaking speed. Occasionally Freddy would slow down, almost to a standstill, and Richard would do the same. It was clear that Richard's concentration was at a maximum and he saw nothing but his brother's rear wheel.

Freddy knew this and, from my viewpoint, I saw his lip curl into an ominous smile. Then, at full speed, he suddenly applied both brakes and the brothers ended up in a mangled pile on the road. Freddy was aware of the consequences of his actions. He knew it was dangerous but didn't care to have such a minor issue intrude on his entertainment. Average people would stand back from a chasm they had inspected and found to be unsafe. Freddy would inspect it just as carefully, then leap. Richard was the same. In games of soccer, he tackled opponents without the least regard to his own safety. They were fearless.

Freddy was laughing so much he had tears in his eyes but Richard was far from amused. He cursed his brother for being an idiot and Freddy accused him of not paying attention. Fortunately, neither was hurt and their bikes suffered no serious damage, but the anecdote is typical of their sibling rivalry.

On the rare occasions I was included in their company, I basked in the rarified glow that surrounded them. It might have been idolatry on my part but I believe I understood why Mr Brian favoured these charismatic brothers, and Freddy in particular.

They and I arrived in the Home at the same time. Richard was my age and Freddy was two years older. When Freddy was ready for high school, Mr Brian personally paid for him to board at a private school in Pretoria and Freddy left the Home. That Mr Brian was taken with the boy was understandable. He probably believed he was assisting a child prodigy and his sponsorship was the stepping stone for Freddy to achieve later greatness.

Unfortunately, Mr Brian's faith in his protegé's academic abilities wasn't justified. Freddy didn't excel at school and he left having completed the legal minimum. Tragically he died a few years later whilst suffering a seizure.

I am in error if I have painted Mr Brian as an ogre. Occasionally he did surprise me and one of my most wonderful experiences was entirely due to him.

I had been in the Home for three years and, by then, was accustomed to its ways. The school day had just ended and it was a warm early afternoon. I walked the half mile back to the Home and made my way down to the House. Lunch, I knew, would be the usual cheese roll and a mug of tea. What was unusual, however, was the appearance of Mr Brian, standing near the tea urn, writing something in a notebook. He was surrounded by a number of clamouring boys.

"Me! Me!" they shouted, trying unsuccessfully to attract his attention.

It was hot and I was tired but I was curious what all the fuss was about.

"Good afternoon, sir," I said quietly to him.

"Good afternoon, Twead," he answered, just as quietly.

I turned away and walked over to a boy on the periphery of the clamouring group.

"What's going on?" I asked him.

"Mr Brian is selecting six boys to go to the Kruger National Park for a week."

I might have been tired but that certainly grabbed my attention. A week in the KNP! That had to be the holiday of a lifetime. I looked up at Mr Brian, who paid me not the slightest heed and I was convinced his favourites were going somewhere very special indeed. There was no point in joining the group, I thought, and walked into the House with a sigh.

Ten minutes later I was called.

"Twead! Report to Mr Brian's flat now!"

I and five other boys stood in his living room, awaiting the reason for his summons.

"I have chosen you boys to go to the Kruger National Park for a week," he said. "You leave today. The Home bus will take you into town in an hour."

I was overjoyed. I was later told (by somebody in the clamouring group) that Mr Brian had noted my silent departure and scribbled my name in his notebook. It turned out that only the boys who did *not* clamour had been selected.

The week in the KNP was one of the most memorable of my life. The bus that carried thirty children, plus several supervising adults to the Park, also had an icebox at the back. Sponsored by a well-known soft drinks company, we were supplied with endless quantities of cola throughout the holiday.

In the Park, we stayed a few nights at Skakuza Camp and the rest of the time in Pretoriaskop. Skakuza overlooked a river and we watched the elephants, hippo, impala, zebras and giraffes, all at the river's edge, in the twilight. Fruit bats hung high in the branches of a tall marula tree, and we unsuccessfully tried to dislodge them with fruit that had fallen to the ground. During the days we travelled the Park roads in the bus, hoping to spot lions, leopards, cheetahs, in fact any wild cats, but we never did. I was content just to see the grazing herds and the occasional baboon begging treats from passers-by.

"Don't feed them," we were told, "you will merely encourage them to eat things they are not meant to."

To my eternal shame, I dropped a sweet for one and received a resounding (and deserved) thump on my back from a supervisor.

It was a wonderful week and I had Mr Brian to thank for it.

* * *

"Is that really all you remember about that trip?" I asked.

Joe thought for a moment.

"No, there's more," he said.

"Like what?"

"Well, you know I said the trip was sponsored by a famous soft drink company?"

"Yes?"

"We had crates and crates of Coke, so much of it that we were sick of it. Then one boy discovered that if you put a stone in the bottle, it fizzed. After that, the Coke just became toys. What fun we had! We sprayed each other, and Coke fights broke out. Everything was covered in Coke and we were all drenched."

"Anything else?"

"Yes, we all stuffed our faces with the marula fruit we found lying on the ground. But it wasn't ripe, and that first night at the camp we suffered the most awful runs."

"Oh my, you boys must have been an absolute nightmare to care for."

"We were diabolical. But it was a tremendous holiday, one I'll never forget."

"So what happened when you stayed at a host's house with Billy? You dropped that thread."

"I was just coming to that."

* * *

"Your hosts will be picking you up from the Home," Mr Brian said.

I was in his flat at the time, sitting on his sofa.

"Thank you, sir," I said, and for want of anything else to say, added,

"Does Billy know?"

"I'm sure he does," Mr Brian said with a smile. "Now off you go, I'm sure you have things to be getting on with."

I had stayed with host families before so was familiar with the arrangement, but I would have preferred to stay with Ma. That was no longer an option but I secretly hoped she would turn up at the eleventh hour. Of course she never did.

I made my way over to Beaton House to find Billy. He beamed a huge smile at me.

"Hey, Joe, you heard then?"

I really liked Billy. A year younger than I, he was short with a complexion as dark as Richard's. Billy's face was a squashed up combination of European and Asian and the twinkle in his slanted eyes belied huge mischief. With Billy, one always had a lot of fun.

"Yeah, Billy, it should be great. I heard they're rich."

"Yeah, Joe, looking forward to it. See you later."

With that, he was away. He was too young for me to hang around with and, anyway, he was in Beaton House.

The Christmas holiday duly arrived and Billy and I were picked up in a large car and driven to Bryanston where Mr and Mrs Maas lived with their daughter, Maureen. She was sixteen, blonde, blue-eyed and very beautiful. Billy and I stared bashfully at her as she and her parents tried to make small talk at the dinner table.

"Do you like your room?" Mrs Maas wanted to know.

"Yes, thank you," we answered shyly.

"Do you think you will like it here?" Maureen wanted to know.

Billy and I tried to look at her but her beauty was too overwhelming. We looked at one another and then at the floor, hoping a huge hole would rescue us. The ladies simply laughed.

It was a glorious holiday. Their house was huge, and the grounds extensive. There was a swimming pool, orchard, paddock (two horses) and three acres of land to play on.

The house was L-shaped and within the angle of the L, they kept their caravan. Billy and I stared at it in wonder. It was large enough to comfortably accommodate at least five people.

"Would you like to spend a night in it?" Mrs Maas asked.

We needed no second invitation and from then on we slept in it exclusively. Mrs Maas was bewildered that we preferred it to the vast rooms and comfortable beds in the house. What she failed to understand was that, in the caravan, Billy and I were kings.

During those bright summer days, Billy and I swam in the pool, kicked a football to one another on the huge manicured lawns, helped Maureen with her horses, and fed to excess on the ripe fruit hanging from the branches in the orchard.

Their dog was a large German Shepherd, with a wonderful nature, and it loved chasing tennis balls. I walloped them away with either a tennis racket or cricket bat. It was all heavenly and I discovered that I had a very sweet tooth for wealth.

One day, half-way through the six week holiday, Mrs Maas called us over.

"You will be staying with some friends of ours for a few days," she said. "We have to be somewhere and I'm afraid we cannot take you with us. It will only be for a few days."

Billy and I were disappointed but we didn't show it. The Home had already taught us to expect the unexpected and we accepted the situation.

Soon we found ourselves living with Mr and Mrs Lawson and their son, Roy. At fourteen, Roy was four years older than I was. Compared with the Maas house, the Lawson's was very modest. Indeed, the Maas's paddock was larger than the Lawson's house. It was one of many, all looking alike, on either side of a leafy road in a suburb near the Home. Despite being tiny, it was homely and comfortable.

Billy and I took to the Lawson's as if they were our parents. Mr Lawson, naturally quiet, was rarely at home and worked in the city. Billy and I followed Roy everywhere, chatting with him, listening to his music, playing with his Scalextric cars, building model aeroplanes and cars. When not following Roy, we sat in the kitchen with Mrs Lawson, listening to her tales about Roy while she baked and cooked.

"When Roy was younger," she told us, "he wore a cap to school as part of his uniform. I taught him to always greet any of our neighbours when he saw them. Then one day Mrs Jones next door asked why he didn't take off his cap when he greeted her. So I told Roy that I would give him a reward every time he took off his cap when he greeted anyone."

"How would you know if he did?" I wanted to know.

Mrs Lawson smiled.

"I told them to tell me if he did," she whispered conspiratorially. "And do you know what he did?"

We had no idea.

"After school he just took off his cap and came home bare-headed, greeting everyone he saw!"

Mrs Lawson laughed at the memory of it.

"And did he get a reward?"

"It wasn't exactly what he was meant to do so, no, he didn't."

If it wasn't tales about Roy, then Mrs Lawson would teach us etiquette and manners.

"Ladies first, always. Always open doors for ladies. Always say 'thank you for having me' after being invited to anyone's home. This is how you lay a table for dinner. The cutlery is laid out from the outside in, in the same order that you eat your courses. Side plates are always to the left of the dinner plate. Place your serviette on your lap, never tuck it under your chin. Do not sit down until invited to do so. Never begin eating until everybody is ready to eat. Always leave a little food on your plate to show that you have had more than enough. Always offer to wash the dishes after eating a meal. Wash the cups and glasses first because the water is cleanest then. Soap dishes first then rinse them under clean water. This is how you drink tea. Don't sip it, wait until the tea is cool enough then drink it as you would water. Always say 'thank you' if anyone does anything for you."

These were just a few of the rules that were regularly drilled into us and which would remain with me for the rest of my life.

The few days we were expected to stay with the Lawsons, turned into the remainder of the holiday.

"Are you sure you would rather stay with us?" Mrs Lawson asked.

"Yes," I said, speaking for Billy and myself. I knew he wanted to stay too. "But what will we say to Mrs Maas? Won't she be angry with us?"

"You leave that with me. I'll speak to her. They are good friends of ours."

The reason Billy and I wanted to stay with the Lawsons was simple. The Maas's house was out of bounds to us and we hardly saw them as we cavorted around their extensive grounds. The Lawsons, on the other hand, had a tiny property and we saw them every minute of the day. They were wonderful, warm approachable people.

"Come into the kitchen and talk with me while I cook," Mrs Lawson would say, and we'd sit at the kitchen table chatting for hours amidst the cooking smells, sampling cakes still warm from the oven. We had a special affinity.

We did see the Maas's again, but only for a brief visit with the Lawsons. Maureen was as beautiful as ever and Mr and Mrs Maas were equally gracious. I have nothing but wonderful memories of them.

So great was the mutual attraction between the Lawsons and us that Billy and I were invited back every Sunday and holiday thereafter. After a year, Billy went his own way and then it was just me.

It would not be unfair to describe the Lawsons as my surrogate parents. Certainly I looked upon Roy as an older brother and I adored him. I loved Mrs Lawson too, but she pressed me in ways I couldn't respond. I was never able to address her as anything but Mrs Lawson.

"Why not try calling me 'Mum'?" she said, after a year.

I could not. It was impossible. Embarrassed, I gazed intently at my feet.

"Alright then, try calling me Aunty Ada."

I couldn't even bring myself to do that. Ma's influence over me extended far beyond what it ought. Even after an absence of more than a year, I always believed she would make a surprise return. Had she done so, I might not have been able to explain my new 'mum' or indeed my mother to Mrs Lawson. No, Ma was my Ma and nobody, not even Mrs Lawson, would usurp her special place in my heart.

At the age of twelve, these were insurmountable difficulties for me. Had I been able to address Mrs Lawson as mum, the subsequent course of my life might have been very different indeed.

19

Annual Migrations

Despite having hosts to stay with during school holidays and permitted Sundays, my life in the Home continued unaltered. The daily routine of reveille, showers, chores, breakfast, school, lunch, play (or more chores), showers, supper, prep, bed, and lights out, continued unabated.

The only reprieve from this relentless schedule (apart from the holidays) was Camp. Camp was truly special. During the first three weeks of July, at the height of the Johannesburg winter, the Home moved *en masse* to a campsite on the south coast. For every boy in the Home this was simply known as Camp.

Situated on the Indian Ocean, about seventy-five miles south of Durban at a place called Twini (pronounced 'tweenee'), the campsite was a clearing not far from the beach. Apart from these three weeks, it was left to its own devices for the rest of the year. This meant that a vanguard of Home personnel was required to prepare it a week ahead of the rest of the Home arriving.

The vanguard, comprising a few energetic Housemasters and volunteers from amongst boys in the Senior Houses, drove down to Twini, taking with them our belongings. Each of us was provided with a canvas sausage bag into which we stuffed whatever we needed for the three weeks. This had to include two blankets taken from our beds. Some of the more fortunate boys had sleeping bags.

A large covered truck was parked just below the Parade Ground and, House by House, we carried our sausage bags to the truck where they were carefully stacked inside. No additional luggage was permitted. The truck was driven to the campsite in convoy with the Home bus containing the vanguard personnel.

The vanguard's task was to cut back the grass and erect World War One bell tents, five per House, with eight boys per tent. Eight rubber ground sheets, for protection against the damp, were tossed inside. An electrical cable, linking them all, entered and exited through flaps at the top of the tents and a single bare light bulb illuminated each interior. We had already been allocated which we would occupy and the vanguard delivered our sausage bags to them.

The Housemasters and their assistants had separate tents complete with fold-up camp beds. Senior House tents were located closest to the site entrance and were separated from the Junior tents by a free-standing rectangular feeding shelter. This had a shallow-peaked roof, supported at regular intervals by brick columns, over a flat cement base. One end of the feeding shelter was a locked, bricked-off room that served two purposes: to store food during Camp time and to store camp paraphernalia (trestle tables, benches and tents) when the site was not used.

Two small barred windows and a locked door guarded the room's contents. The wall on the dining side of the shelter was whitewashed and served as a screen when a movie was shown half-way through Camp. It was a simple and quick affair to remove the trestle tables and arrange the benches, cinema-style, in front of the 'screen'. The door into the storeroom was on one side of this wall and didn't interfere with the picture.

Two ablution blocks, one for the boys and one for the staff, provided shower and toilet facilities. Those for the staff were far more salubrious. In ours there were no mirrors and no hot water. The toilets, too, were un-fronted cubicles that seldom had enough toilet paper. They were located near the Senior House tents and were rarely used at night, except in dire emergencies. Instead of walking through bedewed grass we emptied our bladders on the surrounding undergrowth.

* * *

My first train trip to Camp, in July 1961, began at 11.00 am on the morning of departure and finished at 2.00 pm the following day, covering a distance of just over 400 miles. During all the excitement and activity, I and the other first-timers did not sleep a wink. Consequently, we were exhausted and walked around like automatons when we finally stepped off the train into the warm Natal sunshine.

The journey down was an adventure. The Home was allocated a number of coaches with sleeper compartments. Each compartment (we called them coupes, pronounced koopay) accommodated six boys. The seating in each coupe could be quickly converted into sleeping bunks with three on one side and three on the other. The seats/bunks were covered with a tough, dark-green plastic and bedding was not provided. The evening meal and the next morning's breakfast were served in the buffet carriage and it must have been a very busy time for the African waiters.

The best sleeping bunks were the middle ones because one could stare out through the window into the darkness beyond. Often much time would elapse before even a flicker of light broke the blackness and, shivering at the thought, I wondered what souls inhabited such isolated places.

The initial part of the journey was through the Transvaal which comprised vast, featureless spaces intermittently broken by enormous fields of maize mealies set in endless rows that seemed to take forever to pass by. Then, at about six in the evening, the night set in, plunging everything into darkness.

At the break of day, a new scene would present itself to us, one that was totally different to that of the Transvaal. This was Natal, as green and lush as any Eden anywhere in the world. The terrain, too, was no longer flat and just once I saw something that left me breathless.

I was about fifteen at the time, lucky enough to have a middle bunk, and dawn was just breaking. I looked through the window just as the sun cast its first rays over a valley that, to me, seemed endless. Across the entire vista, hill upon gentle hill jumped into view, each individually picked out by the sun's rays, as if that bright star was presenting them separately to me, inviting me to admire them, one at a time, from a box in which there were a thousand. For a full minute I was transfixed, not daring to look away, not wanting to miss a moment. I stared at the magic picture framed by my window, and would later learn that this was the Valley of a Thousand Hills. I had been most fortunate to see it at its best but, try as I might, I never did see that wonderful spectacle again.

From then on, the journey was through one of the most beautiful Provinces of South Africa. The warm current that washes the soft sandy beaches creates a shoreline of thick undergrowth, or *bundu*. It is also an ideal climate for growing sugar cane and during the three weeks of Camp, we feasted on the stuff. We'd strip the bark off with our teeth to reveal the fibrous, juicy inside. Then we sucked out the sweetness, the delicious juice running down our chins.

Our journey was coming to an end. In the 1960s, Twini comprised a few houses and a small shop that supplied the few inhabitants with their basics. It sat between two rivers across which two bridges were built to accommodate the road and rail traffic. They spanned two lagoons, the rail bridge closest to the campsite being significant inasmuch as we often swam beneath it or used it to cross over the lagoon. At regular intervals niches were built in to protect pedestrians in the event of a train suddenly appearing. The lagoon bridge was also the final bridge to search for from the train carrying us to camp.

"The lagoon bridge!" voices shouted from the leading coaches and a hundred or more heads popped out of the carriage windows.

Then a curious rite followed. Several months prior to the Home's departure for Camp, the boys would spend hours carving two-blade propellers from blocks of wood. These were attached to a shaft so they could spin in a breeze. Some of them were works of art, spinning freely when just breathed upon. Others were barely recognisable as propellers. Ultimately all would suffer the same fate.

Since we travelled down to Camp by train, much of the journey was spent holding our propellers out of the windows. Arriving at the lagoon bridge, the propellors were then tossed into the lagoon. Nobody knew why. It was simply a ritual that had to be done.

A few moments later and we would arrive at Twini station, nothing more than an elevated ramp of concrete with a small open-fronted shelter. But before arriving there, another ritual had also to be practised, usually by the Juniors, the Seniors having seen and done it all before.

Between the lagoon bridge and the station, the train passed by the lone Twini shop. During Camp, this shop did a roaring trade because this was where most of the boys bought their sweets. The most popular were pink and brown ones, individually wrapped. The pink ones were called Pinkies and the brown ones, Nutties. The common practice, for the few that had any money, was to enter the shop, the first day after arriving, and order Nutties and Pinkies. Having done so, one had arrived 'at Camp'.

From the train, the Juniors would shout "NUTTIES AND PINKIES" at the tops of their voices as the train slowly passed the shop before stopping at the station. Sometimes the proprietor would show his face and wave at us. I was never sure if he welcomed or dreaded our annual arrival. Some boys had light fingers and relished the opportunity of lifting what didn't belong to them. I never did but not because I disapproved. There were simply too many other activities to entertain oneself with than thieve from the local shop.

* * *

The south coast boasts miles of some of the most attractive beaches in the world. With the warm Agulhas current washing its shores, one can swim in it all the year round and the shore vegetation is lush and thick, much of it unspoiled except for the small towns along the coast, linked by a single main road and a railway line. The line had yet to be electrified and large steam engines thundered slowly and noisily along its narrow gauge.

Once a year, too, an annual migration occurred along the south coast that was as spectacular as it was interesting. The sardine rush.

Billions of sardines made their way up the south coast in the middle of every July, just when we were at Camp, and it was very easy to identify. Whilst sitting on the beach, we had become accustomed to seeing the gulls diving into the water someway out to sea. It was a commonplace sight but one that always awed me. I loved seeing them float in the air then turn and drop like harpoons into the sea below, folding back their wings at the last moment.

During the sardine rush, their numbers multiplied to such an extent that the sky about a hundred yards out at sea was filled with countless numbers of them. This marked the beginning of the sardine rush and we flocked to the beach. There was no hurry because the event took all day.

Years later, David Attenborough's TV documentaries informed me that there was as much activity below the water as above it. Marauding fish, sharks, dolphins and whales also feasted on the bounty, or each other.

On shore, anybody with any kind of boat would make his way out to the activity, a hundred or so yards out at sea, and, using merely a bucket dipped into the water, pull out vast quantities of sardines that had probably been chased to the surface by predators below. Then they'd bring them back to us on the beach before going out again for another load.

The pile of sardines, some still gasping, would soon cover a five-yard-square area of beach. Not a grain of sand was visible beneath this heap.

We would build a fire or one had already been prepared and lit. Driftwood regularly washed up onto the sand, providing enough fuel to keep the fires burning all day.

The sardines are not the small variety commonly bought in little tins. They are ten-inch whoppers, three of which, when gutted and cooked over a fire, left the eater full to bursting. Gutting the sardines was simple and the entrails were left where they fell. Using a stick, we held our sardines over the fire until they sizzled then feasted.

* * *

"I'd love to see the sardine rush one day, Joe."

"And I'd love to take you. I'd love to show you all the places I remember as a boy."

"Eating fresh fish on the beach and watching the seabirds dive must have been magical."

"It was, and we loved it. But there was a downside. That part of the beach stank for days afterwards. Luckily there were miles of pristine beach on either side so we still had places to romp while the crabs, seabirds and tides finished clearing up."

"Which reminds me. It's your turn to sweep up the fallen grapes under the vine. Every time I walk out there, they squish underfoot."

"What? Would you interrupt a genius at work to carry out such a menial task?"

"Yes. I would."

20

Camp Days and Nights

Camp meant no canings. The alternative punishment, however, was far more potent: being confined to Camp. Should a boy be confined to Camp, he was, amongst many other duties, expected to assist Willy, the Cook.

Willy was a Camp fixture. He was there before I arrived in 1961 and was still cooking well after I had left in 1969. I have no idea where he lived or went to outside the three Camp weeks and I certainly never saw him at the Home. But at Camp he was provided with his own tent, close to the Camp fire, where he supervised all the cooking. Anybody confined to Camp was his personal slave whom he had peeling potatoes, cutting up vegetables, collecting water, or anything else he wanted done.

Every day, one Junior tent was confined to Camp for the day and allocated the chores of washing dishes and cleaning out the feeding shelter after meals. There were four large concrete wash basins, each supplied with piped cold water, where we washed the cutlery, metal plates and cups. The duty boys, together with anyone else unfortunate enough to be confined to Camp, also assisted Willy with the preparation of meals.

Willy was a huge Zulu whose belly Buddha would have envied. He would stand over his huge three-legged cooking pot that straddled a large open fire, gazing intently inside whilst stirring in the ingredients. It was warm work and he sweated profusely, large drops plopping off the end of his nose into the cauldron. The boys accepted that the special 'something' in all their meals was Willy's sweat.

I, like many others, would visit the great man at some time during Camp.

"*Kunjani*, Willy," I would say.

It was the only Zulu I knew and it roughly translated to 'how goes it' or 'hello'.

"*Kunjani, umfana*," Willy would respond.

Umfana was 'young boy'.

Sadly this was the only Zulu I knew and in all my time I never heard Willy converse with another soul at Camp. I think his English was as limited as my Zulu but it never prevented him being understood when barking out orders. If a listener failed to understand his meaning, he mimed the action and understanding quickly followed.

The Camp menu seldom varied. Breakfast was porridge oats with milk and brown sugar, and hunks of white bread, all washed down with tea dispensed from a large urn. Lunch was whatever could be removed from a tin (jam, ham, pilchards) on hunks of white bread, all washed down with tea. Supper was a stew and vegetables with hunks of bread, all washed down with tea. Very basic but it was filling and we loved it.

Meals, and indeed all Camp announcements, were heralded by the Camp bell. This was a triangular piece of metal to which a metal gong was attached and only staff were permitted to ring it. When clanged, all boys assembled in House queues, in numbered tent order, in an area just below the feeding shelter which was called the Parade Area. A tent pole was erected and the Home flag, a red cross on a white background, was hoisted at reveille in the morning and lowered at last post.

Breakfast porridge and the supper stew were always served from robust galvanised billycans, oval shaped, open and with fall-down handles. Each House was allocated one which, together with the plates, cutlery and hunks of bread, was placed at the head of the waiting queue of boys. Father Norman (whom we nicknamed Bee-Bop) would say grace, then food would be served and each boy would find a space at one of the trestle tables in the feeding shelter.

Having eaten his meal, a boy took his plate and cutlery up to the dishwashing area for the duty tent to clean. Any left over food was disposed of in a large open pit, located behind the storeroom in the feeding shelter, that had been dug into the soft soil by the vanguard party. It was a six feet cubic hole in the ground that would be covered at the close of camp.

The staff enjoyed their meals in the staff marquee. This was a large rectangular tent that was situated in a central area, near the feeding shelter, where the Headmaster, Deputy Head, Matron and any visitors had their tents. The sick tent was located close to that of Matron's.

Staff meals were served by two favoured boys and the task was considered a privilege. Whatever the staff left uneaten was a feast to be pounced upon by any boy fortunate enough to see it first, namely the waiters. Rarely did a choice morsel see the light of day before being removed from the marquee. Willy personally cooked all staff meals.

A bugler sounded reveille at 7.00 am every day and breakfast was served an hour later. Thereafter, and before 9.00 am, all tents had to be prepared for Housemasters' inspections. The members of each tent paraded in front of their tent so that each could be inspected for cleanliness. The tents were then inspected and awarded a mark out of ten. The winning tent would win some privilege at the end of Camp, usually a day's excusal from the routine chores that all others were expected to do.

Should anyone become sick, he was put on a stretcher in the sick tent and tended to by Sister McArdle. It was not uncommon to see a boy in the tent, recovering from flu or a cold, but he was never in there for any length of time.

When released from camp at 9.00 am, the boys were allowed to do as they pleased. Some chose to stay in camp, while others went *bundu* bashing. A panga was used to hack away at the thick undergrowth that surrounded the camp on all sides. Some chose to climb the many trees on the edge of the site. A rope hung from one of the branches serving as a crude swing. Accidents did occur but I don't recall any limbs being broken.

Another popular activity was hitch-hiking. There were always a fair number of daily hikers who travelled as far as they could go before turning back. The incentive was adventure, seeing what towns lay further along the coast. It meant a boy would be away from Camp for the entire day but he had to register the fact with his Housemaster who arranged for him to have a packed lunch of a sandwich and an orange.

* * *

"That's unbelievable! You were allowed to go hitch-hiking whenever you pleased?"
"Yes. It wasn't considered unsafe in those days."
"How things have changed!"
"They have," agreed Joe. *"Now, can I carry on?"*

* * *

Years later, when in my later teens, whilst at Camp, I requested permission to hike to the Giants Castle area of the Drakensberg, where the movie, *Zulu*, had been filmed. This was quite an expedition, covering a considerable distance, and could take at least a week to complete. I had no resources, other than a small amount of money and an inordinate amount of confidence that the enterprise would be successful.

The Deputy Head, Mr Ken, favoured me with an audience as I presented my outlandish venture. I greatly doubted he would approve the scheme but that wasn't going to stop me trying. He listened, his head turned to favour his good ear (the other was deaf), and waited for me to finish.

"How long will you be away?"
"About a week, sir."
"And do you intend to go alone?"
"No, sir, I was going to go with a friend."

In fact, I had given no thought whatever to the project. I have always been impulsive and throughout my life I have regularly had to pause to pick up my shattered bones. These moments should have taught me the great value of patience but sadly I never learned that lesson.

* * *

"How true!" I muttered.
"If I wanted your opinion, young lady, I'd have asked for it."

* * *

There were two reasons why I chose the Giant's Castle as my destination. The first was that, at the age of thirteen, I had attended a *Veld and Vlei* (pronounced 'felt and flay') course in that area. This was similar to the Outward Bound programme in Britain. It was the first of its kind in South Africa and it was designed to promote the virtues of teamwork. Fitness, yachting and map-reading were some of the skills that the organisers hoped to instill in us.

We lived in tents that were located on the boundary of a large dam (for yachting skills) situated in the foothills of the Drakensberg Mountains, of which the Giant's Castle area formed a part.

At the conclusion of the course, we climbed those mountains, not with ropes and crampons, but wound our way up one of the perilous passes that occasionally cut through the sheer rock faces. Reaching the summit, we spent a freezing night in a cave before descending the next morning. This was all successfully undertaken when I was thirteen. I now planned to repeat that exercise, three years later, whilst I was at Camp.

My second reason for going, and one that I did not submit to Mr Ken, was that I wanted to escape the restrictions imposed on us by the Home. Being free to do as I pleased always appealed to me.

"And who will be going with you?" Mr Ken wanted to know.

At that moment Johnny W walked by. Despite being a few years younger I always liked him.

"Johnny W," I said to Mr Ken.

He gave me a long hard stare.

"Alright, you can go. Just let us know when you leave and when you get back. Oh, and don't forget to let your Housemaster know and that I gave you permission."

I rushed out and tracked down Johnny W.

"Hey, Johnny, do you fancy going hitch-hiking to the Giant's Castle?"

He stared at me open mouthed, as if I was from Outer Space.

"You what?"

"I've got permission to go, but only if you go, too."

And so that was it. Two boys allowed to hitch-hike a distance of 150 miles to the Drakensberg, climb them, and then return, all without any plan or supplies, depending solely on the good nature of any folk we might meet along the way.

We *were* fed along the way, and handsomely. I even had the audacity to request a meal from the *Veld and Vlei* organisers, who were understandably sceptical.

"Which course did you attend?" a suspicious organiser wanted to know.

"Course Number One," I said, which was true.

"And you want some food?"

"Yes, please."

"Listen, just don't make a habit of this, okay?"

"Of course not. I promise you won't see us again."

A long pause accompanied by a long stare.

"Very well, go to the kitchen. They will give you a plate of food."

We arrived in the Giant's Castle area and made our way to a courtesy hut at the foot of the escarpment. Within was a sign asking us to replace any supplies we might consume. We ate greedily before hastily evacuating the hut when we saw another group of people approaching the next morning. We had no supplies ourselves.

We climbed the same pass I had traversed three years earlier. Arriving at the summit we briefly viewed the icy and barren terrain of Basutoland, then hastily descended back to the warmth of Natal. Soon we were on the road back to Camp and arrived there five days after departing.

One abiding memory of the trip was walking along a road in Durban at 3.00 am in the morning. Despite the early hour, and being the middle of winter, we were wearing T-shirts and I remember thinking how very warm it was.

* * *

But by far the most popular activity at Camp was sitting on the beach and swimming in the ocean. Body surfing was immensely popular and we lived to catch the one wave that would carry us more than just a few feet and then gently deposit us on the beach. Sometimes the waves were just too wild, especially at spring tide, when they could reach a monstrous height. Only the most daring body surfed these. I did try once but was dumped on my head in the sand and never tried it again.

* * *

"What about sharks? Everybody knows that South African waters are teeming with sharks."

"I know, but during all my time at Camp, and we swam nearly every day and often at night, neither I nor anybody else ever encountered a single

121

shark."

"I guess you were lucky."

"Maybe. Mr Derek did tell us to rub carbolic soap onto ourselves, a cheap brand we all used called Lifebuoy."

"I think Lifebuoy still exists."

"Does it? Apparently that would chase any self-respecting shark away. I tried it once but not again. Frankly it was too much of a chore and I couldn't be bothered."

* * *

Our Housemaster, Mr Brian, and his assistant, Mr Derek, sometimes had sleepovers with us on the beach. The sand was as soft as any mattress and certainly more so than the harder ground in the tents. The Milky Way was so bright that one could almost read the words on a page. It was best when there was no moon and we would swim in the silvery light before diving beneath our blankets.

It was wonderful lying on our backs and looking up at the vast firmament above, with the ocean waves crashing down at regular intervals not far from where we lay. Shooting stars tore across the heavens attracting a general shout of, "Shooting star!"

Eventually the shouts were replaced with gentle (and not so gentle) snores as we all fell asleep.

Then, at daybreak (and the real reason why Mr Brian enjoyed sleeping on the beach) the sun would peer over the distant horizon and turn the grey dawn into a multicoloured panorama. Seeing the sun rise on the horizon of the Indian Ocean was magical indeed.

* * *

Sleeping in the tents was fine, provided it wasn't raining. A shallow protective trench was dug around the tent outskirts but rarely (if ever) did it serve its purpose. We were told never to touch the tent canvas when it was wet because its integrity would be compromised. Being told not to do something ensured that we did, and we discovered that this warning was an old wives' tale.

At night, the single low-power light bulb provided enough illumination for us to prepare our beds. The rubber groundsheets were spread evenly to cover all the ground space and one made his bed wherever a space appeared. It did get cold but never enough to be uncomfortable.

Only once was I so cold that I couldn't sleep. I had been swimming all day and had got cold. I lay beneath my thin blankets, awake and shivering.

"I'm freezing!" I whispered to Richard, who was lying beside me in the dark.

Without a word, he threw one of his legs over mine. Within moments I felt his body warmth envelope me and soon after I was blissfully asleep. It was so typical of him to do such a thing and to know exactly what to do.

21

Oddballs and Bad Behaviour

With so many boys at the Home, there were bound to be some oddballs. Macky had an uncanny ability to assign nicknames that stuck to various individuals.

One boy, for example, always tapped his foot on the ground when uncertain about anything, especially when claiming innocence for some misdemeanour of which he was clearly guilty. In *Mad*, a popular magazine doing the rounds, a character (I forget which one) always tapped his foot on the ground. To highlight the behaviour, the cartoonist had inserted *toc, toc, toc* above the character's foot. Macky quickly identified the similarity to that of the boy and from then on the poor chap acquired the nickname of Toc Toc.

To discover if Toc Toc was guilty of a crime, one had only to ask him. For instance: "Toc Toc, were you late for prep tonight?"

If Toc Toc denied the charge without moving a muscle, he was innocent. If he was guilty, his toe would hammer a rat-a-tat on the ground. He would also break out into a sweat and show signs of extreme agitation. The odd thing was, when these traits were pointed out to him, his guilty behaviour escalated to the point where we had to calm the poor chap down.

Another boy, Fonebone, arrived at the Home a few years after I did. Fonebone, also a character in Mad, was the nickname Macky allocated him soon after his arrival. Poor Fonebone suffered from epileptic fits.

Before his arrival, we boys needed to be instructed on how to handle any patient afflicted with the malady. Sister McArdle, the Home's live-in Matron and responsible for all things medical, was on hand to explain everything to us.

"He will behave oddly," she began, "doing strange things like standing in front of a wall and perhaps talking to it. Don't be alarmed. Simply follow him around and make sure he doesn't do anything to harm himself. When the fit is over, he will lie down and sleep. If he is wearing a tie, loosen it and take off his shoes. Make him comfortable. Make sure he isn't lying on his back because he could swallow his tongue. In a few hours he will wake up and carry on as if nothing has happened. He will be fine then until the next attack. Any questions?"

"Why does he have fits?" somebody asked.

"Stress, probably, so try to make things easy for him. I should mention that he might bubble around his nose and mouth. It's just mucous and will need to be wiped away."

We stared uncertainly at one another, unsure that we liked the sound of that.

"Any other questions?"

We had none. When Fonebone arrived we all stared at him as if he was some kind of freak. The expected fit soon arrived and Fonebone behaved just as Sister McArdle had described. We religiously followed him around and, when he frothed, we wiped his mouth and face and when finally he lay down to sleep, we undid his shoes and left him to sleep under a table.

He woke up a few hours later and was soon immersed in another fit. The number of boys that followed him around was halved but, nonetheless, they attentively wiped Fonebone's face and ensured he was safe and comfortable after the ten minutes that the fit lasted.

By the end of the week, Fonebone had had no fewer than thirty but now nobody followed him around. So blasé had we become that we didn't even notice when, during a meal, he would suddenly stand up and face a wall.

After several months, Fonebone had suffered numerous fits. The reactions of unsuspecting bystanders amused us at first but eventually we even wearied of those.

"Is he alright?" a concerned lady would ask at the bus stop, whilst we waited for a bus to take us to school.

Fonebone had begun talking to one of the side walls of the bus shelter.

"Yes, he's okay," one of us would say.

"Are you sure?"

The note of scepticism in the lady's voice was understandable. The white milky froth that had now appeared around Fonebone's nose and mouth, all too familiar to us, must have been terrifying for her. By now the bus had arrived.

"He's going to lie down in a few minutes," the Home boy would tell the lady, "just wipe his nose and mouth and loosen his tie. He'll be okay after a while."

Having said this, the boy would quickly board the bus to school. A few hours later, Fonebone would appear at school as if nothing had happened.

Fonebone often had fits aboard the bus and was left to travel we knew not where before turning up once more at school. Callous, perhaps, but we simply did not want to waste time travelling with him while he recovered. Unfortunately, our indifference sometimes spiralled out of control.

"Hey, Joe! Did you hear what happened to Fonebone at supper?" said Andy, a younger boy.

"No, what?"

"He was sitting at the table with us when he started having a fit. So we pushed him under the table and just started kicking!"

"Is he okay?" I asked, concerned that the boys might have gone a little too far this time. It worried me that the boys' callousness might have raised its ugly head above the parapet and be noticed by the staff. We enjoyed our cruelty too much to let that happen.

"Yeah, he's okay," said Andy and ran off into the night.

Then, at Camp, Fonebone inadvertently committed a crime that had several boys wanting to lynch him.

The Houses were lined up for the evening meal parade outside the feeding shelter. I was in Tent 1 of the Simpson House queue and Fonebone was in Tent 5 at the end of the line. The boys in each House were standing shoulder to shoulder, facing Bee-Bop who always said grace before meals.

Each boy was then given a plate of food and a hunk of bread. The food was served by the Housemaster from the oval billycans that stood steaming on the ground at the head of each queue. The bread, plates and cutlery were collected from a table alongside. Willy always cooked wonderful evening meals and, after a day's swimming or hitch-hiking, we were ravenous.

Nobody moved or spoke whilst Bee-Bop said grace. Anybody that misbehaved during any religious rite might find himself confined to Camp for longer than just a day so it was a big no-no. Imagine our surprise when Fonebone broke rank and started hopping on one foot all the way along our line.

What truly amazed us was his ability to hop on one leg, the other bent at the knee in front of him, his hands hanging limply by his sides. But for grace, his ridiculous antics might have raised a roar of laughter from amongst us. We understood he was in the throes of a fit and the hopping was probably an alternative for no wall being available to talk to. Bee-Bop was aware of Fonebone's behaviour but chose to ignore it, not even pausing whilst reciting the careworn words.

Nobody moved. By the time Fonebone reached the boys in Tent 3, we were becoming a tad concerned. Somebody should have grabbed him and led him away but nobody did. On he hopped and when he reached me, I looked down the line and saw forty heads turned towards us.

Just as Bee-Bop pronounced "Amen", Fonebone's hanging foot came down into our billycan of stew. Still nobody moved, not even our Housemaster, Mr Brian, who stood there open mouthed. They stood facing each other, Fonebone frothing at the mouth and nose, with one foot in the billycan, Mr Brian staring into the maniacally glazed eyes of an epileptic.

Still nobody moved but a low ominous growl, beginning with us in Tent 1, moved down the line. At a stroke, Fonebone had ruined Simpson House's evening meal and nobody could do a thing about it.

Without the rule of law, he would undoubtedly have been lynched. Despite our hunger, none of us was eating stew that night. The thought of eating the remains of food, in which Fonebone had put his foot, was abhorrent even for the least fastidious among us. We were forced to accept tinned pilchards, a poor substitute for Willy's stew, and the boys in the other Houses greatly sympathised with us.

Fonebone was led away to recover, the billycan still attached to his foot. He spent the night in the sick tent, protected by Sister McArdle, who undoubtedly was aware of the animosity the boys harboured against him.

Poor Dirk was another boy who often lit up our lives at Camp.

The dim light bulbs in each tent did not last indefinitely and had to be replaced. They were the bayonet type and replacing them in the dark, without a flashlight, was tricky. Whatever the supply voltage was, anyone having the misfortune to sample it retained vivid memories of the experience for several decades after. I did and can still recall the joy of temporarily joining the National Grid.

The tent leader would allocate the task to one of the boys who, with an inward groan, collected a replacement bulb from Housemaster's tent. He would then fit the new bulb, in the dark and without the aid of a flashlight. Flashlights were rare at Camp, simply because the batteries were too expensive to replace when drained.

Locating the socket at the top of the tent was simple enough. The faulty bulb was easy to find but, being at the top of the tent, it was difficult to reach. It really needed two boys and a friend was called upon to provide a pair of sturdy shoulders on which to sit. It did not take too long to switch them over.

The job of replacing the bulb was entirely up to the tent leader. He would allocate the task to whomever was immediately available but if Dirk was a member of the tent then it was given to him. Often Dirk was given the task by other tents and, if he refused, he was thumped and asked again.

"Dirk!" the tent leader would bark at him.

"Yes, Mike?"

"Go get another lightbulb for the tent."

"Yes, Mike," he would whimper and toddle off.

The sad part was that he had no friends to call upon to help him. Instead, the boys waited in the dark, the tent leader demanding that he move faster.

"I'm really trying, Mike," Dirk would moan and then let out an unearthly scream.

He had, in fact, located the inner lethal electrodes using the tips of his fingers. It was what the boys had been waiting for and they would howl with laughter because Dirk was renowned for it. Never once did he change his method, even when shown how to do it correctly, and it was always a great source of amusement for the boys.

"Hey, do you want to see Dirk change a lightbulb?" was regularly heard at Camp in the evenings.

Dirk, together with other bed-wetters, were usually allocated their own tent. On one occasion the staff, exasperated by his constant bed-wetting, decided that humiliating shock treatment might cure him. They, as well as the boys, believed that laziness was the primary cause of the malady. He and another persistent bed-wetter were ordered to lie on stretchers in the sick tent, throughout the day, encased in their soaking blankets. A sign was hung over the door to the effect that within were bed-wetters and the rest of the boys derided them when they passed by.

* * *

"Joe, you are kidding, right?"
"Sadly, no."
"But that's inhumane!"
"I know. It filled me with shame to write about it."
"Did it work? Did they stop wetting their beds?"
"No, it made not the slightest bit of difference. Who knows, it probably made them even worse."

* * *

All boys love a danger-filled thrill, which is why we loved to run across the face of Splash Rock. Situated half a mile from Camp on a rarely visited part of the beach, it was one huge piece of black basalt, the last remains of some distant volcanic eruption. From end to end it was about ten metres wide and its summit stood five metres above the beach. It was so named because of the white spray caused by the waves regularly smashing against its broad, flat, sea-facing front.

Splash Rock was a formidable structure. From its summit, the rock sloped steeply down its beach-facing side and we loved to sit on top, gazing with awe at the waves crashing against its face and being drenched by the spray. We never climbed the rock during spring tides. Then, the waves were so large that the rock was often completely over-run.

Someone suggested we run across the rock face when the water was receding from the shore. The ten or so metres to safety were not easily gained and had to be timed to perfection. Then somebody else suggested we do it during a spring tide and our sun-tanned faces blanched at the thought. But do it we must because it added credits to our standing amongst the other boys.

Nobody was ever harmed but there were a few near misses. One boy was swept out to sea and the relentless action of the waves threatened to dash him against the rock. Thankfully he managed to break free. I did try but never at spring tide. My nerves never stretched that far.

Other boys, supreme athletes like Rolf, managed it effortlessly, in and out of spring tide. Sometimes Mr Derek invited boys to race to and from Splash Rock, a distance of a mile or so. Rolf always won this too and even had time to run around the rock.

* * *

"Is Splash Rock still there?" I asked.

"I wondered that," Joe answered. "So I researched it."

"And?"

"It's almost completely buried by sand. There's only a small outcrop visible now."

"Gosh!"

"I know, I was surprised. That's all that remains of a Home legend."

"Any other memories of Camp?"

Well, yes, there's one, but it doesn't cover me in glory. I'm pretty ashamed of it really."

"Go on…"

* * *

The Headmaster's son, Michael, often accompanied us to Camp and assisted with the duties as a member of staff. He was a handsome young man, single and an undergraduate at the University of the Witwatersrand (called Wits but pronounced 'Vits'). His primary goal was to be a doctor and in this he eventually succeeded.

I liked Mike because he liked me. I am uncertain why he did but I always returned the affection of any member of staff that liked me.

"Hello, Mike," I would shyly say to him and he would tousle my hair before responding with a smile.

"Hello, Joe, and how are you today?"

"Fine, thank you."

"It's your birthday, soon. I'll see that you get a nice cake."

At the Home, a boy's birthday was celebrated with a cake baked by the kitchen staff. It wasn't as good as one that had been professionally produced but it wasn't bad either. At Camp there were no kitchen facilities and the birthday cakes were bought locally. Michael, as the quartermaster, was responsible for procuring them.

"Thank you, Mike," I would say and then wander away.

That was the extent of it, but I knew I had a rare friend amongst the staff, albeit one that was not permanent and unlikely to influence the opinion of any others.

Michael, responsible for all supplies delivered to the Camp, stored them in the locked room at the end of the feeding shelter. The cans of pilchards and the larger tins of jam and fruit were stacked from floor to ceiling. The meat that Willy would prepare and cook was hung from hooks and fresh bread was brought in daily. The windows were barred on the inside but left open to allow a cooling breeze to pass through.

Because the windows were always left open, anybody had ample opportunity to inspect the supplies inside. But other opportunities also arose when Michael unlocked the storeroom for the boys. Apart from the food, crates of bottled soft drinks were piled in a corner and anybody wanting to buy a bottle had only to ask and Michael always seemed on hand to oblige.

It occurred to me that it might be possible to pilfer the occasional bottle. My plan was simple and initially required my presence in the room. This was not a problem because Michael was quite relaxed about us being inside. Usually, five or more of us entered the room with him. When he was distracted, I quickly snatched a bottle from a crate and transferred it to the window sill of the nearest barred window.

The bars on the windows, although sturdy, were wide enough to allow a hand to reach in. All I had to do was wait outside until the room had been vacated, then reach in and take the bottle.

Much to my surprise the plan worked perfectly. By the time I had stolen three bottles I had become cocky and my fourth attempt proved to be my undoing. I decided to remove the bottle from the sill before Michael had vacated the room, thinking he would be too busy to see me.

"Who's that!" he shouted from within and my heart went cold.

Grabbing the bottle, I made a dash for it, hoping the *bundu* would conceal me. But it was too far and instead I chose to jump into the cesspit behind storeroom, where the food and vegetable matter were disposed of, before being covered at the end of Camp.

The cesspit was an apt place for a thief to hide but it did not save me. Michael gave chase and soon espied my skulking form at the bottom of the fly-infested pit. His expression of utter disappointment and disgust was, for me, a far more painful punishment than the three days I was confined to Camp. Never again did he speak to me and I had lost the only member of staff that I considered a friend.

* * *

"Cheer up. Paco's left a bottle of wine on our doorstep. We'll have it with our supper tonight, shall we?"

Joe yawned and stretched.

"That's a good idea. You never told me how difficult and painful this memoir writing business is."

"I never said it was easy."

"Well, I've just got a couple of paragraphs to write, and this chapter is finished."

"Okay. I'll get supper started, and when you're done, you can open the bottle. Deal?"

"Deal."

* * *

At the conclusion of three weeks, most boys were ready to return to the relative comforts of the Home. Living out of a sausage bag and sleeping on the hard ground was not easy. But return we had to, if only to attend school, the third term of which would begin in less than three days of arriving back.

The train ride back to Johannesburg was always a subdued affair. Despite the pleasures of eating meals in the buffet car, and watching the scenery pass by, the journey back understandably lacked the zest of coming down.

I had the pleasure of attending nine Camps and every one was an adventure. I saw and did things that I might never had if the authorities hadn't stepped in and removed me and my sister from Ma. For that, I suppose, I should be grateful.

22

School Friends

School was a time to get away from the Home and meet non-institutionalised children. We referred to them as day-scholars and rarely did animosity arise between us. Many of my closest friends were day-scholars and I have nothing but the fondest memories of them.

The school year began around mid January and ended the first week of December. It was divided into four terms, each separated by a school holiday. The two longest breaks were the winter holiday in July, when we were at Camp, and the six week summer holiday in December. The other week-long holidays were the autumn break in April and the spring break in October.

The Primary School was within walking distance from the Home and was a single-level L-shaped building that provided tuition for 250 pupils, a fair percentage of which were Home boys.

The great difference between the Home and school was the presence of girls. Here we were given the opportunity to see these rare creatures at close quarters and their virtues were a regular topic of discussion amongst us. Ultimately we would discover that, really, they were quite ordinary and differed from us only in that they wore dresses.

Having spent nearly four years at the Children's Home, and all of them in close proximity with girls, bathing with them and playing with them, they were not much of an enigma for me. Frankly, I liked them. Their gentle ways and natures I always found attractive and, had I been given the opportunity, would much have preferred their company to that of boys. So between the ages of nine and eleven, I was not in the least awed by them.

Come the onset of puberty, at the age of twelve, and all that changed. Women became exotic creatures, full of sexual promise and capable of reducing me to a whimpering tongue-tied mess. This fever would persist for the next forty years and had no known cure.

The Home was not a place in which to be coy. Communal showers, wherein six boys showered at a time, occurred twice a day. Those showering were closely scrutinised by those waiting and any form of modesty was met with derision. It was where we inspected the bruising and flecks of coagulated blood on our bums.

A Patrol Leader was in charge of showers and each group of six was given three minutes to soap and rinse off. The Patrol Leader never used a timing device, depending solely on observation to judge when a group had finished.

"Next!" he would shout and the next six would replace the first.

Anyone wanting longer was forcibly ejected by those following. Time in the shower was precious and malingerers were using what was not theirs. Obstinate refusal was dealt with by the Patrol Leader, usually with a kick or a slap, but this was rare.

The onset of puberty brought with it the accompanying physical transformations that varied from boy to boy and from dormitory to dormitory. Hormones raged. Women's clothing magazines, particularly the underwear sections, could be found in most of the toilet cubicles. Even the characters in girls' comics were not safe from our lusting.

In Standard Two, in the Primary School, I was still three years short of puberty.

On the first day of school, the teacher was calling out the names of the children in our class from the register.

"Churchill."

"Present, Miss," said a day-scholar.

The teacher looked up.

"What's your Christian name?" she asked the boy.

"Winston, Miss."

There was a long pause before she spoke again.

"You have a very famous name, do you know that?"

"No, Miss," Winston replied and the rest of us stared questioningly at each other and at him.

"Who's Winston Churchill?" somebody whispered but nobody knew.

I suppose that, at the age of nine, and in a primary school situated in one of Britain's far flung colonies, one might excuse our ignorance. History was the very last of my interests at that time and I wasn't any different from all the children in my class. All, that is, except Les. I have little doubt but that he knew all about Winston Churchill, preferring to keep such knowledge to himself. I was happiest at school when sitting next to or even near Les.

As a rule, the teachers allocated our seating partners (in the two-pupil desks) never allowing friends to sit alongside one another. Should the teacher discover that he (or she) had placed two miscreants together, it was an easy matter to exchange them for less unruly children.

"Jones, change places with Miss Smith."

"But, Miss," Jones would wail, "I don't want to sit next to a girl!"

I often shared a desk with one of the girls. I didn't mind and generally we ignored each other, keeping any exchanges to a minimum. But sometimes I was forced to consult her.

"Yesterday," said the teacher, "I asked you to read over the section on parts of speech."

Parts of what? What was she talking about?

My mind raced as it searched for the information relating to this latest revelation. I must have been day-dreaming when the teacher mentioned it the day before because my brain persisted in arriving at cul-de-sacs. There was nothing for it but to address the alien beside me.

"What's a part of speech?" I whispered to her.

It was then that I discovered how profound was her hatred of boys and her look shrivelled me to my core. I am told that the opposite of a misogynist is a misandrist and Thelma van Zyl (the girl next to me) was afflicted with misandry from the top of her pretty head to the very soles of her feet.

"You should have done your homework!" she spat, before turning disdainfully away.

"Twead," said the teacher, "what's a noun?"

I glanced at the girl beside me and the small smile on her face was not a pleasant one.

"Um, Miss," I faltered, "it's a part of speech."

I was hoping for a miracle.

The problem was that I might be given additional homework should I fail in this examination. Additional homework interfered with soccer.

"Yes, Twead, it is, but which part?"

"The first, Miss?"

"Can you help him, Miss van Zyl?"

"Miss, a noun is the name of a person, place or thing."

"Excellent, Miss van Zyl. Twead, I want you to write that out a hundred times and have it on my desk first thing tomorrow."

"Yes, Miss," I groaned.

Beside me, Miss Prim smirked as if her life depended on it.

But not all the girls hated me.

Twice a year an event at school merited the spending of one's pocket money at one of the many booths erected for the functions. The two principal events were the School Fête and Sports Day.

On those days, the school was opened to the public. Money raised by the sideshows filled the coffers of the school fund. This was used to pay for projects that local government might deem unnecessary for the maintenance of the school. Lyndsay would leave a small but very valuable silver coin on my desk and then walk away without saying a word. I always quietly thanked her.

The coin would be a sixpence and the only pocket money I had in the Home. I had no difficulty spending my sixpence at one or more of booths that offered everything from tombola to burgers and candy-floss.

Naturally, being a Home boy, no family member came with me, as did those belonging to the day-scholars. I never did spot Lyndsay amongst them and I doubt I would have even acknowledged her had I done so. I have often pondered those bygone days and wish I had more properly thanked her for her many kindnesses. In the hours, days, weeks, months and years that I spent at the Primary School, Lyndsay's generosity has stood out above all others in my memories of the time.

* * *

School wasn't unpleasant but I was always on the lookout for opportunities to escape its monotony.

When I was ten or eleven, the Home was quarantined when an outbreak of scarlet fever was detected. We were off school for three glorious months and everything changed during that time. Mr Brian was more relaxed and the corporal punishment that he usually meted out was greatly reduced. The atmosphere throughout the Home improved considerably and only at Camp did we enjoy such a tranquil environment.

Reveille, usually at 6.00 am every morning, was now at 7.00 am. Duties still had to be performed but now were unhurried. Board games, such as Monopoly, chess, draughts, and snakes and ladders, became the rage and comics were devoured in prodigious quantities. Books by Enid Blyton and Capt. W E Johns were shared by the readers amongst us. Outside, we roamed every corner of the Home, constructed and flew kites, and played sport.

And one day something impossible happened.

It snowed.

We awoke to an outside world of white and the silence was deafening. The usual dawn chorus and the sounds of distant traffic were absent and anything we did hear was muffled. Soon we were treading through the six-inch layer, leaving our footprints as evidence and discovering that, although soft and fluffy, it was also frighteningly cold. Only a few snowballs were thrown before we retreated back to the relative warmth of the House.

But it was impossible to stay indoors and we soon joined the more hardy characters who had stayed out to build snowmen. I was surprised how sticky snow was, seeing a ball grow in size, picking up material when rolled along the ground.

The next morning, apart from a few vestiges of the larger snowmen, all the snow had disappeared. But it had been a memorable experience, especially for boys who had never seen snow before.

All too soon the wonderful period of quarantine passed and we returned to the routine that regulated our lives. School was a major part of it and I found myself again attending lessons and seated at a desk that faced a blackboard and the teacher.

* * *

In 1964, I was in Standard Five, the last year of primary school. I was thirteen years old and had spent the past four years at the school. Now I was preparing for entry to the High School. We would complete our final examinations in early December and the results of these would determine which classes we attended at the High School.

The High School was a bus ride away and accommodated one and a half thousand pupils, drawing its numbers from several surrounding primary schools, one of which was ours. Classes were streamed and students with the highest marks from each primary school were placed in the A stream. This segregation continued down to F stream for Standard Six with fewer streams in successive years. There were thirty pupils in each class.

We would later learn that the streams were not set in stone. Anyone failing to perform well in the A stream might find himself moved down to a lower one and hard workers in the streams below had ample opportunity for promotion.

I was entirely unaware of all this and simply expected to move up to the High School after completing Standard Five. As far as I was concerned, school was school and it never occurred to me that there might be competition for places in the classes.

For the final exam in primary school, and for no other reason than I was bored, I memorized the notes for each subject in the small exercise books we kept. This didn't take long because the subjects were so simple.

In Nature Studies, for example, there were descriptions of lions, ruled by a single male, their hunting methods, their roles as members in a pride, and their habitat. Such information did not take long to memorize because it interested me. When examined, I had merely to regurgitate it and consequently my grades were good.

I arrived at the High School, together with Les, and we were placed in the A stream. This delighted me because I had a friend on whom I could depend for moral support. In fact we soon drifted apart because we found new friends from amongst the day-scholars.

Lenny Holder would become my closest friend and to whom I was most indebted. The students brought sandwiches with them, eaten during the lunch break, and Home boys were provided with packed lunches, usually a sandwich and an orange. Although nutritious, they bore no resemblance to those prepared by the parents of day-scholars. For five years, Lenny shared half his lunch with me.

"My Ma wants to know what you like best," he asked, and I was overwhelmed.

He had removed the guilt I felt in accepting his generosity and he, brilliant boy that he was, understood my feelings.

"Listen, Joe," he said, "it's no trouble for my Ma to make four instead of two sarnies. She likes it that you like her sarnies."

"I love them, Lenny," I said and I meant it.

Sarnies were the name we all used for sandwiches and Lenny's mum made the best. Lenny was like Les in that he was brilliant academically. Always at the top of the class, his thoughtful and modest demeanour made him immensely popular with staff and students alike. Whereas I was regularly caned by almost every member of the male teachers, Lenny never was. I was truly honoured to be his friend.

Lenny, like all the boys in our class, would be my classmate for the duration of the five years we spent at the school and we would get to know one another as well as if we had been in the Home together.

Most of the boys in the Home had a profound dislike of school and very few intended to continue until Standard Ten. They couldn't wait to leave school, and the Home, to earn money.

My lazy nature baulked at the thought of beginning my working life at such an early age. I was enjoying myself far too much and had no intention of exchanging my childhood for the daunting responsibilities of adulthood. So stay at school I did, doing the minimum amount of work to ensure that I remained with Lenny and the other friends I had in my class.

All too soon, however, my school years would end. I left with nothing more substantial than a Standard Ten Certificate. It was lamentably inadequate for the qualification needed to attend Wits University. I always dreamed of being at Wits and believed all graduates were geniuses.

A decade later I did fulfill my dream, but at a university in Britain. I would finally realise that one didn't need to be a genius to attend. At university, I continued my lazy ways and once again squandered another opportunity to excel. Nevertheless that degree was a key to open many doors for me.

23

Animal Encounters

Father Norman arrived in the Home at the same time as me. We nicknamed him Bee-Bop and, like Father Eric, the Headmaster (whom we called the Beak), he was British. Both had moved out to Africa to follow their callings as Anglican priests. The Beak was married with children but Bee-Bop was single.

It was Bee-Bop who introduced me to photography. Converting a spare classroom, he set up a darkroom with blackened windows and when the lights were turned off, it was impossible to see anything at all. Several enlargers enabled us to study the negatives of the photographs we snapped during the day. The film was developed in spools that had to be loaded in the pitch dark prior to filling their containers with developer. Learning to load a film in the dark meant we had to practise the art in the light, and spoiled film was used for that purpose. It didn't take long to master.

"Everyone ready to load their films?" Bee-Bop would ask while his fingers hovered over the light switch.

"Yes," we chorused.

The room would be plunged into a deathly darkness, with only our voices indicating our locations. Outside in the corridor, a red light had been installed to warn against entry when it glowed.

The photographic paper wasn't as sensitive to light as the film and could be worked in a room bathed in red. Cameras, enlargers, film and paper were always available. Well-meaning people donated both their time and equipment and we would often be spoiled with the latest equipment. Mary Oppenheimer, the daughter of South Africa's most wealthy man, donated her enlarger which was fully automatic and a dream to operate.

During the holidays, Bee-Bop would drag his four-berth caravan behind his large Mercedes, ostensibly on a photographic trip. In truth, he loved caravanning. I, together with three other boys, would sometimes accompany him and as a result I saw a fair portion of the country.

We went to Natal and Northern Transvaal, stopping at some scenic spot near a river, where we would set up camp and photograph anything that caught our fancy. In the evenings we would play Monopoly, correctly and according to Bee-Bop's stringent rules, and soon discovered that he was a very sore loser. Heaven help any boy who made a hasty transaction with another.

"You should never have sold Mayfair!" he would snarl. "Michael only won because you sold it to him. Could you not see that he already had Park Lane?"

The offender would look sheepish but Bee-Bop never held a grudge. Moments later we would begin the game again and any transgressions were soon forgotten. Sometimes we played into the early hours of the morning before turning in for the night.

Bee-Bop, being an adult, had the largest of the beds and the rest of us slept comfortably on the converted single beds. The backrest lifted to form a double bunk, much like those in the coupes on the train. One boy usually slept alongside Bee-Bop in a sleeping bag.

One night it was me and he was reading.

"Listen to this," he said, "this writer really knows how to write."

He read a sentence in which the word 'crenellated' was included.

He turned towards me.

"Good, don't you think?"

"Yes, Father. What does crenellated mean?"

"You know the shape of the tops of castle walls, with gaps in them?"

"Yes?"

"Well those are crenellations."

I thought about that for a moment.

"May I read the book after you, please, Father?"

"You can have it now," he said, letting it slide out of his hand into mine, "I've read it three times already."

The book was *Ice Station Zebra* by Alistair MacLean. I read and thoroughly enjoyed it. I was one of a group of readers in the Home and had enjoyed Enid Blyton's marvellous *Famous Five* tales and her wonderful *Adventure* series. I had already devoured many of Capt. W E John's exquisite *Biggles* books. At the age of about twelve, I tried the Hardy Boys and Nancy Drew detective yarns but was lured away by James Hadley Chase, the pseudonym of a Brit who wrote American gangster novels. Now Bee-Bop had introduced me to Alistair MacLean and I became hooked on him. Rarely did I not have a novel in my school or Home blazer pockets.

After leaving school at the age of eighteen, I picked up Charles Dickens's *Pickwick Papers* and could not put it down. One may accuse him of being verbose but I never did.

At school, even our English teacher complained about Dickens.

"I ask you," she wailed, reading from our textbook for the year, *A Tale of Two Cities*, "why can't the man simply write 'he stood up'?"

Dickens had written something like, 'he raised himself to the vertical'. I agreed with her, but once I had read *The Pickwick Papers*, I found it impossible to return to the earlier nonsense by Chase and MacLean.

I have always remembered Bee-Bop's words, that night, so many years ago. The startling fact is that this intelligent and highly educated man never developed his reading skills beyond Alistair Maclean.

* * *

"Ah, that's where you got it from!" I exclaimed.
"What?"
"Your habit of writing a hundred words when only one would do nicely."
"I love words."
"Well, you don't have to wear them out. I think it's just as skillful to find one word that says exactly what you want, rather than describe something using a hundred."
"Oh, listen to you - Miss Know-It-All."
"Well, you sound really pompous. And you don't know if Bee-Bop read other stuff. He may have just chosen Alistair Maclean for the caravanning trip. Anyway, I was just trying to help." I marched off to the kitchen.
"And there's no need to sulk," Joe called after me.

* * *

I loved the caravanning holidays. Every trip was interesting and sometimes they were out of this world. On one occasion, a wealthy friend of the Home invited Bee-Bop to visit his holiday home in a game reserve he owned. Bee-Bop asked if he could bring a few boys with him.

"Bring as many as you like."

About twelve of us travelled to what would be one of the holidays of a lifetime. I preferred travelling with Bee-Bop instead of in the Home bus, and for two glorious weeks we lived in an area of the country that few were privileged to enjoy. It was alongside the Kruger National Park, but fenced off from it, and large enough to house all the wild animals to be found in the Park.

I would spend nights in tree houses, little more than wooden platforms, built into a tree alongside reservoirs of water, where zebra, giraffe and impala came to drink. The reservoirs were a fair size and four of them were dotted around the park. Using telephoto lenses I would snap the animals from the tree houses and later develop the film in the darkroom back at the Home.

When not in a tree house or in the caravan, I would sleep with the rest of the boys in double bunks that were arranged around the walls of a simple rectangular hut. It overlooked a river in which hippo wallowed, staring at us as we cavorted along the shore, just yards away. Dangerous they may have been but we were totally unafraid of them.

Should we choose to walk, rather than travel along the rudimentary sand roads in the provided Land Rover, we were accompanied by African rangers who carried high-powered rifles for our protection.

On one occasion, one of the rangers left our campsite on his bicycle and without a rifle. Within moments he was back, his dark skin ashen. After enquiries we learned that he had just encountered a leopard attacking an impala on the road ahead of him, not far from the camp.

Apparently the leopard and ranger had espied one another at exactly the same moment. The ranger turned and fled but what he didn't realise was that the leopard had made off in the opposite direction, leaving the lifeless impala behind.

By the time we arrived at the kill site, on foot, only the impala remained. Its glassy gaze stared lifelessly at us but it showed no marks of an attack by a predator. It was almost as if the animal had simply laid down on the dusty road to die.

One of the African rangers explained that the leopard had fastened its jaws on the narrow throat of the impala, suffocating it in the middle of the road, when his colleague had chanced upon the scene. Even so, we could see no indications of the attack until the ranger lifted the soft white fur to reveal four neat puncture wounds.

The leopard's loss was our gain and the Land Rover was used to transport it back to camp where it was first hung by its hind legs, to drain the blood, before being skinned. One of the rangers slit the animal open to reveal its insides.

What a biology lesson we were treated to! I expected to see a blood-soaked mess instead of the clean and neatly arrayed arrangement of heart, lungs, liver, stomach and intestines, all exquisitely packed and in perfect condition. More than likely the impala was having a poo when it perished because small balls of dark scat awaited expulsion.

The rangers had seen it all before and smiled at our wide-eyed curiosity. One of them pulled me closer and, using a sharp knife, opened the white lining of the stomach. Within was a fine green pulp, showing how thoroughly an impala masticates vegetation before swallowing. It was all simply fascinating. That night we feasted on the meat that was so fresh that it melted in our mouths and required little chewing.

* * *

The grazing animals were becoming too numerous for the reserve to handle and their numbers had to be controlled. There was a danger they might over-graze and be the cause of greater problems in an area that already suffered from a low rainfall. The head ranger would take a team out at night, to cull carefully selected animals within a herd, and it was not uncommon to hear the report of a high-powered rifle.

One night we accompanied the rangers. They planned to shoot an impala then drag its carcass behind the Land Rover, hoping its scent would attract any wild cats to a tree house in which we would spend the night. The carcass would be suspended from a branch of the tree and we were provided with a high-powered lamp to illuminate any cats that came to feed.

The lamp was first used to illuminate the unfortunate impala which would serve as bait. What surprised us all was how very easy it was to identify and then shoot the animals. When the light was fully upon them, they simply froze, rooted to the spot, standing almost indefinitely like statues. I believe the marksman might have had time for a cup of tea before shooting the animal.

The positive side of it was that the chief ranger, an American who was completing a doctorate relating to the conservation of African game, was able to ensure that the animal being culled was simply an unproductive member of the herd. On several occasions he cancelled one kill to select another.

Eventually one was dispatched and we were dragging its carcass behind our Land Rover. We reached our tree house, pulled up the carcass and sat waiting quietly in the dark for the sound of large teeth sinking into flesh and cracking bones. We waited...and waited.

It is almost impossible for youngsters to sit quietly for any length of time and we were no exception. Somebody had to switch on the lamp (to check it worked), somebody had to speak and be silenced by the rest, somebody had to fidget, somebody had to fart and make the rest of us laugh. In short, it was impossible to maintain silence for a period longer than thirty seconds. The inevitable upshot was that no wild carnivores visited us that night.

One by one we turned in, rolling out our sleeping bags on the wooden base, making ourselves comfortable beneath the branches and the stars. Even as we lay there, our ears were tuned to the sounds of the African night, determined to spring up should one of those sounds come from the vicinity of the free meal hanging below. None did.

Eventually all of us were asleep, until woken by the raucous African dawn chorus. Bleary-eyed, we gazed over the edge.

Not a hair of the carcass remained.

Perhaps our snores had been the signal that it was safe for some lucky beast to make off with the bounty. We would never know when and how it happened but I was left with a profound respect for the patience and cunning of all wild predators.

On another occasion, I was left alone in a tree house with a camera and telephoto lens to capture any animals that might come and drink at the waterhole. I also had with me Colonel Hunt's account of the 1953 conquest of Everest by Sherpa Tensing and Edmund Hilary. I had already snapped a number of zebra, impala and giraffe and sat back to read the book.

I was so absorbed that I didn't notice a troop of thirty or so baboons sitting on the ground looking up at me. My heart went icy cold. I knew they were extremely comfortable in trees and, should they choose, could easily tear me apart. Baboons were fairly common in the reserve and, at night, they terrorised us by barking incessantly just outside the windows of our hut. None of us had the courage to visit the outside latrine once we had turned in for the night.

In the tree house, my imagination had escalated to a point where I was being eaten alive by baboons. The main camp was much too far away for me to scream for help and several hours remained before the Land Rover would reappear to pick me up. I had a vision of them finding just the book when they did turn up.

There was only one thing left for me to do. I decided to bark at them. I quite prided myself on my imitation of a baboon's bark. The trick was to finish the bark with a noisy intake of breath. I had practised it often enough before and now I let rip with the loudest bark I could muster. I must have looked silly, book in hand, barking at baboons on the ground. But, to my amazement, it worked. I wonder what I said? They shot away and gathered under a tree some distance away. I still feel quite proud of myself thinking about it.

The hut we occupied was located alongside a fairly substantial river wherein several hippo spent their days. All we could see of them were their eyes and noses and they stared as hard at us as we did at them. The river was not very wide, about thirty metres or so, but it was deep and the hippos never had any trouble completely immersing themselves.

A large nearby tree provided an ideal branch from which to hang a rope, which we did, and in which knots were tied with a plank fashioned for a seat. It was designed to swing out over the river with the hippos below. Initially just one of us swung out over them but eventually it was tested with all of us swinging at the same time. Had the rope snapped, we intended to swim ashore. We foolishly believed the hippos to be timid and would pose no threat should we suddenly find ourselves in the river with them.

We sometimes tormented them with oranges that we threw at their heads. The hippos simply submerged and reappeared twenty or so yards downriver. One of the more observant among us noted that the location of their reappearance was predictable and an ambush was planned.

Whilst one thrower pelted a poor hippo with an orange, seven of us waited downriver, ready to pounce when it reappeared. On cue the animal surfaced and was bombed by oranges. Irresponsible and stupid, I know, but at the time it was hugely entertaining.

The hippos, frankly, bored me. All I ever saw of them was their eyes, ears and nostrils on the surface of the water. I desperately wanted to capture one gaping on film. So down to the river's edge I went and sat there, not more than a few metres from a number of them. It was approaching evening and I had decided to eat my evening meal with Bee-Bop and the other photographers in his caravan. He was preparing this while I was down at the river.

Hindsight is always wonderful and I now know that hippo are extremely dangerous and that their gape is not a sign of lethargy but one of aggression. Being nocturnal creatures, they leave the water to graze and heaven help anyone or anything that stands between them and their food. Furthermore, they have favoured exit points, from which they leave the river, and I was right in the middle of one.

* * *

"Joe, you idiot!"

"I know that now! We didn't have TV in those days and it was long before David Attenborough educated the masses about the habits of hippos and suchlike."

"So what happened?"

"Patience is a virtue, as you are always reminding me, Vicky. You'll have to wait until I write the next chapter."

24

An Accident

I was blissfully unaware that I was in a hippo path, staring at the eyes and nose of one a very short distance away. Silently we studied one another. I have a tendency to talk to almost any object, animate or otherwise.

"Okay, you fat -------, let's see a yawn," I said. "I haven't got all night and frankly, I'm hungry."

To my astonishment, the hippo did 'yawn' and in my excitement, I almost dropped the camera. The hippo continued to gape and I snapped away like there was no tomorrow. I raced back to the caravan to convey the good news to Bee-Bop.

He was still preparing supper, listening to my babblings, when another boy dived head first into the caravan. Bee-Bop and I were so startled that we both paused to stare at the boy, wondering what would inspire such a unique method of caravan entry.

"Father!" he yelped, "outside!" and he pointed out of the door.

Bee-Bop and I stepped to the doorway and were amazed to find the outer awning in complete disarray. Two camp beds were crushed and the outside flaps had almost been ripped off. The camp beds were for two boys who preferred to sleep outside where it was cooler.

It transpired that the hippo had followed me out of the water and used a well-trodden path over which the caravan's awning had been erected. I have often wondered what might have happened to me had I not hurried back to convey my news.

I couldn't wait to see the negatives in the dark room, when we returned to the Home, and anticipated several award-winning shots. Eventually I did develop the film and stared at the images. Six of them had been shot on the same frame. In my excitement I had forgotten to manually wind on the film. My disappointment was immense.

Bee-Bop, however, had seen some zebra pics on the same roll of film and had a brainwave.

"These are black and white animals," he said, "why not make a positive of the negative and then print that."

"What's a positive?"

"It's exactly like a negative but it's called a positive. We put it into the enlarger, just as we do the negative, but when it's printed it will be only in black and white. There will be no greys. The subject is a zebra, which is black and white, so it should be very striking."

"Sounds great, Father," I said, impressed.

I watched as Bee-Bop quickly created what I thought was a masterpiece. The photograph was then mounted an a white cardboard frame. It was a stunning picture showing two zebra standing at right angles to one another. Twenty inches by sixteen inches in size, purely in black and white and a winner all the way. It won several awards and was donated to the wealthy owner of the reserve who hung it over the fireplace in his house on the reserve. Although I was credited as the author of the work, I knew Bee-Bop deserved all the accolades. I might have taken the photograph, but the winning ideas and imagination were all his.

* * *

"I wonder if that picture still exists? I'd love to see it."

"Yes, I'd like to see it again."

"Who knows? Perhaps somebody might read this book and recognise it, then get in touch with us?"

"We can dream."

* * *

The three weeks at the reserve were the holiday of a lifetime. The freedoms we enjoyed were far beyond those in the KNP alongside. Unlike the Park, we could walk or drive where we liked, protected only by a gun-toting ranger who accompanied us.

One afternoon we were walking through the bush where sporadic islands of acacia trees broke up the sea of surrounding tawny grass. In the distance, about three hundred metres away, we saw the tops of three large black rocks. We decided they were worthy of investigation.

And then the rocks moved.

We were about 200 metres away but our ranger suddenly became very tense and ordered us to stand still and be silent. The moving rocks seemed to sprout up from the ground and grew to an enormous size. They were elephants resting in the grass until they heard our approach.

An elephant never runs, but, should it choose to, it can walk at an incredible speed. I knew this and understood that, should any of those elephants decide to charge us, we stood little chance of survival. The ranger understood this too and was clearly very afraid. The rifle that was slung over his shoulder was suddenly in his hands and he quietly ordered us to retreat without running. We were only too happy to oblige. Luckily, the elephants sauntered away in the opposite direction. It had been terrifying but it was magnificent seeing them in the wild.

On another afternoon's walk, I came across a baby giraffe. It was standing all alone in a group of acacia trees and seemingly unafraid of me. I was very surprised until I saw that it had injured its eye. The eye was swollen and closed and the poor thing was effectively blind on that side. We were just a few metres apart and it was only a foot or so taller than I was.

Then it turned its head and spotted me with its remaining good eye. In an instant it was gone, bolting away in terror. I thought that was the last I would see of it when, to my astonishment, it was charging at me from the direction it had just gone. I stood rooted to the spot but it galloped past, narrowly missing me.

I reported the injury to the American and he was very interested. He wanted to know every detail and clearly intended on some course of action to find and treat the animal. I only hope he found it.

The American lived in the owner's house, which had every modern convenience as well as a swimming pool. At the time, the owner's wife, a lady in her fifties, was staying there too. She had invited Bee-Bop for a meal and insisted he bring a few of us boys with him. Bee-Bop took the photographers.

It is not often that one enjoys cool drinks alongside a swimming pool, surrounded by some of the most dangerous animals in the world. In the evening, the American drove us off-road in an open-backed Land Rover. Bee-Bop was in the passenger seat and we boys were standing in the rear, holding onto a metal cross bar. A large herd of grazing wildebeest, impala, giraffe and zebra had gathered and we drove at speed among them. There were so many that I had only to stretch out my hand to touch one running alongside us. It is one of those experiences that I will forever cherish.

At the meal that night, we were served with the freshest meat, together with exquisitely prepared vegetables, and we feasted. The American ranger was there in body but not in spirit. Before the meal was a quarter finished, he was quietly snoring at the head of the table.

"Please don't mind him," our hostess apologised, "he was out culling impala the night before and hasn't slept in thirty-six hours."

At the house we were also introduced to two orphaned mongooses. They were the cutest little animals and one of them had an alarmingly swollen head. Apparently it had been bitten by a poisonous snake but we were assured that it would soon recover. Its injury certainly didn't do anything to stunt its playful nature because it romped as energetically as its sibling.

* * *

I thought the holiday was unique and that I would never see the reserve again. I was mistaken. Two years later, the owner welcomed us a second time but with the proviso that we help repair some of the damage caused by erosion. Successive rains had washed away the topsoil in certain areas and the land needed barricading against possible floods.

I thought it a small price to pay and immediately volunteered for the expedition. Together with nine other boys and three members of staff, we headed back for another glorious spell on the *lowveldt*.

We piled into the Home bus and headed off on the main road north. The road that branched off from this highway, to our reserve, was just beyond that leading to the Kruger National Park. We had been travelling for the better part of five hours and were keen to see the reserve which was now not far off.

Our driver, Mr Tony, a young Assistant Housemaster, accelerated down the sand road that lead to the reserve. Recent rains had turned it into a dangerous and slippery slope. He applied the brakes but he had lost control of the vehicle. It slid for some distance before cartwheeling onto its roof, jolting William and me out of the back. William, a year younger, had joined me in the back where we had been lying on our backs behind the last row of seats.

He and I slithered down the road, ahead of the bus, unable to stop ourselves. As I slid, I looked back to see the hulk of metal careering on its roof towards me. I desperately tried to escape, clawing at the wet soil, but could gain no purchase. I felt as if I was in a conscious version of those nightmares when one is unable to escape an approaching danger.

Suddenly the vehicle turned sideways and began to roll away from me and finally came to rest against the thick grass alongside the road. One boy was bent double through one of the side windows. The frame had popped out, leaving just the thin metal around the opening, and one more roll must surely have severed him in two.

Then absolute and perfect silence. Out of immediate danger, all I wanted to do was wrap myself in a blanket and sleep. William, nearby, was moaning, blood pouring from a deep gash across his back. I had a small wound on my shoulder, which felt tender, but I had no serious injury. The rest of the boys and members of staff were entirely unharmed.

Mr Tom, an elderly Housemaster, approached me unsteadily.

"Don't sleep, Joe," he said, "you're in shock. I will get you something warm."

He did and I gratefully wrapped the blanket he brought around me. It did not take me long to recover but Willy needed urgent medical attention and we soon found a nearby hospital.

The doctors grudgingly stitched up his wound and, when we returned to Johannesburg, the doctors at the General Hospital were appalled at the handiwork.

It transpired that the *lowveldt* doctors were employed by a European charity. They were there specifically for the needs of Africans. We whites were effectively intruders, the undeserving beneficiaries of their valuable resources. Small wonder then that they dispensed their skills and materials so rudely and reluctantly.

Needless to say, this was an inauspicious start to what should have been an idyllic vacation. We did do some work in the reserve but were never allowed to enjoy the facilities we had the first time. The tree houses were no longer available and even the hippos had moved away.

The bus was a write-off and at the conclusion of our time we had to travel back to the Home by train. The nearest town was Komatipoort, on the border with Mozambique, and the journey was uneventful. We arrived back at the Home, understandably subdued after a holiday that didn't exactly match expectations.

However, including the earlier week-long visit to the KNP, I had spent the better part of two months living with and surrounded by Africa's wildest animals and I am eternally grateful for that.

25

Chapel and Sister MacArdle

Religion was an aspect of Home life that could never be ignored. Except for Bee-Bop's flat, the church, or Chapel as we called it, was by far the tallest structure in the home.

Externally, it was clad in the stone that the architect, Herbert Baker, so favoured, matching those surrounding the Parade Ground. Inside the walls were all unadorned brick that stretched up to a bare wooden structure supporting the external red-tiled roof. Narrow arched windows were the only sources of any natural light.

Attendance was compulsory and every Sunday, Holy Communion was celebrated in the morning and Evensong in the evening.

All new arrivals were taken aside on their first Sunday and the Anglican Church liturgy was explained.

"I, or Father Norman, will conduct the service," said the Beak, Father Eric. "You can follow it in the Book of Common Prayer. There is a copy for each of you and you will find it in the pew you are seated in. If you hear either of us make any mistakes, come and let us know so we don't do it again."

This clever man knew that ardent nine year olds would now attend to every word uttered during future services instead of getting up to mischief. We did but it only lasted a few Sundays before we realised that their rendition was invariably faultless. We also familiarised ourselves with the litany of vocal responses, spoken and sung, the most common of which was a loud 'amen' after every prayer.

In addition to the Book of Common Prayer, we were provided with a hymn book. Staves containing the clefs and musical notes for the hymn, with the first words of the hymn shown between the staves, appeared above the verses. I never did decipher these symbols but enjoyed looking at the patterns.

Home boys always sang the hymns with gusto, accompanied by the organist and choir master, Mr Brian. Before every service, when we awaited the arrival of the choir and officiating personnel, he would regale us with beautiful tunes, usually by Bach, but he played the music of other composers, too. He, of course, could read music perfectly and rolled his torso rather pompously in time to the music.

Everything in Chapel was hushed. Instructions were always whispered and idle chit-chat was forbidden. We would be seated, waiting for the service to begin and I would fight boredom by looking through the prayer book.

Then Mr Brian's organ would blare out the arrival of the procession and we would all stand. Either Bee-Bop or the Beak, together with three altar boys, would lead the choir into Chapel through the back entrance. One boy walked in front, brandishing a crucifix on a long wooden pole. The altar boys wore black cassocks with white surplices and the presiding priest was decked out in a gorgeously arrayed chasuble, sometimes with pure gold tassels, depending on the religious festival being celebrated. They were followed by the choir who were dressed in red cassocks and white surplices.

Occasionally the altar boys and choir wore ruffs around their necks and an altar boy might swing a gold container in which incense smoked profusely.

"Holy Smoke!" somebody muttered and those within earshot giggled.

Bee-Bop stared daggers as a Housemaster who, in a harsh whisper, threatened the boys with dire consequences should they continue to misbehave. Somebody farted loudly and that set the boys off again. More threats and finally discipline was restored but little could be done to prevent shoulders shaking with mirth.

The hour in Chapel was simply too much to endure and I eagerly sought an alternative. I would dearly have liked never to attend but that was not an option. I wished I could bring one of the many comics that abounded in the Junior Houses but that, too, was not possible. Quite simply I had to put up with it. Then I discovered Surgery.

Surgery, the name given to the Home sanatorium, was a haven of quiet seclusion away from the harsh realities outside. Here one was provided with a hospital bed and served three meals a day. There were no chores and nobody was ever flogged. School, too, was avoided and the reading material comprised a prodigious comic collection. Finally, one shared the facility with a number of other malingerers, all of whom were there to escape the external drudgery and routine. Rarely did a boy occupy a bed because he was genuinely sick.

The difficulty was gaining entry into this sanctuary. It was guarded by a formidable lady in her fifties, Sister McArdle, who could spot a skiver simply by a glance. She was ably assisted by another stalwart, Rosy, the African member of the Home's medical establishment.

My first experience of the joys of this refuge was when I was still innocent. I was genuinely ill and Sister immediately ordered me into a bed. I actually didn't want to be admitted because it was during my first days at the Home and I was far too interested in outside events to be locked away in a sick room. But I was ill and my temperature was high and so to bed I went.

I must have slept for some time and Sister had been sufficiently concerned to visit me on several occasions.

"Jeez, Joe," another inmate said from across the room, "Sister has been in and out while you slept. You okay?"

"Yeah, just a cold, I think, but I feel okay now."

However, Sister would not release me until she thought I was sufficiently fit to survive outside.

"I don't want to discharge you too early," she explained, "or you'll just be back again."

For two days I was left to fully recuperate and it was then that I truly appreciated the huge benefits Surgery had to offer. At the end of my spell there, I was reluctant to leave but Sister knew I was ready to go.

"Out! You've been in here long enough now. Out!"

I plotted ways to regain entry but sadly she saw through every trick. I would enter Surgery with sloping shoulders, appearing for all the world as if death was close. When she wasn't looking, I would hold the thermometer against a wall heater before returning it to my mouth.

"One hundred and seven," she said, peering at the reading through her half-moon glasses and then at me.

"I know, Sister," I said, attempting to muster a croak in my voice. "I feel very sick."

"Now, Twead, Anyone with a temperature of a hundred and seven is clinically dead. So I must say that I am surprised that I can hear you speak."

I stared at her and the look on her face clearly showed that she had seen through me.

"Now take you and your sick carcass out of the building and go to school!" she barked.

A trap she set for any unsuspecting shirker was to offer him a plate of pudding. Invariably it was custard and jelly, a rare delicacy in the Home.

"Oh Sister," the charlatan would say, "I feel very bad. Please may I stay in Surgery for a few days?"

"Of course! Would you like a nice bowl of jelly and custard while Rosy prepares a bed for you?"

"Oh Sister, would you?" the poor fool would simper.

"Out!" Sister would roar, "Out! And don't waste my time again! It's Jones, isn't it? You're in Beaton House. I will be reporting you to your Housemaster! Out!"

If a boy held the thermometer against the heater just long enough to give a reasonable 'sick' reading, he was admitted. What he might not realise was that Sister was carefully observing him even after he settled into his bed. The really experienced shammer was aware of this and maintained his subterfuge beyond even a day, wisely lying low. The inexperienced charlatan may have looked and behaved as if he was death warmed up but in bed he suddenly perked up, becoming the life and soul of the ward.

Sister, who had been lurking in the corridor outside, would pounce and eject him. Even long-term patients were ejected earlier than they expected because of raucous behaviour.

In time, I would spend a number of days in Surgery, as well as the General Hospitals in Germiston and Johannesburg, where my tonsils and appendix were removed. And when I was fourteen I did use Surgery as an escape from Chapel but in the process nearly lost my foot.

At some time in the past I had incurred a hairline fracture of the tibia near my ankle. The resulting internal infection resulted in an acute pain in my foot and ankle. It was so sore that even bed linen was an unbearable weight.

During the services in Chapel, we spent a lot of the time on our knees. The pews provided a railing on which to rest our feet when we were seated but it was also used by those seated in the pew ahead. When we knelt, they could rest their toes on it and it was not uncommon to view the soles of their feet when we bowed our heads. Quite often we would playfully twist the foot of a friend seated directly ahead of us.

Kneeling, I lifted my swollen foot and, with a deep sigh of relief, gingerly rested it on the railing. Unfortunately my good friend, Bossy, had no notion of the agony I was in and decided to give my foot a friendly twist. It was during one of the quieter periods of the service when all was calm and still. The scream that escaped my mouth might have been heard in Australia.

Bossy, little expecting such an outlandish reaction, quickly let go of my foot and feigned innocence. I stood up and, despite the service having just begun, limped unchallenged outside and headed for Surgery. Nobody stopped me or even questioned my odd behaviour.

"Jelly and custard?" Sister asked me when I consulted her in the Surgery waiting room.

I didn't bother to reply and before long I was lying in a semi-conscious state on one of the beds. My foot had swollen to an enormous size and all my toes had disappeared. I remember seeing a lot of white coats surrounding me before being taken to Germiston Hospital. There I was given a general anaesthetic and my leg was cut open and drained of the infectious poisons. The relief was immense.

It wasn't long after I entered the Home that I realised that the key to a reasonably quiet existence was endeavouring to endear oneself to either the Housemaster or his assistant. If it was going to make my life any easier, I prepared to become a sycophantic crawler. To this end, I did my best to wheedle my way into Mr Brian's affections but, after my third caning in as many days, I decided to switch my affections to his assistant, Mr Derek.

Mr Derek was in the final year of a degree course and loved any and all forms of sporting activity. He was not a natural athlete but studied and eventually mastered the weird art of race-walking. It was strange seeing him waddle as he walked and he swore it was the most efficient way to walk fast. Naturally, to charm him, I attempted to become a race-walker too but never could abide the waddle so abandoned that approach.

He always encouraged us to do well academically and to that end invited us to read more. At the age of nine I had far better things to do than bury my nose in the dull pages of a book but, if that's what it took to be a favourite, then read a book I must. I reluctantly asked him if he could suggest one.

"Try this, Joe," he said handing me an old hard-cover tome from a dusty bookshelf he had in his quarters.

I hoped he would discuss it with me but he dismissed me with nonchalant wave of his hand. The author was Capt. W E Johns and the book was *Biggles Flies East*. I took it away to read but didn't like it at all and, having read just a page, returned to Mr Derek's quarters.

"Sir, this is too hard. Do you have anything easier?"

"Agh! Get out of my sight!" he snapped and I quickly walked out.

It was not the reaction I had expected and realised that gaining a foothold in his esteem was never going to be easy. I returned to my bed and tried reading the book again. By the end of the first chapter I was hooked. Within a month I had devoured four, often sneaking into Mr Derek's rooms in his absence to exchange the one I had read for another.

"Sir, do you have any more Biggles books?" I asked him, having drained the supply on his shelf.

"That's, how many, eight you've read now?" he said with a smile.

Strangely, without even trying to, I had succeeded in impressing him. But now I no longer had any designs in that direction. During this period he had slapped my face and caned me more often even than Mr Brian had. On one occasion the thin bamboo split my wrist open when I tried to protect my behind with my hands.

"Well, you should have kept your hands in front of you!" he snapped as I stared tearfully at the blood pouring from the wound.

To this day I still bear the scar on my wrist. No, it was not his favour I now craved, but a book to read. The beatings he and Mr Brian had inflicted had made me even more cynical of authority and never again would I attempt to curry their favour. But Mr Derek had inadvertently set me off on an occupation that would last for the rest of my life and for that I was prepared to forgive him.

Now I had a new source of entertainment and one that was ideal for making Chapel a much more pleasant experience. I would smuggle my latest book in either my blazer pocket or, if the book was too large, inside the blazer under my arm. Many fun hours were spent reading in Chapel and I would be oblivious to all about me.

"What's that you're reading?" a quiet voice enquired of me from above as I knelt in the pew one Sunday morning.

I looked up and met the expressionless eyes of Mr Ken, the Deputy Head, and my heart froze.

"I will see you in my office after the service," he whispered before confiscating the precious book.

Mr Ken was renowned for his cuts and I knew I was doomed. All too soon the service finished and I stood outside in the dark corridor awaiting his arrival.

His office was part of the central administrative hub of the Home. Here the Headmaster had a room that adjoined Mr Ken's, separated by a secretary who answered the telephone and typed out their correspondence. She didn't work on Sundays and all was silent within.

Apart from a few boys chatting at the far end of the corridor, near the dining hall, I was alone and fearful. I expected a thrashing and got one. My pleas for mercy echoed around the Herbert Baker infrastructure but went unheeded.

"Read in Chapel again and I will double the punishment. Do I make myself clear?"

Mr Ken never raised his voice and I nodded tearfully. That day, fairly early in my stay at the Home, I learned a valuable lesson. Don't get caught.

I continued to smuggle books into Chapel but now read them with my eyes and ears alert to everything around me. Before I automatically followed those around me when they stood, knelt or sat. Now I constantly sneaked a look over my shoulder and to my left and right. Very likely an observant member of staff might have construed such behaviour as suspicious. But none did and I continued to read illicit literature.

Then the Gideons arrived and handed out a small Bible to each boy. It was a tiny book with the title embossed in gold on a soft red binding. Attached to the spine was a yellow ribbon bookmark. Despite its small size and tiny print, I loved its neatness and it was the first book I ever owned. Furthermore it fitted comfortably in any of my blazer pockets. And the final clincher was that, in Chapel, it had to be valid reading material.

I had some notion of the biblical stories but never paid them much mind. Had anyone asked me to name even one apostle I would have been at a loss. I was familiar with the name Jesus Christ only because I and the boys around me used it often when swearing at one another.

I had never read the Bible before and couldn't wait to get started. I only read it in Chapel and was soon absorbed in its content, once again automatically copying the activities of those around me. Mr Ken did pounce but stopped short when he spotted the book and never bothered me again.

I began at the beginning, reading about the creation, and then about the main characters in what I found to be highly imaginative stories. I searched for the glittering nuggets that I hoped to find, amongst the dreary pages of rules and regulations, and I wasn't disappointed. Hollywood converted many of them to the silver screen, and my favourite was *Samson and Delilah*.

I moved on to the New Testament and read the four Gospels. By the time I reached John's version I was thoroughly acquainted with what Bee-Bop and the Beak were banging on about from the pulpit during their sermons.

The miracles impressed me but not as much as the dialogue. Strange and unclear statements were made that, despite the simple language used, I could not understand. Throughout my remaining years in the Home and, for many decades after, I pondered those statements and arrived at conclusions very different to those I heard spouted at me from the pulpit.

I always wanted to discuss it with Bee-Bop or the Beak but feared they would brand me a heretic. Worse still, they might report me to Mr Ken, or Mr Brian, who undoubtedly would have whacked me. Many years later I did test my ideas on a priest I met. I was in Durham at the time and he was one of those very clever fellows that the church seems to attract.

"How very twee!" he exclaimed, completely deflating me and I vowed never again to attempt the exercise.

My next indiscretion in Chapel was an act of vandalism for which I deserved to be punished. I always kept a round-headed pin in my blazer lapel, for no other reason than I thought it might prove useful in the future. It occurred to me that, while listening to Bee-Bop droning on at the altar whilst I was kneeling, I could use the pin to scratch out my name on the seat of the pew in front of me.

I began, intending merely to etch my initials superficially and in minute characters. The project, however, escalated as did the size of the characters. After six weeks of assiduous labour, I viewed the completed work and was deeply satisfied. JTWEAD was printed in huge letters.

I was not alone. Several other boys also carved their names, including Les. He spent several weeks longer than I did and I was forced to admit his work was of a better quality.

"Not very clever, Joe," the boy alongside me whispered. "They will know who did that, you know."

He was right and in time we would pay dearly for our efforts. For once I had to acknowledge that Mr Ken had every right to flay my behind. But I thought it a small price to pay and when I visited the Home, twenty years after leaving it, I entered the Chapel.

"I see that these are the same pews I sat on when I was here," I told the man who showed me around.

"Yes. We decided to keep the graffiti for historical purposes."

I walked down the aisle and, sure enough, my name was still there, now aged and polished. It was the only mark I ever left on the Home.

* * *

"Gosh, some of the girls did that, too, when I was at boarding school in England."

"I bet they didn't get beaten for it."

"No, you're quite right. They didn't hit us because we were girls. We got lines or punishments instead, but my brother was regularly caned at his boarding school. We had to attend Chapel every evening, and church on Sundays, too."

"Have you quite finished? I'm trying to write."

"You've waited all these years before beginning your book, and now suddenly it's so urgent I'm not allowed to speak?"

"Go away. Go and make coffee or something or I'll be caning you, if you're not careful."

I flounced out with my nose in the air.

* * *

Chapel wasn't totally without its entertainment value. Bee-Bop was almost worth paying to see. He delighted in wearing gaudy vestments and conducting services. He was also a chain-smoker and it was nothing for him to get through sixty a day. Consequently he was prone to coughing bouts that lasted several minutes. It was not uncommon for him to pause between chants while he coughed his lungs out. At other times he would be genuflecting, cough in that position for several minutes, then stand up again. This initially amused us but occurred so often that we tired of it.

An Old Boy, who had left the Home a few years before, returned for a brief visit. Jonah was immensely popular when he was in the Home and we were delighted to see him again. I was fourteen at the time. He regaled us with tales of the British South Africa Police for whom he now worked in Rhodesia.

"Were you ever confirmed?" somebody asked him and he paused to ponder the question.

Confirmation was a year-long course, run by Bee-Bop, culminating in one being permitted to receive the bread and wine during communion services. Anyone agreeing to undertake such a course was endorsing religion in general and Chapel in particular.

Such behaviour was frowned upon by the rest of us and a devotee stood a serious chance of being labelled a 'bible-puncher' and ostracised. The Home was a hard enough place to endure and, being sidelined by one's comrades for religious reasons, might prove too much for even the most ardent devotee.

So it was understandable why Jonah paused before answering. He was well aware that an affirmative reply could prove detrimental to his standing as 'one of the boys' and we awaited his answer with interest. Finally he spoke.

"I like a bit o' grog of a Sunday morning," he said and we fell about laughing.

His tone was facetious and it clearly suggested his contempt for anything religious. He had endured the year-long confirmation course simply so he could enjoy the wine as an appetiser before breakfast. Certainly he lost none of his credibility amongst us.

We might have laughed but the idea struck home. It had never occurred to us that receiving communion on a Sunday morning might have entertainment value. Furthermore, once confirmed, one could participate as an altar boy. This could add an extra dimension to proceedings.

Jonah's flippant remark was instrumental in probably the largest list of confirmation applications in the history of the Home. I, and many of my close friends, endured Bee-Bop's dull attempts to teach us to be better Anglicans and they couldn't wait for their first wine-tasting experience. I say 'they' because it wasn't *my* first taste, but I wasn't going to brag about it. I wisely withheld the fact that I knew where Bee-Bop stored the Chapel wine.

I had already sampled some of Mr Brian's when I sneaked a slug from a bottle he kept in his fridge. It was during one of those very rare times when he allowed us to wander freely through his flat and one of the braver souls opened his fridge to peek inside.

A bottle of sherry was spotted and, with Mr Brian in the next room, it was quickly removed from the fridge and passed around. It was the first alcohol to cross my lips and I loved it. Sweet South African sherry is not to everyone's taste but, for a ten year old, it was nectar.

Then, three years later, I was in the darkroom and discovered that Bee-Bop stored the Chapel wine on top of one of the wall cupboards above the work surface. After careful analysis I decided it might just be possible to use one of the bar-stool chairs we sat on to climb onto the work surface and gain access to the wine on top of the cupboard.

The best time to execute my plan would be when the darkroom was plunged into darkness during the film-loading process. Bee-Bop never turned on the lights until all the photographers had loaded their films and only after he had carried out an audible check on their progress.

"How are you doing, Trevor?"

"Nearly finished, Father."

Trevor's voice would be heard coming from somewhere left.

"Peter?"

"Me too, Father," said Peter, his voice coming from somewhere right.

"Joe?"

Five minutes was ample time for me to accomplish my mission and I would long since have returned to ground level. Had he asked me sooner, my voice would have sailed down from somewhere near the ceiling and on one occasion this almost happened. Soon after switching off the light, he broke the silence.

"Joe, don't forget to rotate the spool in the direction of the load. Do you understand?"

I was standing on the counter and had already uncorked a bottle and taken a slug. Before answering I went down on my haunches, the bottle still in my hand. I have often wondered what he would have said had someone inadvertently switched on the lights at that moment.

"Understood, Father," I said in a boozy croak, bending my head as far down as possible while I spoke.

Fortunately, I was never caught and my nefarious activities only came to light because of my own stupidity. Prior to that, it surprised me that Bee-Bop did not smell the sweet sherry on my breath. He smoked incessantly and perhaps his sense of smell had all but disappeared.

It was confirmation that undid me. In the Anglican Church, like the Catholic church, one must confess all one's sins before the final confirmation service conducted by the Bishop of Johannesburg.

"Write your sins out on a sheet of paper and read them to me in Chapel," Bee-Bop said to us. "You and I will be the only ones present and I will never reveal them to anyone once I have heard them."

I did as he requested and when I came to the bit about the wine in the darkroom, I paused. Should I reveal it and deprive myself of a source of such exciting pleasure? I always was a risk-taker, addicted to the thrill of danger. That, combined with the effect of the few sips I had from the bottle, a warm glow followed by a sense of euphoric relaxation, were pleasures I was reluctant to relinquish.

I placed the wine-tasting sin in parentheses, fully intending to delete it, but forgot to do so. I entered Chapel, armed with my sheet of sins, and marched down to a pew in the choir where Bee-Bop was waiting. I knelt and he placed his hand on my head while I read from my sheet of shame. Then I reached the first parenthesis and stopped dead.

I turned my head beneath his hand and was surprised to see his face alongside mine. He was reading my words as I uttered them aloud. There was nothing I could do but continue with my confession. At its conclusion, I escaped outside into the sunshine, cursing my stupidity.

My confession may have been silently received but action soon followed. Just a day later I was in the darkroom and the bottles of wine had disappeared.

The Bishop duly turned up and baptised us, yet another requisite before one may receive the bread and wine. Then, at the same service, we were invited to enjoy these for the first time. We were required to kneel at a railing that separated the altar area from the rest of the Chapel. The Bishop moved from left to right, placing a wafer in our mouths and Bee-Bop followed with the wine. The bread was a tasteless wafer but the wine was the sweet sherry with which I was already familiar.

"The rule is that you keep your hands behind your back when you are receiving the host," Bee-Bop had explained during a confirmation lesson, "but I don't mind if you steady the bottom of the chalice with your hand."

I found this useful inasmuch as a gentle nudge added an additional quantity of the nectar. But it required care in its execution. Too forceful might attract unwonted attention and too gentle would be ineffectual. It was difficult to gauge and Bee-Bop was ever vigilant of any suspicious activity. I did, however, achieve some success when visiting (and less discerning) clergy assisted at the altar.

My Chapel experience, with the addition of the 'bit o' grog of a Sunday morning', had vastly improved and I didn't let it end there. I volunteered my services as an altar boy and was accepted. It gave me access to the vestry and on one occasion I and a number of other altar boys raided the container in which the wafers were stored.

A single wafer each Sunday was simply too little to appreciate its taste and we decided to try a handful. We needn't have bothered. It was flavourless, clogging our mouths and no amount of water seemed to wash it down. Perhaps it was divine retribution but we never sampled them again.

But Sunday mornings and Sunday evenings were now far more enjoyable because no longer did I listlessly languish in a pew. Now I could prance about unrestricted, assisting the priest in dispensing the bread and wine in the morning, and snuffing out candles in the evening.

My performance as an altar boy lasted just a few years and at the age of sixteen I happily returned to the pews, too old now to be an altar boy. I no longer wanted to be a photographer either. I resigned my club membership and Bee-Bop and I parted ways, occasionally crossing swords in passing.

26

A Bicycle

For four happy years I was part of the Lawson family. Every Sunday that I was allowed out from the Home I spent with them and if I wasn't at Camp or on a photographic trip with Bee-Bop, I was with the Lawsons during the school holidays.

The six-week Christmas holiday was spent mostly in the company of Roy, whom I adored, and I also often sat in the kitchen with Mrs Lawson where she regaled me with tales while baking glorious Cornish pasties. I was always given one to taste and I think she enjoyed seeing me wolf it down.

Then, when I was fourteen and in my first year of high school, I was summoned by the principal, Mr Johnsen. It was near the end of the school day and I entered his office where he was talking to a man I'd never seen before.

"Twead," said Mr Johnsen, "I have spoken to your Headmaster at the Home and he has no objection to your going with this gentleman." Seeing the astonished look on my face and before I could say anything he continued, "I understand you know a Mrs Lawson?"

"Yes, sir."

"Then go with this man who will explain everything to you."

I followed the man to his car and once inside, he immediately came to the point.

"I'm only here because Ada Lawson asked me to pick you up from school. Her husband has died and for some strange reason she seems to think you are part of her family. Personally, I don't think you are and you shouldn't be there at all."

I ignored his comment but was deeply shocked to hear that Mr Lawson had died. We drove in silence and arrived at the house a short while later. Inside, many people were in attendance, all strangers to me despite my four-year association with the Lawsons. Mrs Lawson looked me over and saw that my shoes were in a sorry state. I had intended handing them in to the Home cobbler, who would have replaced them with a second-hand pair had mine been beyond hope. Boys were rarely provided with new shoes.

"I can't have him going to the funeral in those," she said, pointing at my feet, and appealing to the man who had brought me.

"Don't worry," he said, "I'll see to it."

I was bundled back into his car and he bought me a new and very expensive pair. I thanked him but was repaid with a look of grim contempt.

Soon I was back again. Roy was nowhere to be seen and Mrs Lawson was being consoled by several ladies. All I could do was stand quietly in a corner, avoid attracting attention, and await developments.

In truth, the man who brought me was right, I had no right being there. I hardly knew Mr Lawson who was seldom at home and, when he was, he rarely spoke to me. I didn't mind because Roy and Mrs Lawson more than made up for his reserve. I knew he was a man of very few words and I accepted him for that. But I was ever mindful that, because of his generosity, I was honoured to be a member of his lovely family, but did not belong to it.

Other than Mrs Lawson, I knew nobody amongst those assembled in her house and I felt like a total fraud travelling alone to the funeral with her in the primary vehicle of the cortège. We said nothing to each other. She, by now, was dry-eyed and lost in her own thoughts.

In the church she and I sat alone in the front pew staring at the coffin holding the remains of Mr Lawson. I would later learn that he died of a burst appendix. Other than that I knew nothing else regarding the precise circumstances and never dared make enquiries, either of Mrs Lawson or Roy. It would have been grossly insensitive to do so.

Roy suddenly appeared next to me in the pew, accompanied by a young lady I had never met. He had been conscripted into the Army, undertaking compulsory National Service, something all young men were subjected to after they left school. He was almost unrecognisable with his shorn head and I offered him a wan smile in greeting. He simply nodded and sat down with the young woman. I was between him and his mother.

In the four years that I knew him, I had never seen Roy cry. So great was his anguish that the white handkerchief in his hands was torn in two. His grief was silent but palpable and I was grateful for the presence of the young lady who did her best to comfort him. I just wanted the service to be over and to be gone from this place. It did end and I was thankful to be back at the Home. I vowed to myself that, apart from my own, I would do my best to avoid future funerals.

Sundays with Mrs Lawson were now very different. It was as if a light had been switched off in a bright, pleasant room, suddenly darkening all the joyful activity within. No longer did she bake and chat with me at the kitchen table, preferring me to be out of her sight. I would either take Rusty, their golden cocker spaniel, for long walks or ride the bicycle they had given me two years before.

"We have a lovely surprise for you," she had said, when the family gathered one Christmas morning.

In the lounge, a second-hand bicycle was propped against the wall. Mr Lawson, Mrs Lawson and Roy stared at me as I entered the room, no doubt expecting me to express myself in an explosion of gratitude. I was very grateful but I didn't demonstrate the fact. Had I been observant I might have noted the dark shadow that flitted briefly across Mr Lawson's face but I didn't. At the time, nothing was said but the issue would arise again after he died.

It was not long after the funeral and, but for Roy, I might have severed our relationship sooner. Because of his father's death Roy had been allowed home every weekend during his National Service. Consequently I saw him on those Sundays I was allowed out from the Home. Mrs Lawson no longer wanted me around and sought opportunities to discredit me with him.

"I don't care!" I heard Roy fiercely whisper, believing I was out of earshot. "He's my friend and he stays!"

And, unfortunately, stay I did. Roy and I had a special relationship that I was reluctant to bring to an end. After completing his National Service, he continued to live at home but now he worked, thus depriving me of his company during the school holidays. This forced Mrs Lawson to endure me for weeks instead of just the occasional Sunday. The pressure was insupportable and one day it came to a head.

"Mr Lawson didn't like you, you know," she suddenly announced one day.

"Why not?" I asked, deeply hurt but not showing it. I had no idea he harboured me any ill-will.

"Ever since we gave you that bicycle. You never once thanked us for it. He never liked you after that."

I cast my mind back and realised that, as usual, she was right. I had been so overwhelmed that I had simply stared at the bike, analysing its features, making mental notes, planning what changes I would make to its old-fashioned appearance. In the split second that I saw it for the first time, I decided that no self-respecting Home boy would be caught dead on a bike looking like something from the 1920s. These were the ideas that raced through my head, not the gratitude I should clearly have shown. In fact, I was deeply grateful but my failure to demonstrate it was now coming back to haunt me.

During my second year of high school, when I had moved up to Spackman House, the Lawsons and I parted company forever. One day, after school, I was walking past the Parade Ground when my Housemaster, Mr David, called me over.

"Listen, Joe," he said, unusually addressing me by my first name and attempting to soften what he was about to tell me, "don't go to Mrs Lawson this Sunday. She was at the Home earlier today and asked that she never see you again."

I was disappointed but not surprised. Sundays would have to be spent at the Home and a number of boys shared my predicament. I vowed to gather them and arrange soccer matches which I loved playing.

One sunny day, a few years later, I saw Roy playing badminton with a lovely young woman at a popular public outdoor swimming pool. I didn't greet him and I doubt he saw me.

He was my very good friend, the perfect older brother, and he has a special place in my heart. Mrs Lawson, too, is very special in my memories and I can only hope that she eventually forgave me my transgressions. I am forever grateful to the Lawsons for letting me be a member of their family.

27

Housemasters

On 31st of May, 1961, I was just two months short of my tenth birthday when South Africa declared itself a Republic. Prior to that it had been the Union of South Africa.

As the Union, its currency had been pounds, shillings and pence and now as a Republic, it was rands and cents.

I had always greatly admired everything British but am unable to explain why. Now that the country had broken away from Britain, I was greatly disappointed. The national flag changed and each of us was issued with a small paper copy. The celebrations included waving these but I chose not to join in or celebrate.

* * *

At the Home, things were proceeding routinely. Mr Brian had been my Housemaster for three years and I still retain vivid memories of that time. In fairness to him he was a young man, little skilled in the responsibilities required of having charge of forty youngsters aged between nine and fourteen. It was a difficult task even for an experienced Housemaster.

On one occasion he arranged a surprise party that was set for midnight when we were sound asleep.

While we slept, he and his assistant, Mr Derek, quietly prepared the common room for a feast of cakes, biscuits, crisps and soft drinks, set out on the dining room tables. A party hat, party blower and a balloon was provided for each boy and decorations adorned the ceiling.

There was no reason for the party. Perhaps it was inspired by Enid Blyton's tales of midnight feasts, I don't know, but much time and effort, as well as personal cost, must have been spent in its preparation and execution.

The electric House bell that ruled our lives always irritated me. Its strident ring was so loud it could be heard several hundred metres away. It was only activated by the Housemaster who turned it on and off with a switch in his flat. Shorter rings called us for attendance at meals, Home Parades, Chapel and Prep. A continuous ring was a summons for all boys to assemble in the common room for a House Meeting.

Sound at night is particularly loud and at midnight it must have been heard all over the Home. Like automatons we headed for the common room and were dazzled by the spread, staring with disbelief at the colourful display.

"Find a place and sit down," said Mr Brian, "and you can wear the hats if you like."

We did as commanded but sat dolefully staring at the goodies in front of us. Unfortunately the delicious confectionary at that time of the night was the least attractive thing on the planet. All we wanted to do was go back to bed and sleep.

"Go ahead, enjoy yourselves," urged Mr Brian. "What are you waiting for?"

It must have been a strange sight, forty boys staring silently at the feast, reluctant to be there. A similar party was set for all Junior House boys in the gymnasium alongside the pool. It was called Splash and took the place of an evening meal at the end of the year, just before the Christmas break. It was immensely popular and the festivities were so loud that it was difficult to hear one's neighbour seated alongside.

Except for the timing, this party was identical in every respect. But it was an epic misfire and within fifteen minutes we were back in our beds and none of us had seen Mr Brian look more deflated, his well-meaning intentions wasted on us. We were not ungrateful but, as we silently returned to our beds, none of us had the words to frame a suitable apology. At the age of eleven, I certainly could not express my sorrow at disappointing him.

A year later he awoke us again in the middle of the night, tearing us from our beds. We gathered in the common room where he was waiting for us. We stared at him, bleary-eyed, wondering at the reason.

"All bow your heads," he said. "Lord, we pray for the soul of President Kennedy who tragically died today. May he rest in peace. Amen."

I had recently turned twelve and my knowledge of events and people beyond the boundary of the Home was extremely limited. I had no notion who President Kennedy was and didn't care to be awakened to pray for his soul. Why Mr Brian chose such an unearthly hour is still beyond me.

* * *

In his flat, Mr Brian had an impressive radio/record player combination that was the popular style in the 60s. Inside each dormitory and above the doorway was a single speaker that was connected to his record player. At night, when we were in bed, he played popular songs and fairy tales as well as abridged classics such as *Dr Jekyll and Mr Hyde* and *The Snow Goose*. The most popular songs were by Spike Jones whose zany lyrics and music greatly amused us. *Beetle Bomb* was frequently requested but my personal favourite was *Cocktails for Two*.

Mr Brian was a cultured man who enjoyed listening to classical music and we often heard him playing tunes on his piano. Although he favoured Bach, he wasn't averse to hammering out discordant jazz pieces too. In Chapel, he regularly played Bach's *Jesu Joy of Man's Desiring* as the processionary piece before and after services.

Weekly chores were clattered out on his typewriter and these were posted on a notice board outside the House front door. Once a week, on his day off, I always wondered if our noisy activities disturbed his slumber in the mornings.

As the first Housemaster I had in the Home, he and his assistant, Mr Derek, left the greatest impression on me during all the nine years I spent there. It is difficult to explain their influence and I am still uncertain of my feelings towards him. Ambivalent feelings caused me to snap at him rather than extend a hand of friendship when we corresponded with each other fifty years after I last saw him.

I am aware that subsequent Housemasters were equally influential but they entered my life when I was wiser and able to deal with their nonsense. My hide was thicker and, because of the treatment I received at the hands of Mr Brian, my attitude towards authority figures had grown sullen and dark. Furthermore, I became a bully, often emulating his techniques when I was promoted to a position of power during my Senior years.

Mr Brian's willingness to allow the bullying tactics of the older Patrol Leaders on their younger charges in order to maintain discipline was the chief lesson I learned from him. I never forgot it and noticed that it prevailed at all levels throughout the Home. Each Housemaster, together with his small army of subordinates (Headboys, Patrol Leaders and Corporals), continued the theme and during my nine years it never once changed. I employed it when I was given power and no doubt it continued after I left.

* * *

"That way of life sounds so horrible," I said.

"It was very black and white. You knew where you stood all the time. You knew who was higher in rank and lower, and that gave us a kind of security."

"I guess it was a bit like our chickens," I suggested, looking out of the window.

Joe knew exactly what I meant.

"Exactly. We had a pecking order, just like the hens. It was cruel, but it was accepted by us and we passed it on to new boys."

* * *

Mr Brian was preparing to open a Home for disadvantaged black children, often taking his favourites with him when he visited the site.

"You won't believe what happened!" Richard exclaimed, having just returned. "The black kids claimed stairs to sleep on!"

"What do you mean?" I asked.

"One of the kids said, 'I'm sleeping on this step,' and he couldn't believe it when he was told he could have a bed instead!"

The contrast between privileges for blacks and whites was never more forcibly demonstrated. We regarded ourselves as most fortunate when compared to their plight.

Mr Brian did open the Home but was politely informed that, as a result of the official policy of Apartheid, he was forbidden to consort with blacks. The reins were handed over to a black Headmaster and Mr Brian opened a Home for white children in Cape Town.

Our new Housemaster, Mr George, was a thirty-five year old Canadian with a remarkable gift. He spoke several languages fluently, including Zulu and Afrikaans. To hear a Canadian properly pronouncing Afrikaans words always amazed me. The odd thing was that he never studied the languages, merely picking them up by ear. It sounds improbable but when I had difficulty with my school German, he couldn't help.

"Sorry, Twead, I can speak it but I can't read it," he snapped and turned away.

His other gift was that of mimicry and his imitations of Churchill (of whose fame I was now familiar) and Hitler were uncanny. We had heard recordings of their speeches and Mr George's imitations were exact.

Mr George was not Canadian by birth. He was born in South Africa but moved to Canada when he was young. In fact he had been a Home boy in the 1930s and '40s but rarely spoke of his experiences then. Now he had returned as one of its Housemasters. Like Mr Brian and Bee-Bop, he was unmarried and all of these gentleman would remain so for the rest of their lives. Indeed, many Housemasters were single.

I ought to deal with the sexuality of the Housemasters. Homosexuals were referred to as 'rabbits' and the boys knew which Housemasters manifested rabbit tendencies. I should mention that rabbits and rabbit behaviour was, to say the least, highly frowned upon by us boys. Anyone caught indulging them would have been severely dealt with and forever excluded from the company of other boys.

At Camp, when I was twelve, I asked to be included as a member of an expedition that was spending a few nights at Oribi Gorge, a beauty spot situated several miles inland. I was extremely lucky to be accepted because all the other members were Seniors and fraternisation between Juniors and Seniors was discouraged. The Housemaster in charge of the expedition ruled in my favour and along I went. We erected a spare bell tent at a site that overlooked the Mzimkulwana River which ox-bowed far below within the Gorge.

One night I was disturbed from my sleep at an early hour by the boy sleeping next to me. It was Michael, three years older than I was, and doing his best to pull my pyjama bottoms off my rump. It took me a few moments to realise what was going on but I pretended to still be asleep. However, I had to act quickly because I could feel him manoeuvring himself for a final lunge.

Before he could execute his gross intentions, I turned over and successfully cocooned myself within my blanket. It was a neat move and perfectly in keeping with natural sleep behaviour. It also resulted in me being protected for the remainder of the night. Although I was now facing him, the inky blackness prevented him seeing me. I was now safe and returned to my slumbers, listening to him quietly cursing in the dark.

I think he was convinced I had been asleep throughout and the next morning I continued the pretence. Had I reported him I doubt I would have been believed. At worst it might have ended the expedition which we were all enjoying. The climb down to the river, swimming in the dangerous rapids, sweeping downriver and careering between boulders, was just too much fun. We also appreciated being away from the routine at Camp.

It is likely that a Home for boys might attract dubious characters for its staff. Some of its members were rabbits but to accuse them of being deviant is as ridiculous as maintaining that the heterosexual staff were honourable. No member of staff attempted anything as gross as what happened to me at Camp and I have no knowledge of it occurring to other boys.

Bee-Bop was a renowned rabbit and he once stroked my knee. We were alone in his flat, studying some photographs I had developed in the darkroom.

"You know, Joe," he said, "you have very soft skin."

I stared at his hand on my knee and slowly lifted my gaze to his eyes. The icy stare I gave him made him snatch his hand away as if it had been scalded. He never tried his nonsense again with me.

Mr George, too, acted strangely that, in subsequent years, gave me pause for thought. When it happened, I considered it as a touching concern for my wellbeing.

It was shower time in the evening and I was thirteen. Other than a towel I wrapped around my waist, I was naked. I was alone in the dormitory and having showered I was returning to my bed to dress for supper.

"Stand still a moment, Joe," a voice behind me said, that I recognised as belonging to our Canadian Housemaster.

I spun around, surprised at the note of concern in his voice. I stood facing him but wondered what might be the matter.

"No," he said thoughtfully whilst studying my torso and legs, "your stance is okay. I saw you walking just now and you seemed to favour your left side. At the staff meeting this morning, Sister mentioned that some of the boys might have a problem with their walking and that we should send worthy cases to Surgery."

Nobody as yet had ever accused me of walking funny but I was willing to keep an open mind. Being sent to Surgery was very attractive, especially if it meant being absent from school for an indefinite period.

"Listen Joe," he continued, "walk towards me but walk normally."

I did as commanded and when I reached him I stopped.

"No," he said, "it's the towel. I can't see anything with you wearing that towel. Take it off and walk away from me."

I did as ordered and at the end of the dormitory stopped and turned around. I was totally naked and he was closely scrutinising my lower body with his hand on his chin.

"Now walk slowly towards me ... slower!"

How many times I walked naked to and fro I do not recall but at the end of it all he concluded that he was almost sure I had a walking problem although he was unable to identify what it was.

* * *

"Stop laughing!"

"Well, honestly!" I said. "How dumb can you be? Didn't you suspect anything?"

"No, not a thing."

"Even when he asked you to remove the towel?"

"Nope."

"And have you ever had any difficulty with your walking, before or since?"

"Well, no. But, on the other hand, my doubts may be totally unfounded and he may have had valid reasons for studying the gait of a naked thirteen year old boy..."

I snorted, and began laughing all over again.

* * *

Whether he was a rabbit or not, Mr George had an eerie resemblance to the assassinated American President, John F Kennedy. What was more, his Canadian accent sounded American to our untutored ears and his rendition of the President's voice was excellent.

He also had a strange notion about religion and favoured the teachings and writings of the Dalai Lama and Lobsang Rampa. These he often discussed with us and, being very impressionable, we were easily persuaded that the transmigration of the soul, as well as possessing a third eye, were factually possible. The fad didn't last, however, and disappeared altogether when Mr George decided that he had enough of being a Housemaster and was replaced by another whose name was Mr Bland.

My time in Simpson House was coming to an end and I was preparing to move up to a Spackman House. I was now in my first year of high school and I had seen two Housemasters come and go. I would move up to the Senior House with Mr Bland who was to be the new Housemaster there.

Also moving up were Jogs, Bossy, Ticky, Macky and Richard, boys I had grown to know very well during my time in Simpson House. Unlike me, they had more success during their tenure, promoted to positions of power as Headboy (Jogs), Patrol Leaders (Kevin and Richard) and Corporals (Macky and Bossy).

With Richard as their ringleader, they excelled in all aspects of House and Home life and were always popular with boys and staff. I was only too grateful occasionally to be included in their circle.

I was a reasonable soccer player but, much to my disappointment, was never selected to play for the House or for my age group. Macky, on the other hand, was always selected and I considered myself superior to him. To my shame I regularly denigrated his abilities when we played five-a-side games on the sports fields. I never did it openly, spewing my poison with sly hints that he never responded to.

"Go on, James, that's your ball," I would say to the team mate nearest him when Macky received a ball.

The implication was simple: James could easily dispossess Macky. It was a nasty thing to say and, like many nasty things, was born of jealousy. But Macky was above such ugliness and never even mentioned it in our frequent dealings with one another. As a solid member of Richard's inner circle, he was comfortable in the sure knowledge that he would always be selected above me for any team. He had no need to justify his abilities which, in turn, fuelled the green monster within me. Fortunately it came to nought.

We both loved music and one night he and I listened to Jimi Hendrix's rendition of *Purple Haze* over and over again. The Beatles, too, were long established as chart toppers but it was their *Sgt Peppers* LP that wowed us. Simon and Garfunkel were immensely popular too. In fact numerous British and American groups and singers enthralled us throughout the 60s but my absolute favourites were the Beatles.

* * *

Joe closed his computer and leaned back in his chair clasping his hands behind his head.

"You know, Vicky," he said, "until I began writing this tome, I hadn't realised how much happened during the five years I was at Simpson House."

I looked up from the book I was reading.

"It snowed for the first time in many years, the Union of South Africa became the Republic of South Africa, I lost contact with my mother, my grandmother died, I enjoyed an entire term off school, two influential Housemasters came and went, and I nearly lost my foot. I also lost my host family and now had nobody to visit on Sundays and during the holidays."

"Did you feel sorry for yourself?" I asked. "Were you depressed?"

"No! Not at all. I was too alive to be wallowing in self-pity. I was careless of what the future might bring. By now my self-confidence knew no bounds."

"Uh-oh..."

28

Spackman House

Johannesburg, 1966

Mr Bland, our Housemaster in Simpson House, moved up with us to assume charge of the Senior House, Spackman House.

One of the first tasks of a new Housemaster is to introduce himself at an inaugural House Meeting. In Spackman House these were conducted in the lower common room. We were lined in dorm order on three sides of the room and Mr Bland addressed us from the middle.

"I want us to work together," he began, "as a team. This House is like a ship. You should look on me as the captain of the ship and if we work together I am sure we will get on swimmingly."

The rest of his speech maintained the nautical theme and, at its conclusion, he reminded us that his door was always open to anyone with a problem. With that he departed, leaving the Headboy in charge.

It was like being back in Simpson House when we first arrived in the Home. Then the older boys appeared to us as giants. In Spackman House the size differential was not as pronounced but the difference in maturity was. Whereas our eyes were wide with wonder, the older boys exhibited a world-weary wisdom of having seen and heard it all before.

"Right," said the Headboy, when Mr Bland was barely out of earshot, "House Meetings will no longer be held here in the lower wreck. Instead we will have them in the upper wreck."

After a few moments of bewilderment, the brighter ones among us realised the Headboy was stretching Mr Bland's analogy. From then on, the upper and lower common rooms were forever called the upper and lower wrecks.

Taylor House, the other Senior House, was diagonally opposite the Chapel at the far end of the road running past the Parade Ground. Beaton House boys went to Taylor House whilst we in Simpson were promoted up to Spackman.

The area between Spackman and Taylor Houses, and above the playing fields, was vast and unkempt. It was mostly rocky with just a few trees near the road. Early in 1967 we noticed that preparations were afoot to develop the area.

"What's going on?"

"They're here to build two new Houses," we were told. "They'll be Senior Houses called Smuts and Crawford. You'll be moving into Crawford House when it's finished and those in Taylor House will move into Smuts House."

Evidently great changes were in the offing and these would manifest themselves in ways that were much to our advantage. The rule permitting us to visit hosts and loved ones every second Sunday would be greatly relaxed. Initially we were allowed out every Sunday then that was extended to every weekend. Attending Chapel on Sunday morning would become optional and the only compulsory attendance was for Evensong at the end of the weekend.

I was still visiting Mrs Lawson at the beginning of 1967 but that would soon end. When it did, I would have nowhere to go but intended organising five-a-side games on the playing fields. Failing that, I vowed to walk the streets of Johannesburg rather than spend the time in the Home.

But that was all in the future and during my first year in Spackman House, Mr Bland (or more aptly, Captain Bland) decided to leave the Home. He was replaced by Mr David.

This gentleman was quite stout and we nicknamed him Chubby. Chubby was thirty years old, unmarried and from an established British family. He had been educated in a British Public School, the name of which he never divulged to us. In looks he was very similar to the actor Charles Laughton. Chubby's assistant was Mr Sidney, also thirty. Because of his extreme thinness we called him Skidney. Other than that he was Irish, I knew little else about him.

The difference in stature between the two Housemasters was a source of perpetual amusement and comment amongst the boys. So too was their mutual animosity. It may have been for personal reasons but the fact that one was an Englishman and the other an Irishman might have had something to do with it too.

Whilst I was at the Home, I was ignorant of Anglo-Irish history but years later I would learn that the Irish had justifiable cause to detest their English neighbours. Cromwell's murderous campaign to subdue Irish rebels was the beginning of a violent relationship that continues to the present day.

One dusky evening, their mutual enmity scaled dizzying heights. We heard them argue but passed it off as yet another of their usual spats and continued reading comics on our beds. Then one of the boys suggested it could be more serious and we became interested.

The conversation between the two Housemasters was not difficult to follow as the volume exceeded the upper decibel limit of a low-flying jet. We soon understood that Skidney wanted the night off but Chubby wasn't having any of it.

"Try and stop me!" screamed Skidney.

"Just see if I don't!" bawled Chubby.

By now the patio outside the upper wreck was three-deep in us boys who were fascinated spectators in the unfolding drama. In the gloom of the approaching evening we observed Skidney marching out of the Masters' quarters closely followed by Chubby.

Skidney headed down the stairs and out the back where his car was parked on the road. Chubby, completely ignoring us, made his way across the lawn and stood in the middle of the road. We had a grandstand view of events and nobody uttered a word.

Behind the House we heard Skidney's car firing up but all eyes were fixed on Chubby who was standing with legs apart and arms akimbo. By the time the car appeared it was doing at least 30mph with a grim-looking Skidney behind the wheel. Chubby was immovable.

I must confess, given the mind-set of both characters, I averted my eyes. I truly believed that Chubby would probably die. I fully expected to hear the awful sound of metal on crunching bone. Instead, I heard a mass gasp from all around me. I looked up to see Chubby shaking his fist after Skidney's car which sped past the Parade Ground and into the gloom.

"What happened? I couldn't look!" I heard from some of the boys on either side of me.

Those with braver hearts stated that Chubby, at the very last moment, had jumped aside with incredible speed. Had he not done so it is certain he would have been killed. Skidney had not deviated an inch from his intended path and in fact accelerated as he approached the stalwart Chubby. I think it was the closest thing to attempted homicide that those with the courage to look would ever see.

Skidney left the Home soon after that and I don't know what became of him. Chubby stayed on to become the Housemaster of Crawford House when it opened a little time later.

I was in Spackman House for a little over two years. The transition from a Junior House to a Senior House was not nearly as traumatic as when I arrived from the Children's Home. I had already been five years in the Home and knew its ways and understood what was required to survive in the hostile environment.

Initially the Senior House was different inasmuch as the older boys, being stronger, wielded much power over us but rarely abused the privilege. Only once was I socked on the jaw by my Patrol Leader. I had pushed him to the edge of his patience and he snapped and clocked me one.

I detested one of the older boys who wore thick horn-rimmed spectacles, without which he was quite blind. His name was David and he had a dog called Winston. David had a cruel streak, pinching younger boys whilst smiling at them when he did so. On several occasions I observed younger boys yelp in pained surprise when he pinched them. It merely infuriated me and I would lash out with my fist when he pinched me. Of course I had to run after landing a blow, he being much older and stronger than I was.

He pinched me on the train to Camp and we ended up on the floor of the moving train. In a desperate attempt to prevent the ensuing slaughter, I held onto his arms. We were between two carriages and the gap between the coaches was wide enough to admit a view of the track beneath. As I desperately clung to his arms, I remember seeing the wooden sleepers passing below in a blur as the train clacked its way along the rails.

Eventually he managed to free one of his arms and landed a quick blow on my nose before I could stop him. In an attempt to limit the onslaught I was forced to release his other arm and protect my face and head from the unpleasantness about to follow. Then a minor miracle occurred that saved me from what would have been a most severe beating.

In his excitement to be free, David's glasses somehow got knocked from his face and landed close to the gap. I immediately spotted the possibilities and in a superhuman effort prevented him from snatching them up again. The rocking of the train caused the glasses to move ever closer to the gap and David was desperate to save them. At Camp there would be no possibility of finding replacements.

"Okay, Twead, I'll call it quits if you do."

The trouble was I did not trust him and knew that, once he had retrieved them, he would continue with my demolition. So I held him even more tightly. He was desperate but could do nothing. The train rocked and the glasses inched closer. There the two of us lay, clutching each other like lovers, our eyes fixed on the moving pair of spectacles.

They did fall and I released him immediately. I knew the battle was over and he was lost without his glasses. I might have pressed my advantage, knowing how short-sighted he was, but I didn't bother. I left him seated on the carriage floor, a forlorn expression on his face. I never did hear from him again and he spent the whole of Camp on the site, not trusting himself to venture out.

Thankfully, David left the Home before I did and was one of only two boys in the Home whom I loathed. The other was Raymond. He was sly and cunning and his expressionless eyes were like a snake's. One never could see what he was thinking or feeling. It was those eyes that had looked into mine in Simpson House when he quietly challenged me to a fight.

I was fourteen at the time and sitting between two arches that surrounded the Parade Ground. A Home Parade had been called and the boys were milling about prior to forming House lines for the Parade. In my hand was a small inexpensive transistor radio and I was turning the dial, searching for a station.

"Let me see that," said Raymond from above me.

"No," I said, without looking up.

The next instant I saw his foot coming up towards my face, too quickly for me to react. The bridge of his foot split my nose open and I was a bloody mess. A strange bell was ringing in my head and the sunlight seemed to grow a thousand times brighter. In the distance I could hear an angry voice.

"What the ---- did you do that for?"

It was Richard who must have witnessed it.

"He wouldn't let me see his radio," Raymond replied.

"So you kicked him in the face?"

Raymond must have sauntered off because I heard nothing more.

"Joe, you okay?"

I bubbled my gratitude for his solicitude and assured him I was fine.

A week or so later, having stowed my radio away in my locker, I returned to discover it had disappeared. It was a prized possession that I would never see again. I knew Raymond had taken it but couldn't prove it. It was typical of his underhand methods and thankfully he left the Home well before I did. When I later heard that he had died early in his life, I viewed it as divine retribution and did not mourn his passing.

On a lighter note, two older boys, Robert and George, were always plotting mischievous pranks to play on their colleagues. One such came to light only after I narrowly avoided being a victim of their rascally intentions. The prank was aimed at the first boy to enter the House after the evening meal, which happened to be me.

The carpet covering the wooden corridor that linked the dormitories in Spackman House was loose enough to be pulled from beneath the feet of anyone walking over it. It occurred to Robert and George that it would be a fine prank to play on the first unsuspecting soul entering the dark House after supper.

After the meal I hurried back but was overtaken in the darkness by Robert and George. In itself this was normal behaviour and there was nothing in it to arouse suspicion. As I approached the door opening onto the corridor, a tiny doubt arose in the depths of my brain.

Why were there no lights on? I asked myself.

I argued that their haste was due to something they ate at supper and they had fled to the toilets below. Satisfied that I had solved the mystery I opened the door.

The narrow corridor was all that separated me from my dormitory. I needed just two steps to see me inside: one onto the carpet and the second into the dorm. I lowered my foot to step on the carpet. Some inexplicable sixth sense kicked in at the very last instant and I changed my mind. I extended my stride and missed the carpet altogether.

To my right, and in the darkness, I heard the distinct sound of two bodies tumbling down the stone steps leading to the ablutions and lower wreck. Each must have had a corner of the carpet which was pulled with their combined mights to dislodge me. The unexpected lack of resistance had sent them sprawling down the stairs.

I turned on the light to our dorm and, quickly picking up a comic, I lay on my bed pretending to read it. About a minute later I sensed rather than saw Robert and George staring at me from the corridor. I simply couldn't trust myself to look up and not laugh. Had I done so, I am sure I would have been beaten to a pulp. Thankfully, they assumed I was ignorant and walked away.

I was fourteen and a half when I entered Spackman House and in the second year of high school. Richard, Macky, Bossy and Ticky were a year ahead of me in Standard Eight. Jogs had skipped a year and was in Standard Nine. We had all moved up to the Senior House together and were in Dorm 3.

At the beginning of the next year, when I was in Standard Eight, I was delighted to discover that my friends had failed Standard Eight and had to repeat the year. For the first time I would be in the same class with them. I was surprised that Ticky had failed because, unlike the others, he was a reader. Richard, I would discover, had little inclination to be an academic.

"Transpose this formula and make 'r' the subject," said Mr Durie, who we nicknamed Judge and who was taking us for Arithmetic. "When you have done that, bring your books up to me."

It was our first Arithmetic lesson and the formula was the area of a circle with r as its radius. We had covered transpositions in Standard Seven and it didn't take me long to take my book up to Judge. Richard was sitting in the desk in front of me and when I returned he spun in his seat and gave me his book.

"Do mine for me," he said and I did.

What astonished me was that he was so knowledgeable in all subjects but unable to do a simple transposition. More shocking was the fact that he had completed Standard Eight and still couldn't do it. Of course I didn't say anything and within a few months he and Macky, having reached the school-leaving age, left the school and Home.

Ticky, Bossy and I stayed on but Ticky would leave during Standard Nine. Only Bossy and I would eventually finish Standard Ten although Bossy failed Standard Nine leaving me as the sole Home boy during my final year at school.

At the end of my two years in Spackman House, all the older boys had left the Home and been replaced by the Juniors from Simpson House. Of my friends, only Bossy and Ticky remained. None of the boys who had transferred with me from the Children's Home were still around. Karly had long since disappeared, as had Kevin and Joss. Les had left to join his family in Canada.

I recall receiving a letter. This was highly unusual because, until then, I had never had any mail at the Home. I gazed at the envelope and saw my name and the Home's address written in a rough hand. Intrigued, I tore it open and read the contents of the single sheet enclosed. The same hand that had addressed the envelope had written the following, unpunctuated and in block capitals.

HI JOE ITS ME KARLY I AM IN THE ARMY AND I HAVE TO RITE A LETER TO MY FAMLY AND I ONLY NO YOU

I smiled. Karly was undertaking his National Conscription.

29

Musical Instruments and my Father

Cadets was compulsory and occurred every Thursday afternoon after school. It applied only to Senior House boys.

There were two branches of the cadet force: the marchers and the band. Marchers practiced marching drills whilst the band members, led by a drum major, were expected to march as well as play a musical instrument. These included bugles, trumpets and a whole range of percussion instruments. Generally, the marchers performed their drills in time to a pace set by the band.

The instruments were stored in a room beneath the Chapel that previously was an armoury. The weapons had long since disappeared and the room was now known as the Band Room.

The Cadet competition was an annual event in which Johannesburg high schools participated and the standard of marching was assessed by professional soldiers in the South African Army. The squads were unaccompanied by bands and performed a set routine of drills. Every aspect was assessed: marching, manoeuvres, saluting and dress. When well executed, the entire squad acted as a single unit, acting on commands barked out by the senior boy in charge. He was called a Student Officer and, sword in hand, stood to one side whilst shouting out his orders.

The Home took great pride in its cadet squad and only the best marchers were selected. The preparation of the uniform was begun weeks ahead of any competition, with shirts and shorts being ironed until only crisp seams were visible on otherwise unblemished khaki clothing.

Shoes were polished to a mirror-like finish. The polish was applied in tiny circles using index fingers over which thin layers of cloth had been wrapped. Then the same fingers were dabbed in water and the process was repeated. We called it 'boning one's shoes' and only the toe caps and heels were boned. the rest of the shoe was polished and buffed, to achieve a more natural lustre, but the overall effect was stunning. A properly prepared shoe took several days to complete.

Needless to say that on the day of a competition an immaculate turnout was demanded and the Home always excelled at the inspection phase. It did excellently in the marching phases too and regularly claimed first prize in the regional and national competitions.

Not so the band. Members of the band were boys with little ambition, preferring to play an instrument rather than participate in the highly disciplined world of the marchers. It was entered into competitions but rarely performed beyond a mediocre standard.

In my first year in Spackman House, I had to make a choice between the marchers and the band. I had no musical abilities and the far more successful marching squad helped me choose in its favour. We all aspired to be selected for the competition squad and did everything in our power to be noticed. Thirty boys represented the Home and being one of them was a very handsome feather in one's cap.

I did my very best but was always overlooked in favour of another. I silently scolded myself for not trying harder and one Thursday afternoon, when we were stood at ease for a few moments, I glanced down the road that ran past the Parade Ground. At the far end, near the Chapel, the band was idly grouped and there appeared to be none of that urgency and tension which prevailed within our ranks. Unlike our drill-masters, who did nothing but bawl at us, the drum major was relaxed and chatting with the band members.

It suddenly occurred to me that simply marching was both boring and for fools and within a week I had applied for and been accepted as a band member.

"We need a tenor drummer," Michael, the drum major said to me. "Get yourself a set of sticks and learn how to spin them."

The drum sticks were short, with golfball-sized gongs on one end and a leather thong attached through a hole in the other. The thong was tied in a loop just large enough to fit around the middle fingers of one's hand. This allowed the tenor drummer to spin the sticks ostentatiously during play. The skill was getting them to spin in time together and then catching the sticks at exactly the right moment. One had to be ambidextrous and, if not naturally so, much practice was needed. It took me several weeks to master them.

Each tune we played had a different beat count and it was not difficult learning them on the drum that hung against my left thigh. I enjoyed being a tenor drummer but, like the marching, I soon tired of its simplicity and requested to be a side drummer. Side-drummers used a snare-drum and were in the front row of the band. Although they carried their drums as I did, their skills were infinitely greater.

"I suppose so," said Michael, "we always need side-drummers but it's going to take a while to find another tenor drummer. Carry on being a tenor drummer but get a set of practice sticks and start learning how to play. Ask Robin or Trevor to teach you."

Trevor and Robin were close friends with each other and a few years older than I was. They were gifted side-drummers but baulked at having to train me.

"Listen, I don't have the time," Trevor complained. "I'll show you how to do the different rolls but you'll have to practise them yourself."

I was only too happy to oblige and used the practice sticks on every wooden surface I could find. I spent hours teaching myself the single-beat, mama-dadda and paradiddle rolls. I never did master them completely but achieved a satisfactory level of competence before learning to apply them to each piece the band played. It would take me a year to become a fully fledged side drummer and even then, at best, I was average.

Nevertheless, I was where I wanted to be and content to continue my cadet career as side drummer in the band. We maintained the mediocre standard at competitions but that did not seem to concern us and the relaxed ethos of the band was very much to my liking. Eventually I would become the drum major and sadly, if anything, standards deteriorated even further.

On Thursday afternoons I would march the band as far from prying eyes as possible and, after posting sentries against unwanted visits, we spent the afternoons chatting in the cool of a shady arbour. Anyone wishing to practise, I encouraged to do so, presenting a semblance of activity should anyone wonder at the silence surrounding a band practice. Eventually I would insist that several buglers blast away which seemed to work well enough. Nobody ever did visit us and I regarded the tactic as an unqualified success.

* * *

I have made little mention of the Assistant Housemasters, in each House. Mr Derek was the first that I met in Simpson House and his influence was linked to that of Mr Brian. He had a short temper and, when provoked, lashed out, slapping the faces of offenders.

Despite this, he was popular with the boys, always encouraging them to do well at school and at sport. He often spent much time training me to swim faster in the swimming pool and this would eventually pay dividends when I became the Junior *victor ludorum* in the swimming gala.

On the sports field, although he never participated, he was quick to motivate boys to run faster, to be better at soccer, and to play hockey. Hockey was his sport and although I enjoyed it, I always preferred soccer. But hockey was the one sport he actively participated in so I played it too. It was always much more fun when an adult was involved.

One of Mr Derek's gifts was reading to us before bedtime. We squeezed into his small flat and, with standing room only, listened to him read Enid Blyton's *Adventure* Series. His genius was to create a different voice for each character and we especially enjoyed his comical accents for Kiki the parrot.

Other Assistant Housemasters were a different breed altogether. They were very young VSOs (Voluntary Service Overseas) who travelled from Britain and donated their time, efforts and expertise to work for a year in third-world countries. Not that South Africa was a third-world country but I suppose the Home was considered a deserving cause. In essence it was a gap year before they attended tertiary education and was similar to the American Peace Corps. They were paid a pittance which was the going rate for an Assistant Housemaster.

I liked them all and had a particular fondness for Mr Tony whose father, I believe, was one of Britain's top nuclear scientists and one of those responsible for splitting the atom. I sometimes accompanied Mr Tony into Johannesburg where he always headed for the public library before taking me to see a movie.

Another was Mr Adam, a Scotsman, who loved playing the bagpipes. Mr Brian had a particular aversion to this instrument and Mr Adam was ordered to play it (if he must) as far from the House as possible, so as not to offend human ears. At night, whilst we lay in bed, we listened to Mr Adam's mournful melodies drifting up from the playing fields.

On one occasion a VSO mentioned that he had not signed up to work at the Home. We were on the train going down to Camp.

"What do you mean, sir?" we asked. "Don't you like it here?"

"Oh, I like it well enough," he said, a touch of sadness in his voice, "it's just that you boys have it too good. I wanted to work with people who really needed me. You lot don't know it but you have everything. You don't need me."

For the first time I was given an insight into the privileges and advantages that I took for granted. Even so, I would still have preferred taking my chances with Ma.

* * *

Joe finished typing the sentence and stopped. His hands fell into his lap and he stared into space, immersed in his memories. I read over his shoulder and knew exactly what he was thinking.

"Joe?"

Joe returned to the present and looked at me.

"It wouldn't have worked, you know," I said.

"What wouldn't?"

"You know. I've heard you say a million times that you'd rather have stayed with your mother."

"Well, I would have. Ma and I would have managed."

"Joe, you couldn't have managed. She had severe mental issues, she was often homeless and she wasn't capable of looking after herself, let alone

children."

"I'd have looked after her."

"You were five years old! You must understand, you wouldn't have thrived and I know Lizzy would agree with me. Of course being brought up in care is far from ideal, but in your case, I honestly believe you were rescued from a miserable, poverty stricken, unhealthy existence."

"You may be right," Joe said, but he didn't sound convinced.

I let the matter drop and left him to his thoughts.

* * *

All in all, the VSOs were a rich source of information about Britain and I had many opportunities to quiz them about life in their country. I was an unashamed Anglophile and I promised myself that one day I would visit that Promised Land. I learned that television brought news events into people's homes, unlike South Africa where the white Nationalist government had banned TV. I was told that it was possible to be a pilot in the Royal Air Force if one joined its University Squadrons. I always wanted to be a pilot and listened, enthralled, as one VSO described his experiences to me.

"You sit in a glider and a winch pulls you into the air before releasing you. One moment you are on the ground and the next you are a thousand feet up. Very exciting! You would love it."

I never became a pilot but many years later I did experience the thrill of being flung into the air whilst seated in a glider. But that's a chapter in my life that doesn't belong in these pages.

* * *

When I was fifteen I established contact with my father. He had never bothered to contact me and, unlike Ma, I bore him no natural affinity. But I could not resist meeting him properly for the first time when the opportunity arose.

It transpired that my father had grown up with the Home's boxing coach whom everyone knew as Tony. Once a week, Tony visited the Home to train boxers in the gym. I joined but, having no natural ability, I didn't pursue it. I often watched the boys practising on Saturday mornings and so maintained a contact with Tony.

One morning he confounded me by saying that he had known my father. Amazed, I asked him why he hadn't mentioned it before.

"Because you didn't ask me," he slurred.

Tony wasn't the sharpest tool in the box and the many thumps he'd suffered were beginning to tell.

"How could I ask you if I didn't know you knew him?"

"That's your bad luck. Anyway, I still know him. I have his phone number."

This last bit of information blew me away and I couldn't wait to hear any stories Tony had about him. All he could offer me was that Harry was kind-hearted and liked animals.

I did phone my father and the first thing out of my mouth was a question.

"Why did you leave Ma?"

There was a pause before he answered.

"She was making my life miserable. Listen, let's meet this Sunday and we can talk about it."

I agreed and we did. The man who was my father was as tall as I was and extremely ordinary looking. He was clean-shaven and we looked nothing like each other. His clothes were simple, and unlike me, he was quietly spoken. He didn't drive and depended on public transport to commute. He had never remarried and I think he was a cinema projectionist. We ate lunch at one of the numerous cafés to be found in any Johannesburg street.

Understandably we had little to say to one another. At the end of this brief encounter we parted ways and he bunged me a tenner which, in those days, was a lot of money. I never saw him again.

Of the little conversation we had, I can recall only two things. The first was to justify his absence from my life which he explained was due to Ma. She had turned up unannounced at his places of work and had made a nuisance of herself. He didn't explain how she did but said he needed to distance himself as much as possible from her. He feared losing his job and needed to keep his whereabouts secret from anyone connected to her. I presumed his definition of 'anyone' included me.

The other topic was an age-old refrain and I almost fell off my chair when he repeated it.

"Do you have any idea where your sister is?"

"Like I told Ma, I don't know!" I almost bawled at him.

He gave me a surprised look so I explained that Ma had always been on at me about Lizzy.

"As far as I know, she was adopted but I don't know anything else."

He seemed to accept that but it occurred to me that, had he known where she was, there was nothing he could do about it. Never once did he ask after Ma or express any concern over her disappearance from my life. Such was the brief encounter I had with my father, fifteen years after I was born.

30

Surprises and Changes

"Twead, report to Mr Ken in his office," the Headboy of Spackman ordered.

"Am I in trouble?"

"How the ---- should I know? Just get your ---- up to his office and make it swift!"

That was the way he always spoke and I didn't argue. I pondered my fate, wondering why I had been summoned. Visiting the Deputy Head usually implied something sinister. One was called to the Beak's office for a chat whilst Mr Ken's was a place of punishment. I searched my mind for any recent transgressions but could think of none to merit a caning.

"Twead," said Mr Ken, as I stood nervously in front of his desk, "the Home has been contacted by Mr and Mrs Hutton. Do you know these people?"

"No, sir."

"I suppose not. They are your sister's adoptive parents."

Pardon? Lizzy's adopted mum and dad?

"They will be coming to the Home on Saturday at two o'cock. I understand you haven't seen her for some time?"

"It's been ten years, sir."

"Hmmmm. All right, you can go now," he said.

I was happy to escape. The man and his office terrified me.

Saturday arrived and brought with it my long lost sister. Her mum and dad, following initial brief introductions, left us to ourselves. I took her down to the playing fields and we sat alone on the high embankment.

It was wonderful seeing her again and I stared at the pretty thirteen year old who was just three when I saw her last. I was now sixteen. Such changes and yet it was as if we had never been apart. The only difference was that she now belonged to a pair of doting parents whose upper middle class wealth had transformed her circumstances while I still languished in the Home.

"I saw you out of the back window of our car when I was taken away from the Children's Home," Lizzy said. "Do you remember that?"

I explained that I learned she was being adopted but it wasn't from anyone official. It had been a rumour. I told her that a boy in my dormitory had said that the people who had adopted her were outside looking for me. I had run outside but could see nobody. All I had seen was a black car on the road past the back entrance but it was speeding away.

"That was us! You ran after the car but Mom told Dad to hurry in case you caught us."

"Why?"

"I don't know."

Lizzy asked if I remembered posing for a photograph that Matron took of us standing together in the twilight. I did and she retrieved a small picture from a purse she had. It showed us standing together and I had my arm around her shoulder. We were both smiling.

"Matron gave it to Mom."

Lizzy's mum and dad then appeared.

Mrs Hutton, like her husband, was in her fifties. She was somewhat rotund without appearing to be overweight. She was short-sighted and wore her glasses attached to an ornamental chain to prevent them from falling when she removed them from her round hooked nose. Her small dark eyes were shrewd and missed very little. An attractive little hat adorned her flamboyantly coiffured hair. I would discover that she undoubtedly wore the pants in the family and I would get to know her as Aunty Bobbi.

Mr Hutton had the solid build of a man who had participated in many active sports in his youth, and rugby in particular. I would later learn that he represented the Transvaal at tennis and that indeed he had been a rugby player, although not one of note. Those days were now long gone. Not being tall, he looked rather squat and the thirty-odd fags a day that he smoked left him gasping after doing anything strenuous. His sedentary lifestyle as a bank inspector didn't improve matters either.

In appearance, his small grey eyes, set on either side of a rather bulbous nose, looked on the world around him with a kindly tolerance that endeared him to all that knew him. He wore glasses to read, and his thinning short grey hair was plastered neatly over his scalp. A thin pencil-line grey moustache was the only feature on an otherwise clean-shaven face.

I immediately liked this quietly spoken man who always patiently jumped to the commands of his outspoken wife. I would get to know him as Uncle Jim.

From that moment on, my life in the Home improved immensely. Within a short while of being parted from Mrs Lawson, a new family had stepped in to fill the void and they were as close to real family as I was ever likely to get. The new regulations enabling us to visit relatives every Sunday had kicked in and would soon be further relaxed to include the entire weekend.

* * *

Our move to Crawford House was imminent and I was soon to begin Standard Nine at school. As yet I had been given no position of authority. Richard and Macky had left the Home to find work and Jogs was reading Electrical Engineering at Wits University. Only Bossy and Ticky now remained.

A list of the dormitory allocations for Crawford House was pinned to the Spackman House notice board. I discovered that Ticky was to be the Headboy, Bossy the Patrol Leader of Dorm 3, the Junior dormitory, and I was to be his Corporal.

"You will be in Standard Nine," Chubby said to me, "and I am rewarding you for doing well at school. Not many boys even reach Standard Nine."

Crawford House was ready for moving into and was vastly superior to those we had previously occupied. Each dormitory had its own showers and the Headboy, Patrol Leaders and Corporals all had their own rooms. Dorm 1, the Senior dormitory, was entirely single room accommodation. This was unprecedented and afforded the older Seniors the privacy that had never before existed in the Home.

The beds, mattresses and bed clothing were all new. A single thick duvet covered every bed and we were told that well-meaning ladies, led by the Beak's wife, had created them for us. A desk and chair was provided for each boy in Dorm 1, as well as for the Headboy, whose room was larger. The Patrol Leaders and Corporals of Dorms 2 and 3 had secluded rooms within the dorms, one at either end. I now had my own room. The dormitories and single rooms had linoleum floors while the rest of the House had polished stone floors. My last two years at the Home was therefore spent in comparative luxury.

Bossy was eventually transferred to Taylor House, as its Headboy, and I was made the Patrol Leader of Dorm 1. Ticky then left the Home and I was appointed as Headboy. Furthermore, in the Band, I had been promoted to drum major. These events took place during my final eighteen months and provided me with much licence to do as I pleased.

* * *

At school, several strange events occurred. The first would puzzle me for the rest of my life and even today I still think about it. To me, it is inexplicable.

Every day, after school, a classmate of mine, whose name was Akkie, begged and got a lift from me on the crossbar of my bicycle. The school was set atop a substantial hill and the journey down to the bus stop, where I dropped Akkie off, was a thrilling roller-coaster of a bike ride. We both loved it as I swerved around groups of homeward-bound pupils walking down the paved road leading to the school gates.

One night, as I lay asleep in my bed in Crawford House, I had a most vivid dream. In it, Akkie had asked me to give him a lift, a request I never denied. He sat on the crossbar and we set off. On the way down, we swept past the twins, two lovely sisters whom I had a crush on. I looked over my shoulder to give them an admiring glance when suddenly Akkie and I went flying though the air. When we landed in a heap on the road, I woke up.

It was a breath-takingly real dream and so detailed that I could remember every moment of it. That day, after school, the dream was re-enacted for real. Every second was replayed and I still wonder why I did nothing to prevent it from happening. When we crashed, just after I had looked back at the twins, Akkie and I sprawled and slithered down the road before coming to a stop. The odd thing was that not a single person stopped to ask after us, despite us sitting dazed for several minutes in the middle of the road. Even odder was the fact that, other than a few scratches, neither of us was hurt and the bicycle was still totally intact.

* * *

"I know I've heard that story loads of times," I said, "but it really is strange."

"I've never been able to explain it. Why were neither of us hurt and the bicycle undamaged? I remember accusing Akkie of putting one of his feet into the spokes of the front wheel, but he hadn't or they'd have been bent."

"I've never really believed in the supernatural, but sometimes I wonder..."

"Me too," agreed Joe.

"Do you remember old Sancho in the village, and his black cat, Mishi, who followed him everywhere?"

"Of course. Old Sancho walked with a stick and suffered from flatulence."

"That's the one. Well, he died years ago, but I'm sure I still hear old Sancho walking up our street. Tap-tap, parp. Tap-tap, parp."

"Stop your nonsense and let me get on with this wretched book."

"But I do hear him, I promise."

I wasn't lying.

* * *

I had been Headboy of Crawford House for some time and had grown comfortably into the position. I ruled the House with an iron fist and I behaved no differently to Headboys before me. I had been beaten by

Headboys and now I was doing the beating.

My tyranny did not apply to the older boys in Dorm 1. Having been in the Home the longest, they already understood the rules and needed no reminder of the consequences, should they break them. Not so the younger boys whose transgressions were ruthlessly dealt with.

If the offender's Patrol Leader was unable to solve the problem, then he was referred to me. My methods in dealing with the reprobate did not include reasoning. A punch, slap or kick invariably made him see the light. It had been the system during the previous fifty-five years and it was the same in 1968/9 when I was the Headboy.

At school I had no authority. The school appointed Prefects, (whose teeth were as sharp as a hen's), and they were never allowed to raise even a finger against any wrongdoer. They could only report him (or her) to the Headmaster who dealt with the matter. I was not a Prefect and never wanted to be one.

The Headmaster, Mr Johnsen (his first name was John and he was known amongst ourselves as 'Johnny'), summoned me to his office. I should mention that from the moment I turned sixteen, I was never again caned, either in the Home or at school. When I entered, he was with one of the boys from Dorm 3 of Crawford House.

"Twead," said Johnny, "this boy was caught messing about in the corridors and I intend caning him."

The youngster was looking at me, terrified. I must have looked like that when Johnny first caned me when I was in Standard 6. But I had no sympathy for the boy. He had been caught misbehaving and knew the consequences. My difficulty was trying to understand what on earth I was doing there.

"Yes, sir," was all I could think of saying.

I was about to add that he should feel free to lather the hide off the little so-and-so, when he continued.

"Apparently I need your permission to cane him," he said with raised eyebrows.

I stared first at him and then at the boy. I couldn't help feeling that this was some kind of prank being played on me.

My permission?

"You are his Headboy in the Home are you not?"

"Yes, sir, I am."

"Then I need your permission to cane him," he said, somewhat impatiently.

I was tempted to say no, just to see what might happen, but decided against it.

"You have it, sir," I said and I was dismissed.

Half an hour later, Johnny called me back to his office.

"Why didn't you tell me before that you were a Headboy in the Home? You have to tell us these things, Twead, we can't read minds, you know. I've decided to make you a Prefect. You will be awarded a Prefect's badge at tomorrow's school assembly. I can't make you a full Prefect. Had you opened your mouth before, I could have done it but the year is almost over. So I'm making you a sub-Prefect."

Being a full or sub-Prefect meant little to me. I would have preferred to be left alone but the caning incident had raised my head above the parapet. My classmates pulled my leg something rotten despite most of them being full Prefects. Eugene insisted on addressing me as 'sir' which made me laugh. He was still full of mischief and persisted in shopping me to the teachers for misdemeanours perpetrated by others.

"I cannot tell a lie, sir, it was Twead."

Even as I write these lines I can't help smiling.

I was called up to the stage at the morning assembly and ceremoniously awarded a sub-Prefects badge. No additional duties were attached and I accepted it graciously enough.

Johnny now surprised me by calling me regularly down to his office via the intercom in each classroom.

"I'll see Twead in my office," would boom from the loudspeaker box, set above the blackboard.

At first I thought it was to obtain my permission to cane yet another delinquent but I soon discovered it was nothing of the sort. It was simply because he wanted to chat with me.

"I see you have Geography followed by Afrikaans. You can afford to miss those, can you not?"

"And the rest too, sir."

That made him smile.

"Fine. Would you like some tea?"

"Thank you, sir, white, two sugars."

Johnny picked up his phone and ordered the school secretary to bring in the tea. Thereafter our topics of discussion covered a variety of subjects. These included popular music, the Afrikaaner Nationalists, Apartheid, the assassination of Dr Verwoed, reincarnation and even teachers' pay.

"Do you know, Twead, why Mr Bloch no longer teaches Maths?"

I shook my head.

"Because we don't pay him enough. He earned R400 a month as a teacher and was offered R800 in industry."

Mr Bloch had been our Maths teacher and had suddenly left the school half-way through a term. We were without a teacher for the remaining eight months of the year. We had been left the text book and free periods to do as we pleased.

I remember one Saturday morning, having no reading material, picking up the text book and idly turning the pages. To my astonishment, Euclid's Theorems fascinated me. Starting with the first, the rest followed logically, one after the other. I reached Theorem 30 when I was distracted by a five-a-side game that was being organised. Playing soccer always took precedence over everything else.

But the seed had been sowed and Maths, together with English, became my favourite subjects.

Johnny called me from my classes on several occasions and always poured me a cup of tea before choosing a topic to chat about. Despite our friendship, for I do believe that he liked me, I was always wary of him. His mood could turn on a sixpence and I had to tread warily lest I offend him. I did not want to abuse our relationship by being over familiar.

So my last two years in the Home and at school were proving to be very comfortable indeed. Frankly, I was enjoying myself. In the Home, as the Headboy of Crawford House and drum major in Cadets, I had immense power over my subordinates. Unfortunately, the old adage that 'power tends to corrupt and absolute power corrupts absolutely' would soon bear fruit with dramatic consequences.

But before I move onto that, I should relate my progress with the Huttons and Lizzy.

31

The Huttons

The Huttons owned a three-bedroom bungalow in Johannesburg's Southern Suburbs. Uncle Jim's salary ensured that Aunty Bobbi need not work and Lizzy attended a local comprehensive high school that was much like my own.

I had to commute to and from their house but public transport was inexpensive and frequent. Eventually it would become a familiar journey that began on Friday evenings and ended with my attendance at Sunday Evensong in the Chapel.

Every weekend and holiday was spent with the Huttons and Lizzy and I romped. They bought me clothes that I hung in a cupboard in the third bedroom that had become mine while I stayed with them. They even provided me with pocket money to buy gifts at Christmas and for birthdays.

In effect it was as if I had been adopted but with the proviso that I return to the Home during the week. I had no difficulty with this but Lizzy was not satisfied. She wanted to know why her mother and father had not included me in the adoption process.

"Leave it, Lizzy," I said, feeling rather embarrassed.

"No, I want to know," she said, and stood defiantly in front of her mother.

Aunty Bobbi's hand shot out and slapped her hard in the face. I was profoundly shocked but I said nothing.

"Mind your manners, young lady," Aunty Bobbi hissed at her.

All credit to Lizzy, she took the blow without shedding a tear and simply turned sulkily away. Despite this rather vicious rebuff, Lizzy never relinquished her stance and always bombarded her mother with that same question. Oscar Wilde's adage that 'we initially love our parents but later judge them', was never more true.

In fairness to Aunty Bobbi, she tried her best to explain.

"We only wanted one child," she said to Lizzy, "and you wormed your way into our hearts. Would you rather I had left you with your brother in the Children's Home?"

"It would not have worked," she said to me, "you were just too old. Your sister was just right for us and we loved her dearly. I am sorry, Joe, I can't change it now."

I reassured Aunty Bobbi, insisting that she had nothing to apologise for. Lizzy said nothing but I could see that she was not satisfied.

Twenty years after leaving South Africa, I visited Lizzy. Her mum was living nearby and, having aged considerably, was almost blind. Uncle Jim had died several years before.

"Let me feel your face," she said and her fingertips studied my features. "Ah, yes, the same Joe, just a little fuller."

"I still haven't forgiven her for not adopting you," Lizzy said to me when we were out of earshot.

"Let it go, Lizzy," I said. "Your mum and dad treated me very well and I am quite content. Just let it go."

"No," she said flatly, "she should have adopted you too. She should have adopted you when we met again after ten years instead of leaving you in the Home."

Perhaps Lizzy was right. Perhaps I should have been adopted but I wasn't. As I told her, I was content with my lot and the years in the Home had moulded me into a Home boy. Had I joined their family, at the age of sixteen, I doubt I would have adapted to what would have been a very different lifestyle. At best it would have been difficult.

But at age sixteen, I thoroughly enjoyed being with Lizzy again and living in the luxury of her comfortable home. Uncle Jim was placid and Aunty Bobbi would often tell me that he adored Lizzy and, had she demanded the moon, he would have done his utmost to get it for her.

He drove us everywhere because his wife had never bothered to learn. No matter what the road conditions, his speed never exceeded 30mph and more often was even slower. I always sat up front with Uncle Jim, and Aunty Bobbi sat with Lizzy in the back. From there she directed her husband's driving with a shrillness that initially I found amusing but later annoyed me. Unfortunately, I have a hasty temper and her back-seat driving soon had me exploding.

"Look out, Jim!" she screamed one night, when we were on our way to the local cinema.

In the distance, so distant as to be barely visible, even at night, were the headlamps of an approaching car. I had been in a reverie and her shout had given me a fright.

* * *

"*Uh-oh, that was a mistake! I know from bitter experience that if anybody makes you jump, you don't take it kindly...*"

"*I'm afraid that's exactly what happened,*" answered Joe. "*But she really could be most annoying.*"

"Did you snap?"

"I'm afraid I did. Lizzy later told me that my words had made her sink lower and lower into her seat. I was heartily ashamed of myself afterwards."

"What did Uncle Jim say?"

"He said 'You did well, my boy. Perhaps now she'll keep her mouth shut in the car.'"

"And did she?"

"Funnily enough, she did and we had no further incidents of back-seat outbursts." He paused. "Perhaps you could learn from that, Vicky."

* * *

Uncle Jim was not Aunty Bobbi's first husband. She had married a Scotsman, a certain Jock, who hailed from East Wemyss in Fife. He had died early in their marriage and she still greatly mourned his passing. I often listened sympathetically to her tearful recollections of when she and Jock were married.

"Jock and I were so happy, you know," she said, her knitting needles clacking as she spoke, "but we couldn't have children."

She had been one of several women doing secretarial work for some large corporation and blamed her childlessness on a heavy typewriter that needed to be moved between desks in the office.

"After Jock died, Jim and I married. Jim always wanted to marry me but Jock beat him to it. Jim never married. He said he would rather stay single than marry anyone but me."

Uncle Jim, who was in the room when these words were spoken, didn't say a word. I think he had already heard them many times before. He never commented on anything that was said about him by his wife.

Aunty Bobbi was extremely superstitious. Every New Year's Eve the house had to be swept out to remove all the bad luck of the old year. At midnight the whole family had to walk around the house anti-clockwise three times. Coins and bread were then thrown into the house to insure money and food for the coming year. A dark male first-footed across the threshold into the house carrying coal to ensure warmth for the coming year. Although Uncle Jim was now grey, he had been dark-haired in his youth and was an acceptable alternative. Apparently these were Scottish customs taught to her by Jock. I was the second to last one allowed in and Lizzy was last. A blonde woman was considered the curse of Scotland in these matters, or so Lizzy was told. We never did discover the reason.

I don't know why, but one year I completely forgot about her obsession. We had been celebrating the New Year with friends and had returned during the small hours. I climbed out of the car and headed for the front door. I intended switching on the porch and house lights for the benefit of the others. It was purely meant as a courtesy but before I could enter the house I was painfully yanked back by my hair.

"Jim must be the first to cross the threshold!" Aunty Bobbi hissed at me, her face white with anger.

She must have divined my intentions and been hot on my heels as I headed for the front door. Until then I had not truly appreciated the depth of her superstitious nature. Of course I apologised and inwardly cursed myself for my thoughtlessness. Uncle Jim preceded me but not before his wife had checked that he had a piece of coal in his hand. If he didn't, she had some in her handbag.

Her superstitions did not end there. Once a month she visited a fortune teller in Rosettenville, a nearby town. Not being able to drive, Uncle Jim was her uncomplaining chauffeur and Lizzy and I accompanied her on one occasion.

"You do know it's all nonsense," I had the temerity to say to her. "Nobody can tell the future, you know."

Lizzy and Uncle Jim stared at me, no doubt thinking me rash to challenge her deeply held beliefs. Aunty Bobbi was unperturbed and I suspect it wasn't the first time that someone had expressed doubts.

"You can think what you like," she said, rather snootily, "my fortune teller has never been wrong."

I had never visited a fortune teller but had seen their stalls at funfares. Instinctively I dismissed them as charlatans but was not unwilling to give one a chance to prove me right. It seemed an ideal opportunity had presented itself and so I tagged along with them. At the very least it was a new adventure.

"She will have tea with you," Aunty Bobbi explained. "You must drink it all but leave the dregs behind. She will read the tea leaves at the bottom of the cup."

I refrained from laughing and avoided Lizzy's eyes. She and I had formed a special relationship and could read each other's minds simply with a look. I knew she also thought it all nonsense but she tolerated her mother's many harmless foibles.

"Another thing," added Aunty Bobbi, "she will never ask you directly but you must first cross her palm with silver. Here's twenty cents. Before she begins, no matter what she says, put the money in her hand."

Even Hollywood could not have dreamed up a better stereotype. A tea-leaf reading fortune teller whose palm needed first to be crossed with silver was a combination of just about every cliché describing the breed. All that was now needed was a swarthy gypsy lady sitting at a small table in a darkened room.

Instead I was introduced to a sweet white-haired old dear who conducted her services from a brightly lit and spacious dining room. We faced each other across the large table in the centre.

"I understand you are Joe," she said with a smile. "And that you are an unbeliever, or so Bobbi tells me."

I was entirely disconcerted and did not know what to say.

"We shall see," she added, seeing my embarrassment.

Except for one thing, I cannot remember a single thing she told me. I crossed her palm with Aunty Bobbi's 20c and drank the tea she proffered me. When I was finished she took my cup and violently shook the remaining liquid out of the cup. What surprised me was that she did it directly onto her highly polished wooden floor.

I thought her action had dislodged all the cup's contents and envisaged drinking a second cup. Apparently some tea leaves must have survived because she stared at the bottom of the cup for some time before speaking again.

"Make a wish," she said, "but don't tell me what it is. I will speak to you later about it. Do it now."

She stared at me after she had said it and initially I decided not to do it at all. She could not possibly read my thoughts and for a few moments we simply looked at one another. Then, for some reason, I believed she was actually waiting for me to make my wish. Perhaps she was shrewd enough to read the scepticism on my face and knew I hadn't made a wish. Whatever the reason, she refused to say another word until I had made my wish.

So I played along and had to decide between wanting to be a pilot or a writer. My ambitions to be a pilot were already well known to all my acquaintances. I longed to fly one day and idolised Douglas Bader and all the fighter pilots of World War Two. I fully intended joining the South African Air Force (SAAF) who I hoped would help me fulfill my dream.

But my ambition to be a writer was far less well known, something I kept as a jealously guarded secret and withheld from all except those closest to me. I didn't believe that I possessed the necessary skills or intellect to impress any kind of readership. Enid Blyton, Capt. W E Johns, Franklin W Dixon, Carolyn Keene, James Hadley Chase and Alistair MacClean were, in my opinion, artists whose pinnacles of achievement were far beyond my capabilities. I would later learn that Franklin W Dixon (The Hardy Boys) and Carolyn Keene (Nancy Drew Mysteries) were pseudonyms for a plethora of ghost writers.

I chose being a writer and somehow she seemed to know that I had made my wish. She then rattled off a list of events that would take place in my future life but I don't recall a single one. No doubt I was told that I would be going on a long journey and my life would be filled with joys and sorrows, things I would have said to any prospective client had I been in her shoes.

At the conclusion of the reading I was dismissed with no further mention concerning my wish. Although disappointed, I thought it better than to embarrass her so I left the room, passing Lizzy who was next. After Lizzy, Aunty Bobbi and then we were ready to go home. We all stood in the dining room, wishing her farewell, when she suddenly started.

"Young man!" she said, "your wish! I nearly forgot! Not now," she added rather enigmatically, "later."

I had no idea what she was talking about. Did she intend telling me something later? Seeing my confusion, she elaborated.

"Your wish will come true later. Much later."

To emphasise the 'much later', she rolled her hand in small circles to indicate that it would be many years later and I fully understood her meaning.

I was sixteen at the time and, now at the age of sixty-five, these pages comprise my first effort.

Perhaps the old dear was right. It has happened much, much later. Perhaps she really could foresee the future and my reservations concerning clairvoyance were unfounded. Only time will tell and I have precious little of that left.

* * *

Aunty Bobbi always had something to say about everything.

"One day you will find work. When you have a little money to spend you will walk with your head held high. You will see that having money in your pocket makes all the difference."

Then, during the Easter holiday, she ordered me to apply for a student job with CNA, a stationer and bookshop in Rosettenville. It was during my final school year and I saw no harm in it, especially as it would be during the Christmas break which was still some way off. When I had completed and submitted the application form, she reiterated her mantra about me having money in my pocket.

* * *

"Was she right? When the time came, did you walk with your head held high knowing you had earned that money?"

"No! It took me fifteen minutes to spend my first wages. I thought about all those hours I worked to get that money, then how quickly it disappeared. I decided it just wasn't worth it, and Aunty Bobbi couldn't have been more wrong."

"Probably just as well that I look after our finances and pay the bills, then…"

"Definitely."

* * *

Another passion of Aunty Bobbi's was Liberace whom she idolised.

"I just love his clothes and the way he talks to his audience. He sings and plays wonderfully on the piano which usually has a huge silver candle stick holder on top. It holds at least ten candles. I've only been to one of his shows but I loved it. If he ever comes again, I will take you and you will see what I mean."

He did come, and I did go, and I did see what she meant. Although he didn't impress me, I enjoyed Aunty Bobbi's enjoyment of him.

When Billy Graham arrived in Johannesburg, I agreed to accompany the family to the revival meeting that was held at an open air stadium. Thousands turned up to see the man who was cheered by his supporters as he was driven up to the centrally placed podium. Again, Aunty Bobbi enjoyed it, but Uncle Jim, Lizzy and I were less impressed.

I accompanied the family to Durban for a week where we stayed in one of the many high-rise holiday apartments that lined the sea front. We did all the holiday stuff like rickshaw rides, visiting the fun-fair and swimming in the sea. One evening we bumped into an elderly couple whom I had never seen before. They evidently knew Aunty Bobbi and Uncle Jim who were delighted to see them. Lizzy and I walked ahead and I asked my sister who they were.

"Oh, just old friends of Mom's," she said.

I saw them look questioningly at me and then a few quiet words passed between the couples. Lizzy and I joined them and Lizzy introduced me. After that they joined us as we continued our evening stroll through Durban's beautiful Botanic Gardens which we were visiting. This was just prior to attending a live recording of a popular radio programme that Uncle Jim had thoughtfully booked seats for us to attend.

Imagine my surprise when Lizzy was replaced by the gentleman half of the couple that had joined us.

"You're Joe, yes?"

I confirmed that I was.

"Lizzy's brother?"

"Yes." I wasn't sure where this was going.

"If I ever hear that you have let these good people down," here he indicated Aunty Bobbi and Uncle Jim who were walking not far behind, "you will have *me* to answer to, do you understand?"

"*How rude!*" *I exclaimed.*

"*I know!*" *said Joe, wincing.* "*I was so taken aback that I just blustered. I said that nothing could be further from my mind than to disappoint two of the loveliest people I had ever met. I meant it, only Mrs Lawson held a candle to them. She and the Huttons showered me with so many kindnesses and overwhelming generosity.*"

"*I think it was unforgivably rude of that man.*"

"*Unfortunately my relationship with Mrs Lawson had deteriorated, and I had disappointed her, so perhaps he had a point...*"

"*Did you ever fall out with the Huttons?*"

"*No. We did have our ups and downs but nothing to permanently sever our relationship. Not like what happened with Mrs Lawson.*"

"*I'm pleased to hear that.*"

"*Yes, I'm grateful. And their final act of generosity still takes my breath away.*"

"*What did they do?*" *I asked.*

"*By my final year, Camp had lost its sparkle. I was tired of sleeping on the hard ground, living out of a sausage bag and in cramped conditions. That wonderful glow of novelty and adventure had gone.*"

"*What a shame. You loved it so much when you were younger.*"

"*I guess I'd grown out of it. Then Aunty Bobbi announced that she had booked a holiday house not far from the Camp site. It was self-catering and I was free to join them, if I wanted.*"

"*So you stayed there instead?*"

"*Yes! For one glorious week I enjoyed a soft bed and Lizzy and I were on the beach every day.*"

"*Nice!*"

"*Yes, even today I can't believe my good fortune during my stay at the Home. When Ma vanished, I was cared for. Then I had the Lawsons, then the Huttons... Somebody up there was looking after me,*" *he said, pointing up to the heavens.*

"*Yes, it seems so.*"

"*Right, Vicky. My next chapter is about romance. Are you ready for that?*"

"*Of course! Bring it on.*"

32

Lovesick and Seasick

My only notion of romance was gleaned from the silver screen. I was scathing and hissed at any on-screen kissing and couldn't wait for the bullets and fists to fly again.

Then a veil was lifted from my eyes and women and girls became intensely interesting. Girls were closely observed and analysed and I feasted on their beauty.

To stare at any girl was rightly considered as rude and I had to steal my glances when I believed they were unaware of my interest. The only time I could unashamedly stare at a beautiful face was at the movies and Carol Baker in *How the West was Won* epitomised my notion of ideal beauty. I saw that movie when I was eleven. She would be joined by Candice Bergen who appeared in *The Sand Pebbles*, which I saw when I was fifteen.

Both these ladies were blondes and indeed it might be supposed that I preferred blondes but that would not be strictly true. Miss Beveridge, our Arithmetic teacher at the High School, was a dark-haired, blue-eyed beauty with whom I fell in love and whom I might legitimately admire from my seat in the classroom. Nevertheless, it was true that blondes did attract my notice more than non-blondes.

"I want to introduce you to El," Lizzy announced when I visited her for the first time. "She lives two doors down and she's my best friend. She was adopted, just like me, you know. I think she's a year older than you and I know you'll like her."

"When will I meet her?" I asked, with no small interest.

"Today. She said she'll pop round later."

When she did appear, I studied her very carefully indeed.

Her figure didn't attract me at all. In fact it was rather ordinary and without any of the curves and bumps I would have preferred to see. Her loose-fitting, sleeveless yellow dress hung rather limply over a lanky frame and ended at a point halfway down her calves. The little I could see of her legs portended no irresistible urge in me to see more and her flat-heeled slip-on shoes accentuated an inelegant stride when she walked. Her arms were attractive and her hands were beautifully elegant, with long fingers ending in tastefully manicured nails. All this I saw at a glance, the image forever imprinted in my memory.

She had long blonde hair, lank like her figure, that she used to great effect when we were introduced to each other. It hung over her face, obscuring half her features, and she flicked it aside with a wonderful toss of her head. It revealed a face that I found to be simply stunning and my heart was instantly hers to do with as she pleased.

Cleverly applied mascara accentuated her blue eyes, which were perhaps a little too small, but the eye-shadow maximized their impact. Her mouth was a little too wide but the slightly pinked glossy lipstick was perfectly applied over generous full lips. Her nose was thin but in keeping with a face that began with a broad forehead and ended in a small dainty chin. She was an inch or so shorter than I was.

"Pleased to meet you," she said with a smile that revealed perfect teeth.

I shook her extended hand and gazed into her eyes, aware that this was no ordinary girl. I would later meet other girls who were more attractive, but none possessed El's bright intelligence. I could sit for hours chatting with this bird of paradise.

Unfortunately her heart was not free. In later meetings, she showed no inclination to give me any more time than necessary for a perfunctory greeting.

The occasional opportunities to be with her I relished beyond words. Time, however, evaporated alarmingly during those precious moments. More often than not I shared her with Lizzy and Aunty Bobbi, inadvertent chaperones in a drama that began and ended in my head. El would join us when we played card games and I loved seeing her hide behind her hair, using it to screen her face while twirling the ends with her elegant fingers.

Like Lizzy she had been adopted when she was young. Both had been raised in the houses they currently occupied but, unlike Lizzy, her relationship with her parents, and her dad in particular, was less than smooth.

She was 'seeing' a pipe-smoking intellectual that her parents hoped she would marry. Frank was from a good family and completing an arts degree at Wits. Being several years her senior, he was a far more eligible choice than a boy who possessed no prospects and hailed from a Boys Home.

I couldn't have agreed more and when I eventually did meet him, I was further convinced that my chances with El were less than zero. We had been invited by El's parents to a *braai* they were having in their back yard.

Frank was wearing a brown jacket with leather patches on the elbows. His slacks were a slightly different shade of brown, but fitted him perfectly. His socks and expensive leather shoes were complementary shades of brown and a burgundy-coloured cravat was the only article of his clothing with any colour. It was perfectly in keeping with his brown shirt and, indeed, the rest of his brown-shaded turnout.

He wasn't particularly handsome. His short dark hair sat atop a head that sported thick horn-rimmed glasses and his clean-shaven face invited no further comment than having regular features. But his maturity gave him a relaxed confidence that he wore as comfortably as he did his stylish clothing.

When I was introduced to him, he politely shook my hand.

"Pleased to meet you," he said then turned to address somebody more worthy of note.

El's father, Mr Stepford, and Frank did their best to impress each other, both having the same goal in mind. The goal stood alongside her beau, smiling sweetly, looking elegant in her sunny turnout.

I could never match the air of easy familiarity that Frank showed El's parents. His use of a pipe, either to stress a point or indicate an object, was unmatched in its artistry. El often raved about his perfect hands, hands that clasped the pipe bowl and turned the stem to tap the chest of anyone rash enough to oppose an opinion of his. This young man was being groomed to grace either the highest echelons of academia or perhaps the boardroom of some large corporation.

Often, and privately, I studied my own stubby fingers, hoping for some miracle that might change them and so impress El, but I knew it was hopeless. I never would be able to compete with Frank. All I could offer was a yearning heart. I lived for the occasional and all-too-brief moments when I visited the Huttons at the weekends. During holidays, the pain was too great.

At the Easter break I announced that I planned to hitch-hike to Cape Town, a thousand miles away. Aunty Bobbi was shocked.

"Why?" she asked.

"Because I've never been," I answered.

The real reason was it would distance me from El. Living so near her, and not being able to see her, was simply too unbearable for me. I didn't care that I would be totally unprepared and without money. All I wanted to do was escape El's vicinity and distract myself with anything other than thoughts of her.

I had learned about Cape Town during my schooling and wanted to see the silver-leaf trees, Table Mountain, and the huge protea flowers that grew on its slopes. I had also learned about the da Gama Cross, a huge stone cross that had been erected in the fifteenth century by the explorer, Vasco da Gama, when he rounded the southern tip of the continent. It would serve as a navigation aid for vessels heading for India and beyond.

So off I went, and thirty-six hours later I stood in the centre of rush hour traffic, staring up the iconic mountain. It was a grey day and it had been raining. A cold wind blasted through the city and I detested the place. I made an instant decision to turn around and head back to Johannesburg.

Another thirty-six hours later and I stood exhausted in the Hutton's living room. They quickly put me to bed where I slept the sleep of the dead and awoke eighteen hours later, much refreshed.

"Do you remember screaming during the night?" Aunty Bobbi asked me.

"Did I?"

"Yes. You screamed and screamed and screamed. We all came into your room and you were sitting up in your bed. Then you fell back and slept."

"Really?"

I'd no recollection of it. I told them about my journey and they thought me silly to have undertaken it. Secretly I agreed, especially as I had achieved none of my objectives. But I was too proud to admit it.

At school I was so lovesick that it affected my already poor academic performance. Initially I bombarded the ears of anyone who would listen, singing the praises of El's virtues. Then I began hating my closest friends, fearing she would recognise their infinitely superior qualities, imagining she would prefer them to me.

At the Home I ate little and my listlessness did not go unnoticed.

"You okay, Joe?" Chubby asked. "You don't seem your usual self."

I wished I could tell him how profound was my love for El but wisely refrained from doing so.

"Are you in love with her?" Lizzy wanted to know when, for the umpteenth time, I asked her if El was coming over during a weekend.

I should have confessed it but instead blustered a denial. No doubt she knew but said nothing.

El did pop round but all too briefly.

"We're going over to Frank's house," she said. "It's his mother's birthday and he invited us over."

Perhaps the trip to Cape Town knocked some sense into me because from that moment on, my heart began to mend. It had bled for long enough. Lizzy and I enjoyed the rest of the school break together.

I decided to stay away from the Huttons altogether and I planned to revisit Cape Town, but this time in a unique manner. I knew the Beak was a very influential man and planned taking advantage of the fact.

"I was wondering if you could help me, please, Father," I said, standing before the great man as he worked at the desk in his office.

"Joe! Sit down, my boy, sit down!"

I thanked him and sat on the easy chair he reserved for visitors.

"What can I do for you?"

"I was hoping to take a ship to Cape Town. You know, work my passage there. I thought you might have contacts with a shipping line."

It was a long shot and I was delighted when he didn't dismiss me out of hand. He carefully studied me before answering, a small smile on his lips.

"Will you be going alone?"

"No, I was going to ask Rolf to come with me."

Rolf was a few years younger than I was and had entered the Home a few years after I had. He hailed from a German family and could speak very little English when he arrived. Why he was in the Home, he never did explain, but he did tell us that his family worked in a circus.

He was very athletic and his speed of hands, as a boxer, ensured he won a number of trophies in that sport. He was also one of the most personable boys in the Home, immensely popular with us all. It was little wonder I chose him to be my companion for the trip.

"Mmmm...let me see," said Father Eric, "as a matter of fact I do know somebody. I'll write to him and let you know."

Rolf and I did go. With very little cash between us, we hitch-hiked to Durban and worked our passage in the engine room of a cargo ship. At least Rolf did. I was stricken with sea-sickness for most of the time. The Captain did visit me but quickly escaped when I threatened to throw up on him. I worked just one night and greatly regretted not being able to work the whole passage.

* * *

"Seasick?" I asked. "We've been on boats and ferries loads of times and you've never complained of being seasick."

"Um. It may well have had something to do with all the beer the sailors plied us with before we set sail."

"Oh. I see."

* * *

We arrived in Cape Town four days after leaving Durban. As we approached the harbour, the Captain invited us onto the bridge. It was early in the morning and the city was ablaze with light. The face of Table Mountain, too, was bathed in coloured light, illuminated by huge lamps set in the base of the mountain. It was a marvellous sight and I was grateful to witness something so special.

Cape Town did not hold us long enough to see the sights. We hitched back to the Home, having notched up an unforgettable experience.

Some years later I visited Cape Town again and I did see the wonderful silver-leaf tree that shimmered brightly with each breeze. I also saw the beautiful and immense proteas, some so large they had no right to be called flowers. The da Gama Cross I would see twenty years after leaving South Africa, when I returned for a brief holiday from the UK. As for the city, I

206

grew to love it and, together with Durban, regard them as my favourites in all the world.

33

El

I was seventeen and in six month's time my eighteenth birthday would be my last at the Home and at school.

Of course I would spend the Christmas holiday with Lizzy but I planned to try again to get to Cape Town. This time I was more prepared and had accumulated R10, which I thought perfectly adequate for the trip.

I also banked on the generosity of those giving me a ride, a presumptuous tactic that sometimes paid off. I never begged for their help, I was too proud to do that, but hoped they would take pity on what they thought was a penniless schoolboy. It rarely happened but was worth a shot.

I hadn't mentioned my plans to anyone and only intended letting Lizzy know just before I left. Aunty Bobbi was out every morning, working for her church, and Uncle Jim was at work in the bank. I would wait until both had left the house before making my move. I planned my escape to coincide with a Monday. It was the beginning of the working week and I anticipated more traffic on the roads than at weekends. This would increase my chances of getting a ride.

It was Sunday and I intended leaving the next day. Aunty Bobbi and Uncle Jim were out, leaving Lizzy and me alone in the house. This was all perfectly normal and I was happily snoring in my pit when Lizzy shook me awake.

"El's here," she whispered in my ear and my dulled senses absorbed the information. "She's cut her hand and her mom and dad are at church."

Within a millisecond I was wide awake and accompanying Lizzy into the bathroom where El was holding her hand under a tap. There were tears in her eyes and on her cheeks and I had never seen her look more beautiful.

"El, let me see your hand," I said and she offered it to me.

"I was cutting potatoes and the knife slipped," she explained.

It was a deep gash and I seriously considered calling a doctor who could decide if it needed stitching. Lizzy had brought a bandage that I carefully wrapped around her hand, first having padded the wound with gauze soaked in an antiseptic. I was simply delighted to be of service to this adorable creature and, despite the horrid circumstances, did my best to prolong the experience. Perhaps I took more time than was truly necessary.

"Joe, you're very gentle, you know," El whispered to me, and I looked up from her hand into her wet eyes.

Sadly I was overwhelmed and unable to resist taking her into my arms and passionately kissing her lovely mouth. She responded and our tongues locked in an embrace that I wished would never end. It was the first passionate kiss of my life and I know not where I had learned the technique. It just seemed to come quite naturally.

Poor Lizzy. She was an unheeded spectator and simply moved aside as I carried El into the lounge where we continued kissing on the couch.

"I knew you loved her, Joe," Lizzy said when I came up for air, deliriously happy with my lot.

Needless to say that my plans for Cape Town were thrown out the window. El and I, accompanied by a patient Lizzy, floated through the six-week holiday, visiting the cinema, the public pool and each others arms on a regular basis every day.

Never once did I consider El's and my relationship in any other light than as pure and unadulterated. Other than her back and beautiful face, I never touched any other part of her body and indeed found the thought abhorrent. I believed it would have been like defiling an angel.

Just before Christmas day, Lizzy, El and I went into the city to buy presents. I still had my R10 and Aunty Bobbi had generously donated an equivalent sum so I was flush. In addition to several other gifts I had bought for El, I had included a spur-of-the-moment bottle of bath foam that was attractively packaged. I had placed all my gifts in plastic carrier bags, but left the bath foam in its brown paper packaging. During the bus ride home I held it firmly clasped between my thighs hidden beneath the other gifts on my knees.

It wasn't a long ride home and I was enjoying the view from the upper level of the double-decker bus. At some point during the trip the bus drove over some unexpected obstacle. The sudden jolt caused the bottle containing the bath foam to crack and, unknown to me, slowly spill its contents. I felt a warm, wet feeling between my thighs but, being a hot day, I put it down to sweat.

Lizzy, who was seated behind El and me, knew I was guarding something secret and was only mildly interested. However, the growing accumulation of yellow liquid (the colour of the bubble bath) beneath my seat was far more fascinating and she thought I had relieved myself on the bus. This was confirmed when she saw that the front of my trousers was drenched when we reached our bus stop and I stood up.

Only now did I realise my predicament. Unfortunately so did El and Lizzy. They tried nobly to shield me from the gaze of the other passengers but failed miserably. When we got off the bus I tried to explain that the bubble bath was responsible but this only made them to giggle uncontrollably. I got into a huff and walked off ahead of them and they followed, still giggling.

Unfortunately the act of walking began to generate foam which also outlined my buttocks. Their giggles now turned into loud uncharitable guffaws. To their delight the whole back of my trousers began to lather up and bubbles started shooting off my backside in all directions. That finished them off. El and Lizzy collapsed in laughter, too weak to continue walking.

I disposed of the damaged bottle in the nearest bin and made my way back to the house, marking my route with a bubbly mess. Not wanting to be associated with me, El and Lizzy followed, giggling, at some distance behind. I was profoundly mortified and my soul still bears the scars of the experience.

One day, after Christmas and towards the end of the holiday, El decided that Lizzy and I should come round to her house which was two away from the Huttons'. The reason we hadn't done so before was because her father was such a tyrant.

El feared him but wasn't afraid of him. From what I could glean about their torrid relationship, he was not averse to resorting to violence to control her. She knew this and yet she still stood up to him, something I would never have dared do. He was a formidable man.

Lizzy and I looked at one another, wondering why El wanted to exchange our brightly lit and joyous atmosphere for her own dismal abode. I had been in her house and found it to be dark and uninviting. It resembled a church where one might admire the many ornaments but never be allowed to touch them or sit comfortably and relax. Added to that was the hazard of her father returning unexpectedly from work and discovering my presence with his daughter.

That he disliked me was already common knowledge but only because I was a threat to his projected plans of marrying El to Frank. Mr Stepford was unaware of the latest developments and, had he discovered them, I believed I would not have been long for this world. I was not as courageous as El and I feared for my skin.

"Don't worry," she said, reading my mind, "he won't come home today, it will be alright."

Unfortunately he did and in a panic, El stuffed Lizzy and me into a cramped broom cupboard. From within, our hearts hammered, drowning out the muffled sounds from without. Suddenly the door was opened by El.

"You better go home," she said.

Coward that I am, I was only too happy to oblige. Mr Stepford stood silently in the lounge, his back deliberately turned away from us as Lizzy and

I walked past him and out of the house. Only when we had cleared the front gate did father and daughter begin to shout, each vying to have the last word.

I wished El had never suggested Lizzy and I visit her house. Now my fear was that I might never be allowed to see her again. But El went one better and completely disappeared, deciding to run away from home.

Her mum, not being able to drive, begged Uncle Jim to search for her. I have already mentioned that Uncle Jim and I found her, late that night, in the chapel belonging to the Catholic school she attended in Rosettenville.

I was overjoyed to see her but she ignored me. She silently climbed into the back seat of the car and then disappeared into the footwell below. I turned to look for her but, in the darkness, I could make nothing out. Meanwhile Uncle Jim drove us home at his usual sedate pace.

I trailed my arm over the backrest of the front seat, hoping to make any contact with her, whether verbal or tactile, I cared not. About halfway through the half-hour journey, I felt El's long nails dig gently into my arm. In an instant I had swung around and was soon holding her delicate hand between my clumsy paws. I spent the rest of the trip on my knees on the front seat holding my beloved's hand in ecstatic silence.

Uncle Jim accompanied her into her house while I joined Lizzy and Aunty Bobbi in ours. When Uncle Jim returned shortly after he told us that El's father had given assurances that he would control his temper in future.

Sadly, he never did and not long after he and Mrs Stepford parted company forever. They first separated and then divorced. Mr Stepford, driving back from Durban one night, fell asleep at the wheel and nearly killed himself.

The last I heard of him was from Lizzy some years later. She had seen him in the city and had hailed him. He had been pitiful in his gratitude, saying that all his former acquaintances had abandoned him. I have no idea what became of him.

Lizzy was picked up by an international student exchange programme that, following an interview, selected her as an exchange student with an American counterpart. She spent a year living with a family in Salinas, the hometown of John Steinbeck whom I would later admire for his *Grapes of Wrath* and *Cannery Row*.

El, being a year older than I was, would begin her first year of teacher training in Johannesburg. We vowed that our love was eternal and promised to keep in touch through regular correspondence, combined with weekend meetings at the Huttons. Aunty Bobbi would serve as the post mistress, holding my letters for her and forwarding any that she wrote to me.

I fulfilled my side of the bargain, keeping her memory sacred and writing her numerous letters each week. These began stacking up, unread, in Aunty

Bobbi's drawer and only a few arrived from El. When they did, they contained nothing more than a few lines detailing her activities in the College.

Who was I kidding? Her social orbit now included the cream of Johannesburg youth and a young woman with her beauty was bound to attract the attention of a young man her age and with far more prospects than ever I could boast of. Sure enough, a letter arrived, begging my forgiveness but our relationship was at an end. She had met a young man, Lucien, whom she found irresistible. Within a short while she was pregnant and not long after, had married him.

"What shall I do with your letters?" Aunty Bobbi asked me.

"Throw them away," I said.

"Joe? are you sure? There must be at least a hundred here."

"Yes," I said, "please throw them away."

* * *

"Vicky?"

"What?"

"You've gone all quiet."

"No, I haven't."

"Are you jealous?"

"Don't be ridiculous."

"I was just seventeen."

"I know!"

"It was just six weeks, if that!"

"I know, I'm not in the slightest bit jealous."

"Then why have you got a face like a wet weekend?"

"Don't be ridiculous!"

I kicked the chair as I marched out, leaving Joe alone with his insufferable smile.

* * *

I did see El again, when she and Lucien visited the Huttons. I thought Lucien was an excellent choice. He was everything I wasn't: conscientious, ambitious and far better looking than I was. I was also introduced to Monique, their lovely baby girl.

After that, I would never see them again. In March, 1974, when I was twenty-two, I left South Africa for the UK and returned twenty years later in 1994. I stayed for two weeks and spent one of them with Lizzy and her two children, Sandy and Dylan.

"Lucien started his own company and has done very well," Lizzy told me. "He's loaded now. Did you know that, just after you left, they had another baby, a boy?"

That was news to me.

"Yes. His name is also Lucien and he is huge now. He's built like a brick ---- house. I've tried to contact El, to let her know you're here, but she won't answer. I'm sure she'd love to see you again."

Perhaps El felt as I did and did not relish a renewal of our acquaintance.

"No, leave it, Lizzy," I said.

The last I heard was that they had separated and El had moved to Perth, in Australia. But I will never forget the six weeks of bliss that I enjoyed during that summer break. I was disappointed that El preferred another but, once she had, I was not one to bear a grudge. She had opened my eyes to an experience that only poets write about and now, decades later, I still recall those times with more than a touch of fondness.

* * *

"Vicky, stop pulling that face!"
"Well, honestly! Sentimental old load of drivel."
"You ARE jealous!"
"Don't be ridiculous."

34

Walking Away

My final year. Academically I was still under-performing but, in early April, after hearing about El's decision to end our relationship, I was no longer smitten and had returned to my senses.

Chubby was still the Housemaster. His first assistant, Mr Alan, had been immensely unpopular, doing his best to antagonise just about every Senior boy in the Home.

His replacement, Mr Sean, was a far more reasonable chap. He disliked the Home's strict regime and viewed me as the embodiment of all it represented. He wasn't far wrong but, had Bossy been the Headboy, he might have thought me saintly by comparison. Bossy was running Taylor House with an iron fist and nobody dared oppose him.

I never was as strict as Bossy but Mr Sean still thought me a tyrant. He reported my bullying to the Beak who initially preferred not to be involved. At least I concluded as much because I wasn't called into his office to discuss the matter. Then one day I was and he requested I treat the boys less harshly.

"Why don't you use your tongue instead of your fists? You are intelligent enough, surely, to maintain discipline with just a sharp word?"

"Sorry, Father," I said, "but if I don't stamp on them now, they'll just take advantage and who knows what will happen then?"

"Did you know, Joe, that I have never raised my hand against another person?"

I stared at him in disbelief.

"Never, Father?"

"Not once," he said, and the smoke billowed from the pipe he loved to smoke as his grey eyes bored into mine.

Actually I was surprised that I had to justify methods that had been in place for decades past. I was simply behaving as every Headboy had done. Asking me to change my ways was a bit like asking a wild animal to be gentle with its prey. So indoctrinated was I, that in subsequent years I found it difficult not to consider resorting to my fists even during friendly arguments.

Needless to say, his mild request made little impression on me. It was nine years too late. When I entered the Boys' Home, had the environment been like that of the Children's Home, this situation would never have arisen. So I continued as I had learned and Mr Sean ground his teeth and his hatred of me blossomed.

Neither could he expect any support from Chubby. Mr Sean was another Irishman and Chubby's dislike of the race bordered on loathing. No doubt he believed they had been deliberately sent to plague him.

Chubby was an easy-going man who delighted in refereeing soccer matches and coaching the boys to play better football. He was never happier than when he was either in the middle of a football pitch, with a whistle in his mouth, or on the sidelines, cheering on a Home team.

Afterwards we would sit in his flat and discuss the merits (or otherwise) of various players who were in the teams he coached. The conversation would spread further afield and include famous English clubs.

"Joe, if you could only see Arsenal or Spurs playing," he mused, "you would know what I mean about playing properly."

"Have you actually seen them play, sir?"

"Of course! I'm an Englishman, am I not?"

Arsenal would later tour South Africa and thrash the all-white South African team by twelve goals to nil. Tales relating to the Albion always interested me and Chubby was only too happy to speak about his experiences growing up in 'this blessed plot, this earth, this realm, this England'. But the arrival of Mr Sean was perhaps too much for him and he elected to leave the Home.

He was replaced by Mr Pete whose girth was as wide as Chubby's but he disguised the fact by being twice as tall. Always quick to attach appropriate nicknames to Housemasters, the boys eventually labelled him as 'Blob'.

I would miss Chubby, not just as a friend, but also as an ally in my battles with Mr Sean. Chubby didn't exactly approve of my heavy-handed measures but he recognised that he was powerless to stop it. He understood that the violence was traditional, entrenched in the foundations of the Home. Mr Sean refused to accept this.

Chubby was not above wielding his cane, should the need arise, but he had no natural propensity for it as did the Deputy Head, Mr Ken, and most Housemasters. On one occasion, though, he wielded more than just a cane and I was both responsible and on the receiving end.

It was at the breakfast parade on the Parade Ground when the three Senior Houses were lined up for the morning roll call prior to entering the dining hall for breakfast. These occurred every morning and evening and were conducted by any one of the three Senior Housemasters, depending on which was available.

As with all parades, the Houses lined up in dormitory formation with the Patrol Leader at the head of his dorm. When called upon, he would succinctly announce any absentees. If there were none, he simply stated that all in his dorm were present and correct.

Sometimes, boys ran away, in which case they were declared absconded. If an absentee was in the sanatorium he was announced as being in Surgery. Should anybody be absent without a valid reason he was said to be AWOL, or absent without leave.

The Headboy of each House stood behind the line of his House. He was permitted to move freely up and down the line, ensuring the boys conducted themselves appropriately. I had coffee-making facilities in my room and sometimes brought a mug of steaming coffee with me to the parade. This I always laid aside, between the arches, when the parade proper began. One morning I was caught off-guard and decided to hide my mug behind my back. Chubby was conducting the parade.

"We'll wait for the Headboy of Crawford House to finish his coffee," he drolly announced to the parade at large.

"Oh, ta," was my facetious response and I took a sip.

Chubby exploded and ordered me into the Headmaster's office. I sauntered in, carefully nursing my mug of coffee and generally making an idiot of myself. Bossy sniggered as I passed him on my way.

"You're in for it now, Joe!" he whispered with a smirk.

I wasn't worried. All Chubby could do was bawl at me which had no impact whatsoever. I carried my mug into the secretary's office and, sure enough, he started shouting the moment I entered. With a show of deliberate boredom, I raised my eyes to the ceiling (my first mistake) and then slowly raised the mug to my lips to nonchalantly sip the coffee (my second).

I simply did not see it coming. Rarely was I unaware of a slap being aimed at my face by a Housemaster. I had been slapped so many times that I was able to read the signs and take the necessary action to limit any damage. On one occasion, in Simpson House, Mr George aimed a blow that I rode by rolling over backwards.

"That was a bit dramatic, wasn't it, Joe?" somebody said afterwards.

"I know," I said, "I did overdo it a bit, didn't I?" and we both laughed.

But today, Chubby's punch was whipped up with a ferocity and speed that left me sitting on the floor against the office wall. I never did find out what happened to my mug but I doubt it was still in one piece. All I remember was a high-pitched note reverberating through my skull.

When I did regain my senses I discovered that my nose was bleeding profusely and I was alone in the office. I marched myself to Surgery to have my nose repaired and to squeal on Chubby for being a bully. If I was expecting any sympathy from Sister McArdle I was sadly disappointed.

"He should have split your head open instead of just your nose!" she said.

"Bud dee boak by doas," I whimpered.

"And what do you expect me to do, fix it? If it's broken it will mend by itself. Now stuff some cottonwool into each nostril then get out of here!"

Ah Sister, the memory of your compassionate nature still warms the cockles of my heart.

Actually Chubby's behaviour was in keeping with the Home standards of appropriate methods to deal with delinquent behaviour. Frankly, I deserved all I got and never begrudged the blow. I only wished that Mr Sean might have witnessed it and gained some insight into the many positive benefits due to grievous bodily harm as an instrument for maintaining discipline. But he didn't and a storm continued to brew.

A few days after this altercation with Chubby, he and I were on equatable terms once more and it was as if it had never happened. Unfortunately, he could no longer tolerate working with an Irishman and he was replaced by Blob.

Blob and I got on famously. I really liked his expansive nature which so befitted his generous frame. Like Chubby, he was always on the football pitch, refereeing matches or cheering our teams on. He was also a Mathematics teacher at a local high school that some of the boys attended. After school he would return to the Home to assume his Housemaster duties. Like Chubby, he was single and his bespectacled face seldom darkened in anger. He was quietly spoken and rarely interfered or intervened when I was disciplining offenders.

I can only hazard a guess that Mr Sean whispered evil things about me in his ear but I cannot be sure. In any event, I could always depend on Blob for his support and that never changed. But one Sunday, towards the end of the year, matters came to a head.

It happened in Chapel. I was about to take my seat when I observed an extraordinary event. Coops, the Dorm 3 Patrol Leader, was slowly lowering his behind to sit down at the end of a pew. Smitty, one of the youngest boys in the House, and in Coops's dormitory, was already seated alongside him.

While remaining seated, Smitty spun on the pew, simultaneously placing the soles of his shoes against the side of Coops's left buttock. Before Coops had fully sat down, Smitty straightened his leg and Coops found himself sitting on the central aisle carpet. It was a variation of 'pulling out a chair to leave somebody sitting on the floor' routine. It was a neat move, brilliantly executed and caused much mirth amongst those who observed it.

I watched as Coops raised himself up from his embarrassing position in the aisle and sat himself down next to Smitty. What astonished me was that Coops did not even scold the little reprobate. I had been instrumental in his appointment as a Patrol Leader and he had even been a subordinate of mine when I was his Patrol Leader. He should have stamped on any junior who had so disrespected his rank. I was angry with him for allowing the little runt so much latitude.

Smitty looked up and, seeing me, the smirk on his face evaporated.

"See me after Chapel," I hissed at him while glowering at Coops.

But Smitty didn't turn up. Instead he hid behind Mr Sean and that gentleman reported me to the Beak.

"Joe," the Beak said to me in the dining hall, "you will not touch that boy, do you hear me?"

"Yes, I hear you, Father," I said through clenched teeth, "but when I get my hands on the little so-and-so, I'll kill him."

"You'll do nothing of the sort," he said, his steel-grey eyes locked on mine.

I did catch up with the little scoundrel and rapped his skull with my knuckles. He fled in tears to Mr Sean who, once more, reported me to the Beak. I was called into his office.

"I did warn you," he said, "and you chose to ignore me. Pack your things and move down to Simpson House. You are no longer Headboy of Crawford House."

"What? Simpson House?"

"Yes. You can either assist the Housemaster, or do whatever you like, but you cannot stay in Crawford House."

"I would rather leave the Home," I threatened.

"You are well past school-leaving age now and free to do as you please."

"You can't just kick me out onto the streets!"

"I'm not. You can move into Simpson House."

"Well, I'm not staying," I snarled, and walked out of his office in a huff.

I telephoned Aunty Bobbi and asked if I might stay with her. She flatly refused and hung up the receiver. A slight panic began to set in. I had no intention of staying in Simpson House but there appeared to be no alternative.

"Joe," said the secretary, who had been privy to proceedings, "there's a phone call for you."

I stared at her, perplexed. I wondered who might want to telephone me at the Home. Lizzy was in America and Aunty Bobbi had made it abundantly clear that I was not welcome. Perhaps she had changed her mind?

"Hello?" I said into the mouthpiece.

"Joe, it's David."

Chubby?

"Hello, sir," I stammered.

"I heard about your situation. Why don't you come and stay with me?"

I was astounded. He had left the Home a few months back and I had heard nothing about him since. How he had learned about my situation has always been a mystery to me and he never did reveal his source.

"May I phone you back, please? I would just like to talk to Father Eric about it first."

"By all means," he said, and hung up.

I entered the Beak's office and he didn't even look up. I now had a bargaining chip and I hoped somehow to use it to make him change his mind.

"Father," I said, "I will leave the Home rather than move to Simpson House."

"Do as you please," he said, without looking up from his desk.

Nine years earlier, I, together with six other nine year old stamp collectors, had sat on the floor where I now stood, sifting through his stamp collection, choosing the best for ourselves, while he worked at his desk as he did now.

He was great then and he was great now. No other member of staff was more respected than this gentle man who never raised his voice or his hand against a single boy. Yes, he tried to do so with me but it was such a ludicrous failure that his tears of discomfort were only exceeded by mine of laughter at his ineptitude.

It was as if the Home was a culmination of his life's work, to increase its prosperity and to reduce the underlying violence that prevailed throughout, and he did this tirelessly. During his tenure, two new Houses were constructed and the number of disadvantaged boys increased to beyond two hundred. He would introduce married couples, preferably with children of their own, as House Mothers and House Fathers, hoping that, by their example, the boys would recognise a 'normal' family environment.

I am not sure if he ever did exorcise the violence. Years later I would read horror stories, written by boys describing their experiences, who left the Home well after I did. Be that as it may, Father Eric did his best to minimise it.

I was probably the first of the old violent crew to be exiled and I now knew that once he had made up his mind, nothing would change it.

So I walked out of his office for the last time and I telephoned Chubby who very kindly agreed to put me up for the remaining six weeks of the school year. All phone calls were made from the secretary's office and, having replaced the receiver, I turned to walk out forever when Mr Ken appeared at my elbow.

"Joe," he said, "would you mind continuing as the drum major?"

Cadets and the Home band were the most distant topics on my mind at that particular moment but I agreed to do so. Chubby's very comfortable and newly-constructed flat was located a stone's-throw from the Home and it would be no great chore to prepare the band for the Memorial Service and Annual Parade that year.

At the Annual Parade, the last in the cadet calendar, I was awarded the Cadet of the Year trophy but I think Mr Ken was showing me his gratitude for not leaving the band in the lurch. It would have been difficult to replace me at such short notice.

I lived most comfortably with Chubby, who shared his expensive apartment with his mother. I completed my final year at school, emerging with a General Certificate of Education, sufficient to gain entry as a pilot in the South African Air Force.

In the beginning of 1970, just a month after completing school, I and two thousand young men from all over the country were conscripted into the SAAF Gymnasium, Valhalla, to embark on our basic training. The base was located just outside Pretoria and served as a recruitment centre for pilot selection. Soon after our arrival, an officer addressed our intake.

"Anyone interested in applying for pilot training, report to Hangar A."

In Hangar A, rows of desks filled the floor space and when we were all seated, very few desks remained untaken. It seemed I wasn't alone in having stars in my eyes where aircraft were concerned. On each desk was an application form, together with a multiple choice questionnaire.

"First complete the application form then the questionnaire," the officer said, addressing us from the front of the hangar. "Beware. Some of the questions may seem silly to you but do not underestimate them. During the next month, you will be undergoing a number of intelligence, psychological and fitness tests to assess your aptitude to be a pilot. If you pass those tests, and I do mean *if*, because only a few of you will, a psychiatrist will interview you. He will ask you to explain why you chose the answers you did in today's questionnaire. Believe me when I tell you that it will be *his* decision whether you are selected or not."

He was right. Only a few of us were selected and I was fortunate to be one of them. I was about to embark on a new life and a new career

But that's another story.

* * *

Joe closed his laptop and leaned back in his chair.

"Well, that's that then," he said.

"You've finished?" I asked

"Yes. Writing a memoir is a painful process, isn't it? I'm ashamed of so many things. It was very painful to drag up all those old memories."

"I know. Life dealt you a rough hand, it wasn't your fault. If you'd been

born to ordinary parents as part of an ordinary family, things would have been very different."

"Yes," Joe said, "but then I'd have never have met you."

"Steady on" I said, "you're sounding almost romantic."

Joe smiled and stood up, then put his arms around me.

"Come on, Beaky, let's pour ourselves a wine and go up to the roof terrace and watch the sun go down over the mountains."

Epilogue

I left South Africa in March 1974 and followed my dream to visit Britain, eventually becoming a British national. In 1994, I revisited my country of birth.

Much had changed.

The white Nationalist government had just handed over power to the black Nationalists and nobody quite knew what would happen next.

Following a joyful reunion with Lizzy, I made a beeline for the two places that most affected me during my formative years.

Much to my surprise, the Boys' Home had become a private school. I suppose it was to be expected, being ideal with all the necessary infrastructure already in place, and no doubt the Anglican Church needed the money. I believe the Home still exists, but in a different guise, having splintered into several separate locations and now catering for both girls and boys.

Johannesburg Children's Home continues as it did when I was there, nearly sixty years ago. It was established before the turn of the 20th Century and is the oldest orphanage in Johannesburg.

Of the Housemasters in the Boys' Home, I only know of a few that are still alive today. Mr Brian and Mr Derek are still in South Africa, as is the Beak, who is 104 as I write these words. He was sent a letter of congratulations by Her Majesty the Queen when he turned one hundred.

Of the significant boys in this memoir, Bossy, Richard and his brother, Freddy, are dead. The rest live either in South Africa or in Australia.

Ma died in 1989 and her ashes were scattered out at sea in Durban, or so I am told. Lizzy sent me pictures of a number of relatives who attended her funeral. I am told that Ma never wanted to hear any mention of Lizzy or me when she lived near Durban.

Lizzy learned where our father, Harry, was living and paid him a visit. Following their shock reunion, he told her she bore an uncanny likeness to Ma. He wrote me a letter but I was still too resentful to reply politely. In the letter, amongst other things, he advised me to check for prostate cancer when I was older. I always remembered that and, fortunately, followed his advice.

Uncle Jim had already died when Lizzy introduced my father to her adopted mother, Aunty Bobbi, for the first time. Lizzy says the pair got on very well with each other. My father would die a few years later, as would Aunty Bobbi.

Lizzy became a doctor and taught at a university in Johannesburg. She is semi-retired and has moved down to the South Coast, near Twini. I still consider that area to be almost paradise on earth and hope to find it not too much changed. One day I want to take Vicky and show her the landmarks of my childhood, and visit Lizzy.

Joe Twead, Australia, 2016

If you enjoyed *One Young Fool in South Africa*, Joe and Victoria would be forever grateful if you would consider leaving a review. Thank you!

1

The Five Year Plan

"Hello?"

"This is Kurt."

"Oh! Hello, Kurt. How are you?"

"I am vell. The papers you vill sign now. I haf made an appointment vith the Notary for you May 23rd, 12 o'clock."

"Right, I'll check the flights and…" but he had already hung up.

Kurt, our German estate agent, was the type of person one obeyed without question. So, on May 23rd, we found ourselves back in Spain, seated round a huge polished table in the Notary's office. Beside us sat our bank manager holding a briefcase stuffed with bank notes.

ʇʇʇ

Nine months earlier, we had never met Kurt. Nine months earlier, Joe and I lived in an ordinary house, in an ordinary Sussex town. Nine months earlier we had ordinary jobs and expected an ordinary future.

Then, one dismal Sunday, I decided to change all that.

"...heavy showers are expected to last through the Bank Holiday weekend and into next week. Temperatures are struggling to reach 14 degrees..."

August, and the weather-girl was wearing a coat, sheltering under an umbrella. June had been wet, July wetter. I sighed, stabbing the 'off' button on the remote control before she could depress me further. Agh! Typical British weather.

My depression changed to frustration. The private thoughts that had been tormenting me so long returned. Why should we put up with it? Why not move? Why not live in my beloved Spain where the sun always shines?

I walked to the window. Raindrops like slug trails trickled down the windowpane. Steely clouds hung low, heavy with more rain, smothering the town. Sodden litter sat drowning in the gutter.

"Joe?" He was dozing, stretched out on the sofa, mouth slightly open. "Joe, I want to talk to you about something."

Poor Joe, my long-suffering husband. His gangly frame was sprawled out, newspaper slipping from his fingers. He was utterly relaxed, blissfully unaware that our lives were about to change course.

How different he looked in scruffy jeans compared with his usual crisp uniform. But to me, whatever he wore, he was always the same, an officer and a gentleman. Nearing retirement from the Forces, I knew he was looking forward to a tension-free future, but the television weather-girl had galvanised me into action. The metaphorical bee in my bonnet would not be stilled. It buzzed and grew until it became a hornet demanding attention.

"Huh? What's the matter?" His words were blurred with sleep, his eyes still closed. Rain beat a tattoo on the window pane.

"Joe? Are you listening?"

"Uhuh..."

"When you retire, I want us to sell up and buy a house in Spain." Deep breath.

There. The bomb was dropped. I had finally admitted my longing. I wanted to abandon England with its ceaseless rain. I wanted to move permanently to Spain.

Sleep forgotten, Joe pulled himself upright, confusion in his blue eyes as he tried to read my expression.

"Vicky, what did you say just then?" he asked, squinting at me.

"I want to go and live in Spain."

"You can't be serious."

"Yes, I am."

Of course it wasn't just the rain. I had plenty of reasons, some vague, some more solid.

I presented my pitch carefully. Our children, adults now, were scattered round the world; Scotland, Australia and London. No grandchildren yet on the horizon and Joe only had a year before he retired. Then we would be free as birds to nest where we pleased.

And the cost of living in Spain would be so much lower. Council tax a fraction of what we usually paid, cheaper food, cheaper houses... The list went on.

Joe listened closely and I watched his reactions. Usually, *he* is the impetuous one, not me. But I was well aware that his retirement fantasy was being threatened. His dream of lounging all day in his dressing-gown, writing his book and diverting himself with the odd mathematical problem was being exploded.

"Hang on, Vicky, I thought we had it all planned? I thought you would do a few days of supply teaching if you wanted, while I start writing my book." Joe absentmindedly scratched his nether regions. For once I ignored his infuriating habit; I was in full flow.

"But imagine writing in Spain! Imagine sitting outside in the shade of a grapevine and writing your masterpiece."

Outside, windscreen wipers slapped as cars swept past, tyres sending up plumes of filthy water. Joe glanced out of the window at the driving rain and I sensed I had scored an important point.

"Why don't you write one of your famous lists?" he suggested, only half joking.

I am well known for my lists and records. Inheriting the record- keeping gene from my father, I can't help myself. I make a note of the weather every day, the temperature, the first snowdrop, the day the ants fly, the exchange rate of the euro, everything. I make shopping lists, separate ones for each shop. I make To Do lists and 'Joe, will you please' lists. I make packing lists before holidays. I even make lists of lists. My nickname at work was Schindler.

So I set to work and composed what I considered to be a killer pitch:

• Sunny weather
• Cheap houses
• Live in the country
• Miniscule council tax

- Friendly people
- Less crime
- No heating bills
- Cheap petrol
- Wonderful Spanish food
- Cheap wine and beer
- Could get satellite TV so you won't miss English football
- Much more laid-back life style
- Could afford house big enough for family and visitors to stay
- No TV licence
- Only short flight to UK
- Might live longer because Mediterranean diet is healthiest in the world

When I ran dry, I handed the list to Joe. He glanced at it and snorted.

"I'm going to make a coffee," he said, but he took my list with him. He was in the kitchen a long time.

When he came out, I looked up at him expectantly. He ignored me, snatched a pen and scribbled on the bottom of the list. Satisfied, he threw it on the table and left the room. I grabbed it and read his additions. He'd pressed so hard with the pen that he'd nearly gone through the paper.

Joe had written:

- CAN'T SPEAK SPANISH!
- TOO MANY FLIES!
- *MOVING HOUSE IS THE PITS!*

For weeks we debated, bouncing arguments for and against like a game of ping pong. Even when we weren't discussing it, the subject hung in the air between us, almost tangible. Then one day, (was it a coincidence that it was raining yet again?) Joe surprised me.

"Vicky, why don't you book us a holiday over Christmas, and we could just take a look."

The hug I gave him nearly crushed his ribs.

"Hang on!" he said, detaching himself and holding me at arm's length. "What I'm trying to say is, well, I'm willing to compromise."

"What do you mean, 'compromise'?"

"How about if we look on it as a five year plan? We don't sell this house, just rent it out. Okay, we could move to Spain, but not necessarily for ever. At the end of five years, we can make up our minds whether to come back to England or stay out there. I'm happy to try it for five years. What do you think?"

I turned it over in my mind. Move to Spain, but look on it as a sort of project? Actually, it seemed rather a good idea. In fact, a perfect compromise.

Joe was watching me. "Well? Agreed?"

"Agreed…" It was a victory of sorts. A Five Year Plan. Yes, I saw the sense in that. Anything could happen in five years.

"Well, go on, then. Book a holiday over Christmas and we'll take it from there."

So I logged onto the Internet and booked a two week holiday in Almería.

Why Almería? Well, we already knew the area quite well as this would be our fourth visit. And I considered this part of Andalucía to be perfect. Only two and a half hours flight from London, guaranteed sunshine, friendly people and jaw-dropping views. It ticked all my boxes. Joe agreed cautiously that the area could be ideal.

So the destination was decided, but what type of home in Spain would we want? Our budget was reduced because we weren't going to sell our English house. We'd have to find something cheap.

On previous visits, I'd hated all the houses we'd noticed in the resorts. Mass produced boxes on legoland estates, each identical, each characterless and overlooking the next. No, I knew what I really wanted: a house we could do up, with views and space, preferably in an unspoiled Spanish village.

Unlike Joe, I've always been obsessed with houses. I was the driving force and it was the hard climb up the English property ladder that allowed us even to contemplate moving abroad. In the past few years, we had bought a derelict house, improved and sold it, making a good profit. So we bought another and repeated the process. It was gruelling work. We both had other careers, but it was well worth the effort. Now we could afford to rent out our home in England and still buy a modest house in Spain.

"If we do decide to move out there," said Joe, "and we buy an old place to do up, it's not going to be like doing up houses in England. Everything's going to be different there."

How right he was.

双双双

Like a child, I yearned for that Christmas to come. I couldn't wait to set foot on Spanish soil again. We arrived, and although Christmas lights decorated the airport, it was warm enough to remove our jackets. Before long, we had found our hotel and settled in.

The next morning, we hired a little car. Joe, having finally accepted the inevitable, was happy to drive into the mountains in search of The House. We had two weeks to find it.

Grumpy's Garlic Mushrooms Tapa
Champiñones al Ajillo
Serves 4

50ml (2 fl oz) extra virgin olive oil
250g (8oz) fresh mushrooms (sliced)
4-6 cloves of garlic (chopped or sliced)
3 tablespoons dry Spanish sherry
2 tablespoons lemon juice
Large pinch of dried chili flakes
Large pinch of paprika
Salt, freshly ground pepper
Chopped parsley to garnish

Method
• Heat the oil in a frying pan and fry the mushrooms over a high heat for 2 or 3 minutes. Stir constantly.
• Lower the heat and add the garlic, lemon juice, sherry, salt and pepper.
• For a milder flavour you can leave it at that if you like. But if you like a few 'fireworks', now is the time to add the dried chili and paprika as well.
• Cook for another 5 minutes or so until the garlic and mushrooms have softened, then remove from the heat.
• Sprinkle with chopped parsley and divide up into pre-heated little dishes.
• Serve with plenty of fresh, crusty bread to mop up the seriously garlicky juices.

Note: Tapa means 'lid' or 'cover' in Spanish. It's thought that the name originally came from the practice of placing slices of meat on top of a sherry glass, to keep out flies. The meat, often ham or chorizo, was characteristically salty, inducing thirst. Bartenders saw this and began serving a variety of tapas which increased alcohol sales. Thus a new tradition was born.

Yet again the mountains seduced us. The endless blue sky where birds of prey wheeled lazily. The neat orchards splashed with bright oranges and lemons. The secret, sleepy villages nestled into valleys. Even the roads, narrow, treacherous and winding, couldn't break the spell that Andalucía cast over us.

Daily, we drove through whitewashed villages where little old ladies dressed in black stopped sweeping their doorsteps to watch us pass. We waved at farmers working in their fields, the dry dust swirling in irritated clouds from their labours. We paused to allow goat-herds to pass with their flocks, the lead goat's bell clanging bossily as the herd followed, snatching mouthfuls of vegetation on the run.

Although we hadn't yet found The House, we were positive we'd found the area we wanted to live in.

One day we drove into a village that clung to the steep mountainside by its fingernails. We entered a bar that was buzzing with activity. It was busy and the air heavy with smoke. The white-aproned bartender looked us up and down and jerked his head in greeting. No smile, just a nod.

Joe found a rocky wooden table by the window with panoramic views and we settled ourselves, soaking in the atmosphere. Four old men played cards at the next table. A heated debate was taking place between another group. I caught the words 'Barcelona' and 'Real Madrid'. Most of the bar's customers were male.

Grumpy, the bartender, wiped his hands on his apron and approached our table, flicking off imaginary crumbs from the surface with the back of his hand. He had a splendid moustache which concealed any expression he may have had, and made communication difficult.

"Could we see the menu, please?" asked Joe in his best phrase book Spanish.

Grumpy shook his head and snorted. It seemed there was no menu.

"No *importa*," said Joe. "It doesn't matter."

Using a combination of sign language and impatient grunts, Grumpy took our order but our meal was destined to be a surprise. A basket of bread was slammed onto the table, followed by two plates of food. Garlic mushrooms - delicious.

We cleaned our plates and leaned back, digesting our food and the surroundings. In typical Spanish fashion, the drinkers at the bar bellowed at each other as though every individual had profound hearing problems.

"We're running out of time," said Joe. "We can carry on gallivanting around the countryside, but we aren't going to find anything. I very much doubt we'll find a house this holiday."

Suddenly, clear as cut crystal, the English words, "Oh, bugger! Where are my keys?" floated above the Spanish hubbub.

Read more in

Chickens, Mules and Two Old Fools
by Victoria Twead
(Wall Street Journal Top 10 bestseller)

Contact the Authors and Links

Email: TopHen@VictoriaTwead.com
(emails welcome)

Facebook: https://www.facebook.com/VictoriaTwead
(friend requests welcome)

Website: www.VictoriaTwead.com

Free Stuff and Village Updates newsletter
http://www.victoriatwead.com/Free-Stuff/

Twitter: @VictoriaTwead

Chickens, Mules and Two Old Fools book trailer:
http://youtu.be/1s9KbJEmrHs

•

Books by Victoria Twead

The Old Fools Series

Chickens, Mules and Two Old Fools by Victoria Twead (Wall Street Journal Top 10 bestseller)

Two Old Fools ~ Olé! by Victoria Twead

Two Old Fools on a Camel by Victoria Twead (thrice New York Times bestseller)

Two Old Fools in Spain Again by Victoria Twead

One Young Fool in Dorset (The Prequel) by Victoria Twead

Also by Victoria Twead

- How to Write a Bestselling Memoir
- A is for Abigail (Sixpenny Cross 1)
- B is for Bella (Sixpenny Cross 2)

Ant Press Books

You may also enjoy these other Ant Press titles:

MEMOIRS

Midwife - A Calling by Peggy Vincent

Midwife - A Journey by Peggy Vincent

Into Africa with 3 Kids, 13 Crates and a Husband by Ann Patras

More Into Africa with 3 Kids, some Dogs and a Husband by Ann Patras

Fat Dogs and French Estates ~ Part I by Beth Haslam

Fat Dogs and French Estates ~ Part II by Beth Haslam

Simon Ships Out: How One Brave, Stray Cat Became a Worldwide Hero by Jacky Donovan

Smoky: How a Tiny Yorkshire Terrier Became a World War II American Army Hero, Therapy Dog and Hollywood Star by Jacky Donovan

Instant Whips and Dream Toppings: A True-Life Dom Rom Com by Jacky Donovan

Heartprints of Africa: A Family's Story of Faith, Love, Adventure, and Turmoil by Cinda Adams Brooks

How not to be a Soldier: My Antics in the British Army by Lorna McCann

Moment of Surrender: My Journey Through Prescription Drug Addiction to Hope and Renewal by Pj Laube

Serving is a Pilgrimage by John Basham

FICTION

Parched by Andrew C Branham

CHILDREN'S BOOKS

Seacat Simon: The Little Cat Who Became a Big Hero by Jacky Donovan

The Rise of Agnil by Susan Navas (Agnil's World 1)

Agnil and the Wizard's Orb by Susan Navas (Agnil's World 2)

Agnil and the Tree Spirits by Susan Navas (Agnil's World 3)

Agnil and the Centaur's Secret by Susan Navas (Agnil's World 4)

Morgan and the Martians by Victoria Twead

Chat with the author and other memoir authors and readers at
We Love Memoirs:

https://www.facebook.com/groups/welovememoirs/

Manufactured by Amazon.ca
Bolton, ON